WHO
RULES
AMERICA?

WHO
RULES
AMERICA?

CHALLENGES TO CORPORATE AND CLASS DOMINANCE

SIXTH EDITION

G. WILLIAM DOMHOFF
University of California, Santa Cruz

 **Higher Education**

Boston   Burr Ridge, IL   Dubuque, IA   New York
San Francisco   St. Louis   Bangkok   Bogotá   Caracas   Kuala Lumpur
Lisbon   London   Madrid   Mexico City   Milan   Montreal   New Delhi
Santiago   Seoul   Singapore   Sydney   Taipei   Toronto

Higher Education

Published by McGraw-Hill, an imprint of The McGraw-Hill Companies, Inc., 1221 Avenue of the Americas, New York, NY 10020. Copyright © 2010. All rights reserved. No part of this publication may be reproduced or distributed in any form or by any means, or stored in a database or retrieval system, without the prior written consent of The McGraw-Hill Companies, Inc., including, but not limited to, in any network or other electronic storage or transmission, or broadcast for distance learning.

This book is printed on acid-free paper.

1 2 3 4 5 6 7 8 9 0 DOC / DOC 0 9

ISBN-13: 978-0-07-811156-3
MHID: 0-07-811156-0

Vice President and Editor in Chief: *Michael Ryan*
Publisher: *Frank Mortimer*
Sponsoring Editor: *Gina Boedeker*
Managing Editor: *Nicole Bridge*
Development Editor: *Craig Leonard*
Marketing Manager: *Pamela Cooper*
Production Editor: *Brett Coker*
Design Manager: *Margarite Reynolds*
Production Supervisor: *Tandra Jorgensen*
Composition: *Macmillan Publishing Solutions*
Production Service: *Lynn Lustberg, Macmillan Publishing Solutions*
Printing: *45# New Era Matte Plus by Quebecor Fairfield*

Credit: © *Jim Bourg/Pool/Getty Images*

Library of Congress Cataloging-in-Publication Data

Domhoff, G. William.
  Who rules America?: challenges to corporate and class dominance / G. William Domhoff.
  — 6th ed.
     p. cm.
  Includes bibliographical references and index.
  ISBN-13: 978-0-07-811156-3 (alk. paper)
  ISBN-10: 0-07-811156-0 (alk. paper)
  1. Elite (Social sciences)—United States. 2. Power (Social sciences)—United States.
  3. Social classes—United States. 4. Corporations—United States—Political activity.
  5. United States—Politics and government. I. Title.
  HN90.E4D652 2009
  305.5′20973—dc22

                                                                    2009007940

The Internet addresses listed in the text were accurate at the time of publication. The inclusion of a Web site does not indicate an endorsement by the authors or McGraw-Hill, and McGraw-Hill does not guarantee the accuracy of the information presented at these sites.

www.mhhe.com

Contents

Preface

This sixth edition of *Who Rules America?* is completely updated to capture the dramatic changes in the United States since the previous edition appeared in mid-2005. It reflects the fact that the Bush Administration's hubris and miscalculations have entrapped the country in two unpopular wars while at the same time generating a major economic crisis. These mistakes opened up the possibility of replacing the Republicans' corporate-conservative coalition with a centrist-liberal-labor coalition led by the first African-American president in the nation's history, Barack Obama.

This new edition stresses that the current historical moment is the first time the Democrats have been in control of the White House and Congress without having a conservative Southern wing to keep them from enacting changes that might move the country in a more egalitarian direction. Whether the centrist Democrats want to go in that direction, or can be pressured to take that direction if the Republican ultraconservatives in the Senate can be overcome, is one of the questions that will be under debate throughout the country while this book is being read.

This edition pays special attention to the historic election of Barack Obama to the presidency to see if and how his victory accords with key sociological ideas. It shows that he has touched all the right bases in his climb to the top and that he has all the attributes of a successful American politician. It finds that his most important financial supporters were moderate conservatives in the corporate community. It concludes that his Cabinet and White House staff have less corporate involvement and more government experience than past government appointees to these positions, which might be a positive sign for those hoping for economic reform. The book now ends with a new chapter on the possibilities for egalitarian social change that have been created by the ongoing wars in Iraq and Afghanistan, the loss of jobs and homes in the economic meltdown, and a new administration that was elected based on the claim that change is possible.

This edition, which marks the forty-second consecutive year that *Who Rules America?* has been available to readers, draws on recent studies in sociology and political science to update information on corporate interlocks, social clubs, and the charitable foundations, think tanks, and policy-discussion groups through which the corporate rich strive to shape public policy. It depicts the continuing disjuncture between the general public's liberal policy preferences on a variety of economic issues and the lack of attention to these preferences by elected officials in order to highlight the minimal to nonexistent role of public opinion unless it is embodied in a social movement. It uses the replacement of Republicans with Democrats in the 2006 and 2008 elections to stress once again that elections can register citizen discontent with political decisions. To update and extend information on the large flow of money from corporations and foundations to think tanks, policy-discussion groups, and opinion-shaping organizations, the new edition draws on the grants section of the *Foundation Directory Online* for invaluable and timesaving compilations.

As before, the book is supplemented by a website at www. whorulesamerica.net that is updated when major new studies appear. It includes a library of online articles and chapters, with links to methodological tools. The key documents on the site are noted at appropriate points in the text to remind readers that further analyses on particular topics are available. "Wealth, Income, and Power," a document that was created after the fifth edition appeared, has become a popular destination for students and members of the general public seeking information on the large gaps between the very rich and everyone else in America. Whorulesamerica.net now houses the methodological information on how to do power structure research that formerly appeared in the book as the Appendix. This change allows for more detail on methodology for those who want to do their own studies and at the same time makes the book shorter and leaves more space to discuss substantive issues.

There is one change in conceptual emphasis from the previous three editions. In those editions I said that the basic power conflict in American society is between the "corporate-conservative coalition," lodged in the Republican Party, and the "liberal-labor coalition," which has a place at the table in the centrist-dominated Democratic Party. Although past editions said that some members of the corporate community continue to play a key role in the Democratic Party through campaign contributions and appointments to cabinet positions, as demonstrated by the corporate nature of the Clinton Administration, that point was not stressed enough. In this sixth edition the central power conflict is framed as one between the overall corporate community and the liberal-labor coalition, with some members of the corporate community supporting the Democrats even though they oppose unions and much of the liberal-labor agenda.

Although the current moment is filled with even more uncertainty than is usually the case, it is an exciting time to be thinking about the question of "who rules America," or indeed, about who might be ruling the country a few years from now. I hope readers have as much fun reading this book as I had writing it. I also hope it proves useful in understanding some of the events that will unfold during the new post-Bush era.

In closing this preface, I want to extend my deepest thanks to the several colleagues around the country who gave me information and feedback that made it possible to finish this revision in a timely fashion: Dean Baker, Center for Economic and Policy Research, Washington, D.C.; Val Burris, Department of Sociology, University of Oregon; Diana Kendall, Department of Sociology, Baylor University; Leah Rogne, Department of Sociology and Corrections, Minnesota State University; Clifford Staples, Department of Sociology, University of North Dakota; and Richard L. Zweigenhaft, Department of Psychology, Guilford College. I am also grateful to the many colleagues who took the time to provide very helpful anonymous suggestions in response to a survey on how to improve the current edition based on their use of the previous edition in their courses.

Introduction

THIS IS THE IDEAL HISTORICAL MOMENT TO BE READING THIS BOOK

Do corporations have far too much power in the United States? Three-fourths of Americans have answered "yes" to that question for the past twenty years. This book explains why their answers are accurate even though the United States has freedom of speech, the possibility of full political participation, and increasing equality of individual opportunity due to movements for civil rights and women's rights. In other words, the book attempts to resolve a seeming paradox: How is it possible to have extreme corporate domination in a democratic country? This paradox is made all the more striking because in most other democratic countries, corporations do not have as much power. The wealth and income differences between people at the top and the bottom are smaller and the safety net for those who are poor, ill, or elderly is stronger. Why does the richest nation in the world also have the most poverty compared to Canada, Western Europe, and Japan? And why did all those gaps in wealth, income, and security increase between 1980 and 2008 (Baker 2007)?

Using a wide range of systematic empirical findings, this book shows how the owners and top-level managers of large companies work together to maintain themselves as the core of the dominant power group. Their corporations, banks, and agribusinesses form a *corporate community* that shapes the federal government on the policy issues of interest to it, issues that have a major impact on the income, job security, and well-being of most other Americans. At the same time, there is competition for profit opportunities within the corporate community; this can lead to highly visible policy conflicts among rival corporate leaders, conflicts that are sometimes fought out in Congress. Yet the corporate community is cohesive on the policy issues that affect its general welfare, which is often at stake when organized workers, liberals, or strong environmentalists organize sustained political challenges. The book therefore deals with another seeming paradox: How can a highly competitive group of business leaders cooperate enough to work their common will in the political and policy arenas?

None of this means the corporate chieftains have complete and total power, or that their success in each new policy conflict is a foregone conclusion, or that they never lose. For example, lawyers and other highly trained professionals with an interest in consumer or environmental issues have been able to use lawsuits, lobbying, or publicity to win governmental restrictions on some corporate practices and even to challenge whole industries. They also have had great success in winning millions of dollars for employees and consumers who have suffered from corporate wrongdoing, which led to efforts by corporate lawyers and Republicans to put limits on corporate liability. In addition, wage and salary workers, when they are organized into unions and have won the right to strike, can gain pay increases and such social benefits as health insurance. Even the most powerless of people occasionally develop the capacity to bring about some redress of their grievances through sit-ins, demonstrations, and other forms of strategic nonviolent disruption.

Moreover, one of the great triumphs of the Civil Rights Movement, the Voting Rights Act of 1965, began a process that made it possible for liberal, black-brown-white voting coalitions to challenge the corporate community in the electoral arena. Although this book demonstrates that the corporate community became even more powerful after the 1960s, in good part due to a reaction by many white Americans against the changes brought about by the civil rights, feminist, gay and lesbian, and other social movements, it also shows that the potential for limiting corporate power developed at the same time. The Democratic Party has been gradually transformed from the political arm of the Southern rich and big-city political machines to the party of corporate moderates, liberals, minorities, women, and labor unions. And thus another paradox: During the period from 1965 to 2007, when the salaries of top executives went from 42 times greater than an average worker's pay to 344 times as much, new political openings for egalitarian social change nonetheless developed, openings that were never exploited until 2008 (Anderson, Cavanagh, Collins, Pizzigati and Lapham 2008). The nature of these openings, and the reasons why liberals and labor are still not able to take full advantage of them, are explained throughout the book.

Partly because the owners and high-level managers within the corporate community share great wealth and common economic interests, but also due to the political opposition to their shared interests, they band together to develop their own social institutions—gated neighborhoods, private schools, exclusive social clubs, debutante balls, and secluded summer resorts. These social institutions create social cohesion and a sense of group belonging, a "we" feeling, and thereby mold the owners and top managers in the corporate community into a *social upper class*, which is described in Chapter 3. In addition, the corporate owners and managers compensate for the fact that they are few in number by financing and directing a wide variety of nonprofit organizations, such as tax-free foundations, think tanks, and policy-discussion groups, to aid them in developing policy alternatives that serve their interests. The highest-ranking employees in these nonprofit organizations, those who serve on the organizations' governing boards, become part of the *power elite*, the leadership group for the corporate community and the upper class. The composition of the power elite is explained in more detail at the end of Chapter 4.

Corporate owners and their top executives enter into the electoral arena first and foremost through their large campaign contributions to candidates in both political parties, especially in party primaries. They also provide financial support to a wide variety of patriotic, antitax, and single-issue organizations that celebrate the status quo and warn against "big government." Their efforts have led to pro-corporate presidents and a pro-corporate majority in both houses of Congress since corporations became the dominant institutions of American society in the 1870s. Historically, the pro-corporate majority in Congress consisted of Northern Republicans and Southern Democrats, but that arrangement changed gradually after the Voting Rights Act made it possible for a coalition of African-Americans and white liberals to push the most conservative Southern Democrats into the Republican Party. At the same time they slowly replaced eighteen other white conservative Democrats in House districts in the South with African-American legislators.

Since the last quarter of the twentieth century, due in part to the changes in the South, most corporate leaders have developed a strong preference for the Republican Party, where they are joined by a wide range of highly conservative middle-class Christian organizations concerned with a variety of social issues, including abortion, prayer in schools, and gay marriage. However, the moderate conservatives within the corporate community still maintain a significant presence in the Democratic Party, as most recently demonstrated by the major financial backing that they have provided to President Barack Obama since he first ran for the Senate in 2004.

The corporate community's ability to transform its economic power into policy influence and political access makes it the most important influence on the federal government. Historically, its key leaders have been appointed to top positions in the executive branch in both Republican and Democratic administrations. Its allies in Congress listen carefully to the policy recommendations proposed by the experts it employs at foundations, think tanks, and policy-discussion groups. This combination of economic power, policy expertise, and continuing political success makes the corporate owners and executives a *dominant class,* not in the sense of complete and absolute power, but in the sense that they have the power to shape the economic and political frameworks within which other groups and classes must operate. They therefore have won far more often than they have lost on the issues of concern to them, at least up until the end of the Bush Administration.

Despite their preponderant power in the federal government and the many necessary policies it carries out for them, leaders within the corporate community are constantly critical of it because of its potential independence and its ability to aid their opponents. They know they need government, but they also fear it, especially during times of economic crisis when they need it the most. Although the corporate community focuses its complaints on taxes and government spending, the deeper issue is power. In particular, its leaders are wary of the federal government due to its capacity to aid average Americans by (1) creating government jobs for the unemployed, which might make people less likely to take low-paying or dangerous positions in the private sector; (2) making health, unemployment, and social security benefits more generous, which also might make people less willing to work in low-paying jobs; (3) helping employees gain greater workplace rights and protections, which would make it more difficult to control the workplace; and (4) investing tax dollars in publicly controlled enterprises, which might compete with private corporations. The corporate community generally opposes all of these possibilities on the grounds that they might increase taxes, impede economic growth, or limit freedom. Most of all, however, corporate leaders oppose any government support for unions because unions are a potential organizational base for advocating a whole range of polices that threaten corporate power. In a phrase, *control of labor markets* is a crucial issue in the eyes of the corporate community.

In the context of the current economic crisis, the corporate community also is concerned that government leaders could take permanent control of the banks, mortgage companies, and automobile manufacturers it had to rescue in the last four months of 2008. Moderate conservatives within the corporate community are holding their breath and praising the efforts of the Obama Administration, but the ultraconservatives are loudly announcing their fear of "socialism," which is the term they use to express the fact that a strong government can control the economic sector, as it does in many countries that are far from socialist. They know that bailouts and financial rescues have occurred in the past—to save the fraudulently managed savings and loan industry in the 1980s, for example—but they worry that the current bailout may be too large and last too long for them to regain their former degree of dominance.

The corporate community's main opponents—union leaders, locally based environmental organizations, most minority-group communities, liberal churches, and liberal university communities—sometimes work together on policy issues as a *liberal-labor coalition*. However, this coalition is often extremely difficult to hold together because its members have divergent and sometimes clashing interests. It usually has far less money to spend on political campaigns than the corporate leaders, although this difference has been altered slightly because money in small sums can now be raised on the Internet. Despite the fact that unions have represented a declining percentage of working people since the 1950s, with a precipitous drop from 1975 to 1996 and the loss of several hundred thousand more members since that time, labor unions still had 15.7 million members at the end of 2008 (Greenhouse 2008). They remain the largest and best-financed part of the coalition. They also cut across racial and ethnic divisions more than any other institutionalized sector of American society.

Today, the liberal-labor coalition also includes a few men and women from well-to-do business and professional families who are critical of the corporate community despite their comfortable financial circumstances. This is often because they do not like—and in some cases fear—the alliance many corporate conservatives have forged with the Christian Right within the Republican Party. The presence of people from privileged social backgrounds in the liberal-labor camp suggests that unexpected formative experiences, including the shock of encountering extreme poverty, religious intolerance, or racial prejudice, can lead to liberal social and religious values that can be as important as class in shaping political orientations. Historically, there are many examples inside and outside the United States of liberal, reformist, and even revolutionary leaders who came from wealthy social backgrounds. The presence of wealthy liberals and leftists among the opponents to corporate dominance adds another level of complexity to the power equation: There is class domination in the United States, but not all members of the upper class support class domination.

The liberal-labor coalition enters into the electoral arena through the liberal wing of the Democratic Party, sometimes fielding candidates in party primaries to stake out its policy goals. Contrary to the strident warnings of ultraconservatives and the fond hopes of liberal commentators, this coalition never has had a major voice in the Democratic Party at the national level and never even had the possibility of such a voice when the Southern rich were a key element in the party. Although there is now the potential for new political openings, union leaders and liberals probably had more impact from the late 1930s to the early 1970s than they have had ever since. In the 1990s, unions spent tens of millions of dollars on political campaigns in presidential election years and by 2008 that figure had reached several hundred million, if all levels of government are included. They also deploy their paid organizers and members to work at the grass-roots level—making telephone calls, stuffing envelopes, and going door-to-door to get out the vote. However, their political clout has been hurt since the 1970s, not only by their decline in membership, but by the fact that many of their members disagreed with liberals over a variety of issues: affirmative action and busing, the Vietnam War, women in the workplace, and environmental protection. More-over, there are disagreements within the union movement itself over the degree to which it should function like a social movement and be more aggressive in its organizing efforts. Generally speaking, unions for service workers, teachers, and government employees often seek changes that have been resisted by some industrial and building trades unions, at least until very recently.

The liberal-labor coalition is sometimes aided by the organiz-ing and social movement skills of political leftists, who in the past played a significant role as socialists and communists in the struggle for women's suffrage in the Progressive Era, the building of industrial unions in the 1930s, and the development of the Civil Rights Move-ment in the 1960s. However, the leftists, who now tend to identify themselves as progressives, libertarian socialists, or anticapitalists, are also strong critics of the liberal-labor coalition because of their grave doubts about the possibility of reforming corporate capitalism to any significant degree. They also criticize the liberals for limiting themselves to an emphasis on improving representative democracy instead of pushing for more participatory democracy. In addition, they often support left-wing third parties with the hope of replac-ing the Democrats, a strategy strongly rejected by the liberal-labor coalition. Moreover, a small percentage of them believe that smash-ing windows, tearing down fences, and entering into confrontations with police units are useful tactics in some situations, as seen in what transpired at the demonstrations and rallies carried out by the global justice movement between 1999 and 2001 (e.g., Yuen, Burton-Rose and Katsiaficas 2001; Yuen, Burton-Rose and Katsiaficas 2004). As a result, there is a far larger and more contentious gap between the liberal-labor coalition and the various types of leftists than any dif-ferences that are present in the corporate–Christian Right coalition within the Republican Party.

The major policy conflicts between the corporate community and the liberal-labor coalition are best described as *class conflicts* because they concern the distribution of profits and wages, the rate and progressivity of taxation, the usefulness of labor unions, and the degree to which business should be regulated by government. The liberal-labor side wants corporations to pay higher wages to employees and higher taxes to government. It wants government to strengthen regulations on a wide range of business practices and help employees organize unions. The great majority in the corporate community rejects all these policy objectives, claiming they endanger the freedom of individuals and the efficient workings of the economic marketplace. The conflicts these disagreements generate can manifest themselves in many different ways: workplace protests, strikes, industry-wide boycotts, massive demonstrations in cities, pressure on Congress, and voting preferences.

Social conflict over abortion, same-sex marriage, gun control, and other social issues favored by liberals and vigorously opposed by strong conservatives are not part of this overall class conflict. They are separate issues related to genuine differences in moral values (Lakoff 1996). They also may relate to the very different outlooks toward life in general that characterize strong liberals and strong conservatives. These differences are not reducible to economics or the class structure, and they encompass more than political and social issues, but their origins are not fully understood (Altemeyer 1996; Jost and Sedanius 2004; Tomkins 1964). Whatever the way in which the various social issues are dealt with, they do not directly affect the power of the corporate community. However, they are an important part of the competition between the Republicans and Democrats in the electoral arena.

To help familiarize readers with the six main political orientations in the United States, Table 0.1 on page xviii presents the views of the Christian Right, ultraconservatives in the corporate community, moderate conservatives in the corporate community, trade unionists, liberals, and leftists on the key issues that differentiate them. The critical issues that separate the three conservative orientations from liberals, leftists, and organized labor are the conservatives' shared opposition to labor unions and their desire for the smallest possible involvement of government in the economy and everyday life. However, there are degrees of difference between corporate moderates and corporate ultraconservatives on support for social benefit programs such as Social Security and in their acceptance of liberal social initiatives such as abortion, affirmative action, and civil rights for gays and lesbians. These differences lead some moderate conservatives to feel more at home in the moderate wing of the Democratic Party, but it bears repeating that they are strongly opposed to unions even though they are Democrats. Thus, the Democratic Party has more fundamental disagreements internally than does the Republican Party.

Table 0.1 The Policy Preferences on Several Key Issues for Six Political Orientations

	Christian Right	Ultra-Conservatives	Moderate Conservatives	Trade Unionists**	Liberals	Leftists/Progressives
Favor private ownership and private profit?	yes	yes	yes	yes	yes	no
Oppose unions?	yes	yes	yes	no	no	no
Oppose government regulation?	yes	yes	yes*	no	no	no
Oppose government social benefits?	yes	yes	somewhat	no	no	no
Oppose liberal social agenda?	yes	yes	somewhat	no***	no	no

*With the important exception of environmental regulations, which they now accept.

**Some trade unionists are also liberals or leftists.

***In the past, some trade unionists opposed aspects of the liberal social agenda.

On the other side of the divide, the liberal, left, and trade unionist orientations are supportive of unions, seek greater government involvement in the economy, and advocate a liberal social agenda. However, as noted earlier, there is a major disagreement between the liberal-labor coalition and the leftists on the degree to which capitalism can be reformed to bring about greater economic equality and the usefulness of third parties, leading to very different economic programs and political strategies. These differences can cause conflicts that benefit the Republicans under some circumstances, as discussed in Chapter 6.

Neither the corporate community nor the liberal-labor coalition elicits the strong loyalty of a majority of the American population. They are therefore in constant competition for the allegiance of the general citizenry, most of whom are focused on the positive aspects of their everyday lives when things are running smoothly: love and concern for their families, the challenges of their jobs, or the enjoyment of a hobby or athletic activity. The typical American usually pays little attention to most policy issues, focuses on political candidates only around the time of elections, and has a mixture of liberal and conservative opinions that seems contradictory—and annoying—to the relative few who have strong conservative, liberal, or leftist orientations. As work based on a 2007 national survey puts it, Americans are conservative egalitarians. They are wary of big government and they cherish individual freedoms, but they are also supportive of many economic initiatives that are labeled as liberal, and they are willing to pay higher taxes so that everyone has better economic opportunities (Page and Jacobs 2009).

In the electoral arena, the importance of average centrist citizens—who usually define themselves as moderate Democrats or independents when it comes to political preferences—can be seen through surveys reporting the percentage of liberals and Democrats in the country. According to a 2008 survey by the Pew Research Center for the People and the Press, one of the largest and most reliable nonprofit polling organizations in the country, only 21 percent of Americans consider themselves liberals, compared to 36 percent who say they are moderates and 38 percent who describe themselves as conservatives; this is not very different from how they labeled themselves in 2000 and 2004 (Horowitz 2008). On the other hand, 39 percent of voters described themselves as Democrats in exit polls in 2008, 29 percent said they were independents, and 32 percent said they were Republicans, which means that President Barack Obama and other Democrats had to gain support from many moderate Democrats and independents in order to win a majority of the popular vote.

Many media commentators and popular pundits claim that most American citizens are apathetic and lacking in knowledge about the political process, but they are wrong. The cautious way in which ordinary citizens approach politics actually makes sense for several reasons. To start with, there are difficulties in bringing people into agreement on new policy initiatives, which can lead to endless meetings, interpersonal tensions, and frustration. Even when there is agreement on a new direction, it can take years to change policies at any level of government; it is therefore hard to maintain enthusiasm and momentum unless the situation is very dire. It thus seems more sensible and practical to focus on the many time-consuming necessities and pleasures of everyday life, those that have the virtue of leading to feelings of personal accomplishment and satisfaction. Put another way, the pull of everyday life is overwhelming for most people. But in times of turmoil, all bets are off. People pay attention and they express themselves clearly. The ongoing wars and the economic crisis have made the years 2009 through 2012 into a critical juncture during which the American public could play a significant role.

The usual focus on everyday life changed suddenly and unexpectedly in the 2006 congressional elections when independents turned against the war in Iraq and voted 59 percent for the Democrats and only 40 percent for the Republicans, creating liberal-leaning Democratic majorities in the House and Senate. In 2008 independents and new voters turned out in larger numbers to express their fears about the economy and their continuing distaste for the war by increasing the Democratic margins in both houses of Congress and by electing an articulate and open-minded centrist Democrat to the presidency. Does this mean that the corporate domination of the country might end, or that corporations might at least be tamed? Could a liberal-labor-left coalition have a real impact?

As you read this book sometime between 2009 and 2012, issues of economic reorganization and political strategy will be under debate left, right, and center, and the answers to the questions asked at the end of the previous paragraph will begin to appear. You will have a ringside seat as the drama unfolds, making it possible to see for yourself if the power analysis presented in this book has any accuracy or relevance. Or you may decide that you want to join the fray by contributing to one political movement or another, in which case you might end up shaping the power structure that will be analyzed in the 2013 edition of this book.

1

Class and Power in America

Class and *power* are terms that make Americans a little uneasy. Concepts such as *dominant class* and *power elite* immediately put people on guard. Even though there is widespread concern about the extent of corporate power, the idea that a relatively fixed group of privileged people might shape the economy and government for their own benefit goes against the American grain. But what exactly do everyday Americans and social scientists mean when they talk about class and power, and how do their views compare? This chapter answers those two questions. It also explains the methods used to study class and power, while providing a preliminary look at the American upper class and an outline of how the rest of the book will unfold.

WHAT IS A SOCIAL CLASS?

For most Americans, class implies that people have permanent stations in life, an idea they do not like because it flies in the face of beliefs about equality of opportunity and seems to ignore the evidence of upward social mobility. Even more, Americans tend to deny that classes might be rooted in wealth and occupational roles. They talk about social class, but with euphemisms like "the suits," "the blue bloods," "Joe Sixpack," and "the other side of the tracks."

American dislike for the idea of class is deeply rooted in the country's colonial and revolutionary history. Colonial America seemed very different from other countries to its new inhabitants because it was

1

a rapidly expanding frontier country with no feudal aristocracy or inherited social statuses. The sense of difference was heightened by the need for solidarity among all classes in the war for freedom from the British. Revolutionary leaders from the higher classes had to concede greater freedom and equality for common people to gain their support. A historian states the power equation succinctly: "Leaders who did not fight for equality accepted it in order to win" (Palmer 1959, p. 203). In other words, outside enemies bring a people together, at least for the time being.

Although large differences in wealth, income, and lifestyle already existed in revolutionary America, particularly in port cities and the South, these well-understood inequalities were usually explained away or downplayed by members of the middle classes as well as by the merchants, plantation owners, and lawyers who were at the top of the socioeconomic ladder. As shown by a historical study of diaries, letters, newspapers, and other documents of the period, Americans instead emphasized and took pride in the fact that any class distinctions were small compared with Europe. They recognized that there were rich and poor, but they preferred to think of their country "as one of equality, and proudly pointed to such features as the large middle class, the absence of beggars, the comfortable circumstances of most people, and the limitless opportunities for those who worked hard and saved their money" (Main 1965, pp. 239, 284).

The fact that nearly 20 percent of the population was held in slavery and that 100,000 Native Americans lived in the colonies as well was not part of this self-definition as a middle-class, egalitarian society (Mann 1993, p. 137). It is clear, however, that the free white majority nonetheless defined itself in opposition to the potentially dangerous slaves on the one hand and the allegedly warlike "savages" on the other. This made their shared "whiteness" a significant part of their social identity. In fact, race is another factor that makes the class-based nature of American society less salient than it might otherwise be.

Even members of the upper class preferred this more democratic class system to what had existed for many centuries in Europe. To emphasize this point, a study of the democratic revolutions in North America and Europe begins with a letter written from Europe in 1788 by a young adult member of a prominent American upper-class family. After the young man registered his disgust with the hereditary titles and pomp of the European class system, and with the obsequiousness of the lower classes, he stated his conviction that "a certain degree of equality is essential to human bliss." As if to make sure that the limits of his argument were clear, he underlined the words *a certain degree of equality*. He then went on to argue that the greatness of the United States was that it had provided this degree of equality "without destroying the necessary subordination" (Palmer 1959, p. 3). That is, class dominance should be as subtle and reasonable as possible.

Two hundred years later, in response to sociologists who wanted to know what social class means to Americans, a representative sample of the citizenry in Boston and Kansas City expressed ideas similar to those of the first Americans. Although most people were keenly aware of differences in social standing and judged status levels primarily in terms of income, occupation, and education (but especially income), they emphasized the openness of the system. They also argued that a person's social standing is in good part determined by such individual qualities as initiative and the motivation to work hard. Moreover, many of them felt the importance of class was declining. This belief was partly due to their conviction that people of all ethnic and religious backgrounds are being treated with greater respect and decency regardless of their occupational and educational levels, but even more to what they saw as material evidence for social advancement in the occupations and salaries of their families and friends. In short, a tradition of public social respect for everyone and the belief in social mobility (from which racial minorities were excluded until the last forty years) are also factors in making class less important in the everyday thinking of most white Americans (Coleman, Rainwater and McClelland 1978). People are very aware of basic economic and educational differences and they can size up social standing fairly well from such outward signs as speech patterns, mannerisms, and style of dress, but the existence of social classes is nonetheless passed over as quickly as possible.

People of the highest social status share the general distaste for talking about social class in an open and direct way. Nevertheless, they are very conscious of the fact that they and their friends are set apart from other Americans. In the study of Boston and Kansas City residents, an upper-class Bostonian said: "Of course social class exists—it influences your thinking." Then she added: "Maybe you shouldn't use the word 'class' for it, though—it's really a niche that each of us fits into" (Coleman, Rainwater and McClelland 1978, p. 25). In a classic study of social classes in New Haven, Connecticut, a person in the top category in terms of neighborhood residence and educational background seemed startled when asked about her class level. After regaining her composure, she replied: "One does not speak of classes; they are felt" (Hollingshead and Redlich 1958, p. 69). As part of a study of thirty-eight upper-class women in a large Midwestern city, a sociologist bluntly asked her informants at the end of the interview if they were members of the upper class. The answers she received had the same flavor of hesitation and denial:

> "I hate (the term) upper class. It's so non–upper class to use it. I just call it 'all of us,' those of us who are wellborn."
>
> "I hate to use the word 'class.' We're responsible, fortunate people, old families, the people who have something."
>
> "We're not supposed to have layers. I'm embarrassed to admit to you that we do, and that I feel superior at my social level. I like being part of the upper crust" (Ostrander 1980, pp. 78–79).

SOCIAL CLASS ACCORDING TO SOCIAL SCIENTISTS

Social scientists end up with just about the same understanding of social classes as do typical Americans, but only after two important theoretical issues are dealt with first. They begin with a crucial analytical distinction between *economic classes,* which consist of people who have a common position in the economic system, such as "business owners" or "employees," and *social classes,* which consist of people who interact with each other, develop in-group social organizations, and share a common lifestyle. They also stress that class is a relationship as well as a set of positions within the social structure. It is therefore a double-edged concept, so to speak, denoting both the relationship between people in different economic roles and the specific positions within the overall relationship. To use the earlier example once again, business owners and wage earners constitute separate economic classes, but the concept of class also encompasses the relationship between them.

The distinction between economic classes and social classes is important because class as an economic relationship is always operating as part of the social structure, but the people in any given economic position may or may not develop their own social organizations, live in the same neighborhoods, and interact socially. The degree to which a given economic class is also a social class therefore can vary widely from place to place and time to time, which matters because members of an economic class may be limited in the degree to which they can exercise political power if they do not think of themselves as being members of a social class with common interests (Weber 1998; Wright 1998).

The systematic study of whether or not people in a given economic position are also members of a social class begins with a search for connections among the people and organizations that are thought to constitute the social class. This procedure is called "membership network analysis," which boils down to a matrix in which social

Table 1.1 A Hypothetical Membership Network Using Schools and Clubs

Individuals	Organizations			
	School 1	*School 2*	*Club 1*	*Club 2*
Person 1	X			X
Person 2		X	X	
Person 3	X		X	X
Person 4		X	X	X
Person 5				

Note: Person 5 is an "isolate" with no connections. He or she is not part of the social class.

organizations such as schools and clubs are arrayed along one axis and individuals along the other. Table 1.1 provides a hypothetical example of such a matrix.

As can be seen in Table 1.1, the boxes, called *cells,* created by each intersection of a person and an organization, are filled in with information revealing whether or not the person is a member of that organization. This information is used to create two different kinds of networks, one organizational, the other interpersonal. An *organizational network* consists of the relationships among organizations, as determined by their common members. These shared members are usually called *overlapping* or *interlocking* members. An *interpersonal network,* on the other hand, reveals the relationships among individuals, as determined by their common organizational affiliations. (These and other methodological issues are explained further with the help of diagrams and tables in the document on "How to Do Power Structure Research" on www.whorulesamerica.net.)

To provide a more complete example of the type of analysis that appears throughout the book, suppose a researcher had the alumni lists for dozens of private schools and Ivy League universities, along with membership lists for many clubs and guest lists from debutante balls. By determining the names that overlap on two or more of these lists, it would be possible to determine which of these organizations are part of the same social network. In addition, it could be shown that the most central organizations in the network are determined by the fact that they share members with many other organizations, whereas a peripheral organization might have members in common only with organizations that are also one or two steps removed from the central organizations. Furthermore, some organizations may have no members in common with any of the others, which reveals that they are not part of the social network. In the end, those organizations that are part of the network would be defined as the social upper class.

A membership network analysis is in principle very simple, but it is theoretically important because it contains within it the two types of human relationships of concern in sociological theorizing: inter-personal relations and memberships in organizations. Thus, these networks contain a *duality of persons and groups* (Breiger 1974). For analytical purposes, the interpersonal and organizational networks are often treated separately, and some social scientists talk of different "levels of analysis," but in the reality of everyday life the two levels are always intertwined. Hence the useful phrase: a duality of persons and groups.

This network-based way of thinking about a social class as a duality of persons and groups fits well with earlier definitions of social class. For example, in one of the first empirical investigations of social class in America, a study of caste and class in a southern city in the 1930s, the sociological researchers defined a social class as:

> The largest group of people whose members have intimate access to one another. A class is composed of families and social cliques. The interrelationships between these families and cliques, in such informal activities as visiting, dances, receptions, teas, and larger informal affairs, constitute the structure of the social class. A person is a member of the social class with which most of his or her participations, of this intimate kind, occur (Davis, Gardner and Gardner 1941, p. 59n).

A political scientist who conducted a classic study of class and power in the city of New Haven, Connecticut, wrote that similar "social standing" is defined by "the extent to which members of that circle would be willing—disregarding personal and idiosyncratic factors—to accord the conventional privileges of social intercourse and acceptance among equals; marks of social acceptability include willingness to dine together, to mingle freely in intimate social events, to accept member-ship in the same clubs, to use forms of courtesy considered appropri-ate among social equals, to intermarry, and so on" (Dahl 1961, p. 229). A Marxist economist provides a similar definition when he concludes that a "social class, then, is made up of freely intermarrying families" (Sweezy 1953, p. 124).

As these converging definitions from different disciplines show, there is a general agreement among social scientists that there are social classes in America and that each of them has its own social orga-nizations, in-group activities, and common lifestyles. Indeed, it may be the only concept on which there is widespread agreement when it comes to studying power. The first problem for power analysts begins with the question of whether the top social class, the upper class, is also an economic class based in the ownership and control of large income-producing properties.

IS THERE AN AMERICAN UPPER CLASS?

If the owners and managers of large income-producing properties in the United States are also a social upper class, then it should be possible to discover a very large network of interrelated social institutions whose overlapping members are primarily wealthy families and high-level corporate leaders. These institutions should provide patterned ways of organizing the lives of their members from infancy to old age and create a relatively unique style of life. In addition, they should provide mechanisms for socializing both the younger generation and new adult members who have risen from lower social levels. If the class is a sociological reality, the names and faces may change somewhat over the years, but the social institutions that underlie the upper class must persist with only gradual change over several generations.

Four different types of empirical studies carried out several decades ago established the existence of such an interrelated set of social institutions and social activities in the United States to the point where there have been only a few new studies in recent years: historical case studies, quantitative studies of biographical directories, open-ended surveys of knowledgeable observers, and interview studies with members of the upper-middle and upper classes. Taken together, they suggest that the upper class includes somewhat less than 1 percent of the population, but for the purposes of keeping statistical analyses simple in this book, the figure 1 percent will be used. These studies not only demonstrate the existence of an American upper class. They also provide what are called *indicators* of upper-class standing, which are useful in determining the degree of overlap between the upper class and the corporate community, or between the upper class and various types of nonprofit organizations. Social indicators can be used to determine the amount of involvement members of the upper class have in various parts of the government as well.

In the first major historical case study, the wealthy families of Philadelphia were traced over the period of 200 years, showing how they created their own neighborhoods, schools, clubs, and debutante balls. Then their activities outside of that city were determined, which demonstrated that there are nationwide social institutions where wealthy people from all over the country interact with each other (Baltzell 1958). This study led to the discovery of an upper-class telephone directory called the *Social Register,* published for thirteen large cities from Boston to San Francisco between 1887 and 1975. The guide to the thirteen city volumes, the *Social Register Locator,* contained about 60,000 families, which made it a very valuable indicator of upper class standing until many members of the upper class lost interest in it in the 1970s. This loss of interest reminds us that customs can change in the upper class, just as they do in other classes, and that there is always a need for new studies.

Using information on private school attendance and club membership that appeared in 3,000 randomly selected *Who's Who in America* biographies, along with listings in the *Social Register,* another study provided a statistical analysis of the patterns of memberships and affiliations among dozens of prep schools and clubs. The findings from this study are very similar to those from the historical case study (Domhoff 1970, chapter 1). Still another study relied on journalists who cover upper-class social events as informants, asking them to identify the schools, clubs, and social directories that defined the highest level of society in their city. The replies from these well-placed observers revealed strong agreement with the findings from the historical and statistical studies (Domhoff 1970, chapter 1).

A fourth and final method of establishing the existence of upper-class institutions is based on intensive interviews with a cross-section of citizens. The most detailed study of this type was conducted in Kansas City. The study concerned people's perceptions of the social ladder as a whole, from top to bottom, but it is the top level that is of relevance here. Although most people in Kansas City can point to the existence of exclusive neighborhoods in suggesting that there is a class of "blue bloods" or "big rich," it is members of the upper-middle class and the upper class itself whose reports demonstrate that clubs and similar social institutions as well as neighborhoods give the class an institutional existence (Coleman, Rainwater and McClelland 1978). (The specific schools and clubs discovered by these and related investigations are listed in Appendix A.)

Although the social indicators derived from these studies are a useful tool for research purposes, they are far from perfect for any specific individual. They are subject to two different kinds of errors that tend to cancel each other out with large samples. *False positives* are those people who qualify as members of the upper class according to the indicators, even though further investigation would show that they are not really members. Middle-class and scholarship students at private secondary schools are one example of a false positive. Honorary and performing members of social clubs, who usually are members of the middle class, are another important type of false positive. *False negatives,* on the other hand, are people who do not seem to meet any of the criteria of upper class standing because they do not choose to list their private school or their club affiliations in biographical sources and shun social registries.

Private schools are especially underreported in publicly available biographical sources. Many prominent political figures do not list their private secondary schools in *Who's Who in America*, for example, and George H. W. Bush removed his from the 1980–1981 edition when he became vice president in the Reagan Administration. More generally, studies comparing private school alumni lists with *Who's Who* listings suggest that 40–50 percent of corporate officers and directors do not list their graduation from high-prestige private schools. Membership in social clubs may also go unreported. In a study of the 326 members of a prestigious private club with a nationwide membership who are listed in *Who's Who in America*, 29 percent did not include this affiliation (Domhoff 1983).

The factors leading to false positives and false negatives raise interesting sociological questions, some of which are given tentative answers in later chapters. Why are scholarship students sought by some private schools, and are such students likely to become part of the upper class? Why don't some members of the upper class list private schools and clubs in biographical sources? Why are some middle-class people taken into upper-class clubs? Merely to ask these questions is to suggest the complex social and psychological reality that lies beneath this seemingly dry catalogue of upper-class indicators. More generally, the information included or excluded in a social register or biographical directory is a *presentation of self* that has been shown to be highly revealing concerning religious, ethnic, and class identifications (e.g., Zweigenhaft and Domhoff 1982).

The most important false positive in the United States today is President Barack Obama, who graduated from Punahou School in Honolulu, one of the ten wealthiest private schools in the country, even though he is not a member of the upper class. He was able to attend Punahou because his maternal grandfather, a furniture salesman, and his maternal grandmother, one of the first female vice presidents in a large Honolulu bank, wanted him to have a good education. In addition, his grandfather's employer, an alumnus of the school, urged the admissions office to accept him (Mendell 2007, p. 36). As a result the future president spent eight years mingling with the children of wealthy business leaders and highly educated professionals (90 percent of the students were white) while receiving an excellent education in a setting very similar to prep schools elsewhere in the country. With its impressive theaters and buildings, situated on several acres of green fields surrounded by a fence, largely out of the public view, it is "so idyllic that it resembled a Hollywood set" according to the

Chicago Tribune reporter who visited the school as part of his research on a biography he wrote on President Obama (Mendell 2007, p. 37).

In addition to an ideal college preparatory education from a school that stands for quality and class in the eyes of college admissions officers, the future president developed valuable "connections" with individuals who possess wealth and other resources. Such connections are now called *social capital* by sociologists because wealthy friends and their parents can be helpful in many ways, such as putting in a good word with an employer, passing on useful information about investment opportunities, or even lending money for an investment. Perhaps even more important, President Obama acquired the style and tastes of the upper class, now called *cultural capital* because the right sensibilities can be useful in creating a sense of ease and familiarity when meeting members of the upper class (Bourdieu 1986).

In other words, President Obama's status as a false positive on one upper-class indicator provides useful information on why the son of a Kenyan father and a white mother (who worked in Indonesia as an anthropologist during his childhood and teen years) could think about a political career. After four years in Indonesia with his mother, stepfather, and half-sister, he lived in Honolulu from ages ten to eighteen in a white household where both of his (Republican) grandparents worked in business settings, so he was comfortable in the white middle class and took the possibility of a business career for granted. (In the first year after he finished his undergraduate education at Columbia University, he worked for Business International Corporation in Manhattan, which publishes newsletters on the global economy and provides consulting services to American companies with international operations [Mendell 2007, p. 62].).

Attending Punahou added something in addition to his familiarity with the white middle class: It gave him the opportunity to study in an elite white setting from the fifth through the twelfth grades, providing him with the social and cultural capital to interact with members of the corporate community and social upper class in a relaxed and graceful way. President Obama exudes a self-assured manner that resonates with other prep-school graduates. However, like many private school graduates who decide to pursue a career in politics, he does not list his graduation from a private school in his biographical sketch in *Who's Who in America*.

IS THE UPPER CLASS AN ECONOMIC CLASS?

It may seem obvious that members of the upper class must have large amounts of wealth if they can afford the tuition at private schools, the fees at country clubs, and the very high expenses of an elegant social life. However, it is a difficult matter to demonstrate that they do have greater ownership wealth than other people because the Internal Revenue Service does not release information on individuals and most people are not willing to volunteer details on this subject. The search has to begin with aggregate information on the wealth distribution, followed by the study of lists of rich individuals compiled from the work of journalists and biographers.

In considering the distribution of wealth in the United States, it first needs to be stressed that the wealth and income distributions are two different matters. The wealth distribution has to do with the concentration of ownership of *marketable assets*, which in most studies means real estate and financial assets (stocks, bonds, insurance, bank accounts) minus liabilities. The income distribution, on the other hand, has to do with the percentage of wages, dividends, interest, and rents paid out each year to individuals or families at various income levels. In theory, those who own a great deal may or may not have high incomes, depending on the returns they receive from their wealth, but in reality those at the very top of the wealth distribution also tend to have the highest incomes, mostly from dividends and interest.

Numerous studies show that the wealth distribution has been extremely concentrated throughout American history, with the top 1 percent owning 40–50 percent in large port cities in the nineteenth century (Kesiter 2005). It was fairly stable in the first seventy years of the twentieth century, although there were small declines in inequality in the aftermath of the New Deal and World War II, and then a further decline in the 1970s, in good part due to a fall in stock prices. (That is, most people did not become richer, but the wealthy lost some of their wealth, at least until the stock market went up again.) By the late 1980s, however, the wealth distribution was almost as concentrated as it had been in 1929, when the top 1 percent had 36.3 percent of all wealth. In 2004, the last year for which good estimates are available, the top 1 percent owned 34.3 percent of all marketable wealth (Wolff 2007, Table 2). Moreover, it is very likely that these figures are underestimates because there are ways to hide wealth, including secret bank accounts in other countries. In 2008, for example, the Internal Revenue Service forced a Swiss bank to close 18,000 American accounts containing $18 billion that was not disclosed on tax forms, thereby avoiding $300 million in taxes each year (Browning 2009).

Since none of the studies on wealth and income distributions include the names of individuals, other types of studies had to be done to demonstrate that people of wealth and high income are in fact members of the upper class. The most detailed study of this kind showed that nine of the ten wealthiest financiers at the turn of the twentieth century, and 75 percent of all families listed in a compendium of America's richest families, have descendants in the *Social Register*. Supplementing these findings, another study discovered that at least one-half of the ninety richest American men in 1900 have descendants in the *Social Register* and a study of ninety corporate directors worth $10 million or more in 1960 found that 74 percent met criteria of upper-class membership (Baltzell 1958; Domhoff 1967; Mills 1956). However, the degree of overlap between great wealth and membership in the upper class has attracted little further research attention because the earlier findings are now generally accepted.

These findings establish that the social upper class is an economic class based in the ownership and control of income-producing assets. However, they do not show that the upper class controls the corporate community, because stock holdings in any one company may be too dispersed to allow an individual or family to control it. This issue is dealt with extensively in Chapter 3.

WHAT IS POWER?

American ideas about power have their origins in the struggle for independence. What is not so well known is that these ideas owe as much to the conflict within each colony over the role of ordinary citizens as they do to the war itself. It is often lost from sight that the average citizens were making revolutionary political demands on their leaders as well as helping in the fight against the British. Before the American Revolution, governments everywhere had been based on the power and legitimacy of religious leaders, kings, self-appointed conventions, or parliaments. The upper-class American revolutionary leaders who drafted the constitutions for the thirteen states between 1776 and 1780 expected their handiwork to be debated and voted upon by state legislatures, but they did not want to involve the general public in a direct way.

Instead, it was members of the "middling" classes of yeoman farmers and artisans who gradually developed the idea out of their own experience that power is the possession of all the people and is delegated to government with their consent. They therefore insisted that special conventions be elected to frame each colony's constitution, and that the constitutions then be ratified by the vote of all free white males without regard to their property holdings. They were steeled in their resolve by their participation in the revolutionary struggle and by a fear of the potentially onerous property laws and taxation policies that might be written into the constitutions by those who were known at the time as their "betters." So the idea of the people as the constituent power of the new United States arose from the people themselves (Palmer 1959).

In the end, the middle-level insurgents only won the right to both a constitutional convention of elected delegates and a vote on subsequent ratification in Massachusetts in 1780. From that time forth, however, it has been widely agreed that "power" in the United States belongs to "the people." Since then every liberal, leftist, populist, or ultraconservative political group has claimed that it represents "the people" in its attempt to wrest arbitrary power from the "vested interests," the "economic elite," the "cultural elite," "the media," the "bureaucrats," or the "politicians in Washington." Even the Founding Fathers of 1789, who were far removed from the general population in their wealth, income, education, and political experience, did not try to promulgate their new constitution, designed to more fully protect private property and compromise some of their fundamental disagreements, without asking for the consent of the governed. In the process they were forced to add the Bill of Rights to ensure the constitution's acceptance. In a very profound cultural sense, then, no group or class has "power" in America, but only "influence." Any small group or class that has power over the people is therefore perceived as illegitimate. This may help explain why those with power in America always deny they have any (Vogel 1978, for a full analysis).

THE SOCIAL SCIENCE VIEW OF POWER

Most social scientists believe that power has two intertwined dimensions. The first involves the degree to which a community or nation has the capacity to perform effectively in pursuing its common goals, which is called *collective power*. Here, the stress is on the degree to which a collectivity has the technological resources, organizational forms, population size, and common spirit to achieve its goals. In that sense, many nations have become more powerful in recent decades than they were in the past, including the United States. Moreover, the collective power of the United States has grown because of its ability to assimilate immigrants of varying economic and educational levels from all over the world as productive citizens. The gradual acceptance of African-Americans into mainstream social institutions also has increased the nation's collective power.

The second dimension of power concerns the ability of a group or social class within a community or nation to be successful in conflicts with its rivals on issues of concern to it. Here, the stress is on *power over*, which is also called *distributive power*. Paralleling general American beliefs, most social scientists think of distributive power in the sense of great or preponderant influence, not in the sense of complete and absolute control. More specifically, a powerful group or class is one that can realize its goals even if some other group or class is opposed (Olsen and Marger 1993; Wrong 1995). This definition captures the sense of struggle that is embodied in the everyday meaning of power and it readily encompasses the idea of class conflict defined in the Introduction. It also fits with the main goal of this book, which is to show that a social upper class of owners and high-level executives has the power to institute the policies it favors even in the face of organized opposition from the liberal-labor coalition.

Generally speaking, the ability of a group or class to prevail begins in one of the four major social networks—economic, political, military, and religious—that can be turned into a strong organizational base for wielding power (Mann 1986). Although economic and political networks have been the main power networks in the United States for historical reasons that are discussed in Chapter 8, the four power networks have combined in several different ways in other countries to create widely varying power structures. For example, military force has led to the capture of the government and control of the economic system in many countries past and present. In other countries, such as Iran in the 1970s, a well-organized religious group has been able to develop popular support and demonstrate the ability to exercise force if need be in maintaining control over the government.

Due to the variety of power outcomes that the historical record provides, most social scientists believe there is no one fundamental basis for distributive power from which the other types of power can be derived. The four basic power networks have existed since hunting and gathering societies developed and they have always been intertwined (Gendron and Domhoff 2009, pp. 194–196). This means that the concept of distributive power is a fundamental one in the social sciences, just as energy is a fundamental concept in the natural sciences for the same reason: No one form of energy or power is more basic than any other (Russell 1938; Wrong 1995).

However, a definition of distributive power does not explain how a concept is to be measured. In the case of distributive power, it is seldom possible to observe interactions that reveal its operation even in small groups, let alone to see something as large and diffuse as a social class producing effects on another social class. People and organizations are what can be seen in a power struggle within a community or nation, not rival social classes, although it may turn out that the people and organizations represent the interests of social classes. It is therefore necessary to develop what are called *indicators of power*.

Although distributive power is first and foremost a relationship between two or more contending groups or classes, for research purposes it is useful to think of distributive power as an underlying trait or property of a group or social class. As with any underlying trait that cannot be observed directly, it is measured by a series of indicators, or signs, that bear a probabilistic relationship to it. This means that not all of the indicators necessarily appear each and every time the trait is manifesting itself. It might make this point more clear to add that the personality traits studied by psychologists to understand individual behavior and the concepts developed to explain findings in the natural sciences have a similar logical structure. Whether a theorist is concerned with friendliness, as in psychology, or magnetism, as in physics, or power, as in the case of this book, the nature of the investigatory procedure is the same. In each case, there is an underlying concept whose presence can be inferred only through a series of diagnostic signs or indicators that vary in their strength under differing conditions. Research proceeds, in this view, through a series of *if-then* statements based on as many independent indicators as possible. *If* a group is powerful, *then* at least some of the indicators of power should be measurable in some circumstances (Lazarsfeld 1966, for a classic statement of this approach).

THREE POWER INDICATORS

Since an indicator of power may not necessarily appear or be measurable in each and every instance where power is operating, it is necessary to have several indicators. Working within this framework, three different types of power indicators are used in this book. They are called (1) Who benefits? (2) Who governs? and (3) Who wins? Each of these empirical indicators has its own strengths and weaknesses. However, the potential weaknesses of each indicator do not present a serious problem because all three of them have to point to the owners and managers of large income-producing property as the most powerful class for the case to be considered convincing.

Who Benefits?

Every society has material objects and experiences that are highly valued. If it is assumed that everyone would like to have as great a share of these good things of life as possible, then their distribution can be utilized as a power indicator. Those who have the most of what people want are, by inference, the powerful. Although some value distributions may be unintended outcomes that do not really reflect power, the general distribution of valued experiences and objects within a society still can be viewed as the most publicly visible and stable outcome of the operation of power.

In American society, for example, wealth and well-being are highly valued. People seek to own property, to have high incomes, to have interesting and safe jobs, to enjoy the finest in travel and leisure, and to live long and healthy lives. All of these "values" are unequally distributed, and all may be utilized as power indicators. In this book, however, the primary focus with this type of indicator is on the wealth and income distributions. This does not mean that wealth and income are the same thing as power. Instead, high income and the possession of great wealth are simply visible signs that a class has power in relation to other classes.

The argument for using value distributions as power indicators is strengthened by studies showing that such distributions vary from country to country, depending upon the relative strength of rival political parties and trade unions. One study reported that the degree of inequality in the income distribution in Western democracies varied inversely with the percentage of social democrats who had been elected to the country's legislature in the first three decades after 1945. The greater the social democratic presence, the greater the amount of income that goes to the lower classes (Hewitt 1977).[*] In a study based on eighteen Western democracies in the same era, it was found that strong trade unions and successful social democratic parties are correlated with greater equality in the income distribution and a higher level of welfare spending (Stephens 1979). Thus, there is evidence that value distributions do vary depending on the relative power of contending groups or classes.

Closer to home and the present moment, the highly concentrated wealth distribution highlighted earlier in this chapter provides the first piece of evidence that the American upper class is a dominant class. The fact that the top 1 percent of households (the upper class) own 34.3 percent of all marketable assets and that the next 9 percent, most of whom are high-level managers, professionals, successful small business owners, professional athletes, and entertainers, own 36.9 percent, means that 10 percent of the population owns 71.2 percent of all marketable assets. This leaves 28.8 percent for the 90 percent of the people who are lower-level managers, supervisors, teachers, clerical workers, production workers, and service workers (Wolff 2007, Table 2). These numbers provide a stark x-ray of the distribution of power in the United States. In addition, the increasing concentration of both the wealth and income distributions between the 1980s and 2004 implies that the upper class

[*]Social democrats come from a tradition that began with a socialist orientation and then moved in a more reformist direction. For the most part, social democratic parties have only slightly more ambitious goals than the liberal-labor coalition in the United States; the left wing of the liberal-labor coalition would feel at home in a strong social democratic party in Western Europe.

and corporate community gained increasing power over everyday wage earners during that time period. (You can read the document "Wealth, Income, and Power" on www.whorulesamerica.net to learn more details on the wealth and income distributions and their relationship to power.)

The ratio of average yearly income for chief executive officers (usually called CEOs) of major corporations compared to average factory workers is another excellent indicator in the *Who benefits?* category. As briefly mentioned in the Introduction, this ratio rose from 42:1 in 1960 to 344:1 in 2007. The ratio was even higher in 2007 for the managers of private investment funds, where the average annual earnings for the top officers at the fifty largest firms was $588 million— that's 19,000 times as much as the average worker (Anderson et al. 2008). At that point, Wall Street financiers truly were the rulers of the universe.

Who Governs?

Power also can be determined by studying who occupies important institutional positions and takes part in important decision-making groups. If a group or class is highly overrepresented or underrepresented in relation to its proportion of the population, it can be inferred that the group or class is relatively powerful or powerless, as the case may be. For example, if a class that contains 1 percent of the population has 30 percent of the important positions in the government, which is thirty times as many as would be expected by chance, then it can be inferred that the class is powerful. Conversely, if it is found that women are in only a small percentage of the leadership positions in government, even though they make up a majority of the population, it can be inferred that women are relatively powerless in that important sector of society. Similarly, if it is determined that a minority group has only a small percentage of its members in leadership positions, even though it comprises 10 to 20 percent of the population in a given city or state, then the basic processes of power—inclusion and exclusion— are inferred to be at work.

This indicator is not perfect because some official positions may not really possess the power they are thought to have, and some groups or classes may exercise power from "behind the scenes." Once again, however, the case for the usefulness of this indicator is strengthened by the fact that it has been shown to vary over time and place. For example, the decline of landed aristocrats and the rise of business leaders in Great Britain has been charted through their degree of representation in Parliament (Guttsman 1969). Then, too, as women, African-Americans, Latinos, and Asian-Americans joined movements to demand a greater voice in the Unites States in the 1960s and 1970s, their representation in positions of authority began to increase (Zweigenhaft and Domhoff 2006).

Who Wins?

There are many issues over which the corporate community and the liberal-labor coalition disagree, including taxation, unionization, and business regulation. Power can be inferred on the basis of these issue conflicts by determining who successfully initiates, modifies, or vetoes policy alternatives. This indicator, by focusing on relationships between the two rival coalitions, comes closest to approximating the process of power contained in the formal definition. It is the indicator preferred by most social scientists. For many reasons, however, it is also the most difficult to use in an accurate way. Aspects of a decision process may remain hidden, some informants may exaggerate or downplay their roles, and people's memories about who did what often become cloudy shortly after the event. Worse, the key concerns of the corporate community may never arise as issues on the political agenda because it has the power to keep them in the realm of *non-issues* (i.e., most people know there is a problem, but it is never addressed in the political arena) through a variety of means that are discussed in Chapter 5.

Despite the difficulties in using the *Who wins?* indicator of power, it is possible to provide a theoretical framework for analyzing governmental decision-making that mitigates many of the methodological problems. This framework encompasses the various means by which the corporate community attempts to influence both the government and the general population in a conscious and planned manner, thereby making it possible to assess its degree of success very directly. More specifically, there are four relatively distinct but overlapping processes (discovered by means of membership network analysis) through which the corporate community tries to control the public agenda and win policy victories on the issues that do appear on it. These processes are based in four power networks, which are discussed in more detail in later chapters.

1. The *special-interest process* deals with the narrow and short-run policy concerns of wealthy families, specific corporations, and specific business sectors. It operates primarily through lobbyists, company lawyers, and trade associations, with a focus on congressional committees, departments of the executive branch, and regulatory agencies. The lobbyists are often former elected officials or former aides and advisers

to elected officials who can command very large salaries in the private sector because their information and connections are so valuable to corporations.

2. The *policy-planning process* formulates the general interests of the corporate community. It operates through a policy-planning network of foundations, think tanks, and policy-discussion groups, with a focus on the White House, relevant congressional committees, and the high-status newspapers and opinion magazines published in New York and Washington. It is the place where corporate leaders meet with academic experts and former government officials to discuss differences and prepare themselves for government appointments.

3. The *opinion-shaping process* attempts to influence public opinion and keep some issues off the public agenda. Often drawing on policy positions, rationales, and statements developed within the policy-planning process, it operates through the public relations departments of large corporations, general public relations firms, and many small opinion-shaping organizations, which direct their attention to middle-class voluntary organizations, educational institutions, and the mass media. Many advertising executives, former journalists, and former government officials are employed by the organizations in this network. Sometimes the process works through harsh media attacks on opponents of the corporate community.

4. The *candidate-selection process* is concerned with the election of politicians who are sympathetic to the agenda put forth in the special-interest and policy-planning processes. It operates through large campaign donations and hired political consultants; it is focused on the presidential campaigns of both major political parties and the congressional campaigns of the Republican Party.

Taken together, the people and organizations that operate in these four networks constitute the political-action arm of the corporate community and upper class. Building on the structural economic power of the corporate community, which is explained in the next chapter, and the status power of the upper class, which is explained in Chapter 3, and then the expert power developed within the policy planning network, which is explained in Chapter 4, this political-action arm is the final step on the path to corporate and class domination of the federal government.

WHAT DO OTHER SOCIAL SCIENTISTS THINK?

Although most sociologists and political scientists agree that the corporate community has had more influence than any other group in American society in recent decades, many doubt that the owners and managers of these corporations have the policy cohesion, scope of vision, and degree of power to be considered a dominant class. They tend to favor one of three alternative theoretical perspectives—*pluralism, historical institutionalism*, or *elite theory*. Based on studies of the relationship between public opinion and government decisions, pluralists argue that the general public has power on many issues through forming into interest groups that shape public opinion and lobby elected officials. They point to the successes of non-business groups, such as labor unions from the 1930s to the 1960s, or environmentalists and consumer advocates in the 1970s, as evidence for their claim. Even more important, citizens are said to have the power to influence the general direction of public policy by voting for the candidates and political parties that are sympathetic with their preferences. Most pluralists also believe that corporate leaders are too divided among themselves to dominate government. They further claim there are divisions between owners and managers of large corporations and that corporations are only organized into narrow interest groups that sometimes argue among themselves.

Approaching the matter from a different angle, historical institutionalists assert that predominant power is located in government, not in the general citizenry or a dominant social class. Following European usage, advocates of this theory often employ the phrase "the state" rather than "government" to emphasize the government's independence from the rest of society. This state independence, usually called "autonomy," is said to be due to several intertwined factors: (1) the state's monopoly on the legitimate use of force within the country; (2) its unique role in defending the country from foreign rivals; and (3) its regulatory and taxing powers. Thanks to these powers, government officials can enter into coalitions with those social classes or interest groups in society that share the same goals as the state at that juncture. Historical institutionalists also argue that independent experts, who have few or no connections to corporations or labor unions, can be powerful because they have information that is valuable to state officials. In the final analysis, historical institutionalists, who also call themselves *state autonomy theorists,* conclude that government officials have the capacity to impose their views on the corporate community and the rest of society no matter how united the corporate leaders or citizen groups might be.

The third alternative, elite theory, intersects with class-dominance theory, agreeing with it on some crucial points, but disagreeing on others. Elite theorists begin with the idea that all modern societies are dominated by the leaders (called *elites*) of large bureaucratically structured organizations, whether corporate, nonprofit, or governmental. The people who hold these top positions have the money, time, contacts with other organizations, and authority over lower-level employees to shape political and many other outcomes outside their organizations. Although corporations are one important power base according to elite theorists, they do not see the corporate community as predominant over other organizational leaders in the United States, as class-dominance theorists do. More generally, elite theory puts far less emphasis on classes and class conflict than a class-dominance theory does.

Because the analysis presented in this book challenges some basic American beliefs and is met with skepticism by those who hold to one of the three competing theories, it is necessary to proceed in a deliberate fashion, defining each concept as it is introduced, and then providing empirical examples of how each part of the system works. By approaching the problem in this manner, readers can draw their own conclusions at each step of the way and decide for themselves if they think the argument fails at some point.

HERE'S THE PLAN

Using membership network analysis as a starting point, each chapter presents one aspect of a cumulative argument. The next chapter provides evidence for the existence of a nationwide corporate community that includes Wall Street banks, military contractors, agribusinesses, accounting firms, and corporate law firms as well as large and well-known corporations like ExxonMobil, General Electric, and IBM. Chapter 3 uses alumni lists, club lists, and memberships in other social organizations to show that the owners and top-level executives in the corporate community form a socially cohesive and clearly demarcated upper class that has created its own social world and a distinctive lifestyle. The chapter argues that the social bonds developed by the corporate owners and managers merge with their common economic interests to make it easier for them to overcome policy disagreements when they meet in the policy-planning network. In a phrase, social cohesion helps bring about policy cohesion.

Chapter 4 demonstrates that members of the intertwined corporate community and social upper class finance and direct a network of foundations, think tanks, and policy discussion groups that provides policies and plans to deal with newly emerging problems faced by the corporate community. It is through involvement in the policy-planning network that corporate leaders gain an understanding of general issues beyond the confines of their own narrow business problems, discuss policy alternatives that are in their interests as a class, and come to know and work with specialists and experts on a wide range of topics. Chapter 5 describes how several of the organizations in the policy-planning network link with public relations firms, the public affairs departments of large corporations, and middle-class voluntary groups in an effort to reinforce the individualistic and antigovernment dimensions of the American value system, thereby trying to influence public opinion on specific issues.

Chapter 6 explains the nature of the American electoral system and why it is not as responsive to the preferences of the general public as the electoral systems in other democratic countries. It also explains why campaign donations can play an important role in American politics, making support from wealthy donors essential for a successful candidacy at the national level and in highly populated states. It pays special attention to the major corporate fundraisers for President Obama.

Chapter 7 examines the network-based processes through which corporate leaders are able to dominate the federal government in Washington on issues of interest to them. It begins with an examination of the special-interest process, but it only provides a few examples of how it operates because all theorists agree that such a process exists and that corporations have the predominant role within it. The chapter then outlines the several avenues through which the results of the policy-planning process are incorporated into government policy. It next examines the social, educational, and occupational backgrounds of Cabinet appointments and top staff appointments in the White House, showing that they have come disproportionately from the corporate community and policy-planning network. It goes into detail regarding top appointments in the Obama Administration to show that there are significant differences with those of past administrations.

Chapter 8 summarizes the theoretical framework that fits best with these findings, the *class-domination* theory, and then discusses the empirical shortcomings of pluralism, historical institutionalism, and elite theory. It also explains why the corporation-based upper class is so powerful in the United States compared to other industrialized democracies by examining American and European history within the framework of the four interrelated organizational networks mentioned earlier in the chapter: economic networks, political networks, military networks, and religious networks.

Chapter 9 explains the transformations in American politics that have brought the country to its present juncture. It briefly overviews some of the issues that will give an indication of which way the Obama Administration is leaning in the conflicts between the corporate community and the liberal-labor coalition. It discusses the positions on various issues that the liberal-labor coalition might be advocating. Many readers may know the outcome of some of these arguments by the time they read this book.

2

The Corporate Community

It may seem a little strange at first to think about the several hundred big corporations that sit astride the American economy as any sort of community, but in fact corporations have many types of connections and common bonds. They include shared ownership, longstanding patterns of supply and purchase, the use of the same legal, accounting, advertising, and public relations firms, and common (overlapping) members on the boards of directors that have final responsibility for how corporations are managed. Then, too, large corporations share the same goals and values, especially the profit motive. As noted in the introduction, they also develop a closeness because they are all opposed and criticized to some degree by the labor movement, liberals, leftists, strong environmentalists, and other types of anticorporate activists.

For research purposes, the *interlocks* created when a person sits on two or more corporate boards are the most visible and accessible of the ties among corporations. Since one's membership on a board of directors is public information, it is possible to use membership network analysis to make detailed studies of interlocking patterns extending back into the early nineteenth century. The organizational network uncovered in these studies provides a rigorous research definition for the term *corporate community*: It consists of all those profit-seeking organizations connected into a single network by overlapping directors.

However, it is very important not to overstate the actual importance of these interlocks. They are valuable for the dissemination of organizational innovations among corporations; they give the people who are members of several boards a very useful overview of the corporate community as a whole; they contribute to political cohesion; and they seem to have modest effects on some of the financial practices of the interlocked corporations (Burris 2005; Mizruchi 1992; Mizruchi 1996). But for purposes of this book, corporate interlocks should be thought of as one of the starting points that outsiders can use to understand the overall corporate community.

Once the bare outlines of the corporate community are established through an examination of interlocking directorates, it is possible to extend the membership network analysis to find the other types of organizational affiliations maintained by corporate directors. Such studies show that members of the corporate community create two types of organizations for purposes of relating to each other and government. First, they develop trade associations made up of all the businesses in a specific industry or sector of the economy. Thus, there is the American Petroleum Institute, the American Bankers Association, the National Association of Home Builders, and hundreds of similar organizations that focus on the narrow interests of their members and bring their concerns to government through the special-interest process discussed briefly at the end of the previous chapter.

Second, the corporate community is pulled even closer together by several overarching business associations that look out for its general interests and play a role in the policy-planning process that will be discussed in Chapter 4: the National Association of Manufacturers, the U.S. Chamber of Commerce, the Conference Board, the Business Council, and the Business Roundtable. In the case of the National Association of Manufacturers and its many state affiliates, for example, its foremost concern since 1903 had been all-out opposition to labor unions in any part of the economy. It routinely opposes any increase in the minimum wage or any other legislation that might give more power to its employees. In early 2009, it resisted two bills introduced into the House of Representatives to deal with pay discrimination against women on the grounds that they would "open the floodgates to unwarranted litigation against employers at a time when businesses are struggling to retain and create jobs" (Pear 2009). The U.S. Chamber of Commerce encompasses all American businesses, not just manufacturing, and is therefore much larger in size and reaches into more communities through its state and local affiliations than does the National Association of Manufacturers, with which it shares many views in common.

The Conference Board has a fact-gathering and information-dissemination role, publishing many studies about business conditions and consumer confidence of interest to all members of the community.

The Business Council, on the other hand, is primarily an occasion for formal but off-the-record meetings with top appointees in the executive branch of the federal government. As for the Business Roundtable, it is the organization that has coordinated the corporate community against a wide range of challenges from the liberal-labor coalition since the 1970s. In 2008, the Business Council, with 112 members, and the Business Roundtable, with 143, shared 53 members in common.

The close relationships among these five general corporate groups has been demonstrated through studies of their overlapping directors (Burris 2008). However, the relationships are even closer than individual director interlocks show because there are numerous company-based interlocks among these five organizations as well. That is, one top executive of a corporation may be a director of one organization and another executive may be a director of one of the other organizations. Company-based interlocks show that vice presidents and legal advisers from the largest corporations, especially vice presidents for public relations or government relations, along with chief executive officers in smaller companies, direct the National Association of Manufacturers and the U.S. Chamber of Commerce. In 2008, six companies had top officers on the boards of four of the five groups: AT&T, Dow Chemical, Merck (pharmaceuticals), Pfizer (pharmaceuticals), PricewaterhouseCoopers (a worldwide accounting firm), and State Farm Insurance.

Studies of individual and company-based interlocks, in conjunction with case-study information, establish that the Business Roundtable is at the center of this five-group network. It is command central in the corporate community. It is also central in the policy-planning network discussed in Chapter 4. Its viewpoints and impacts will come up later in this chapter and in other chapters as well.

THE UNEXPECTED ORIGINS OF THE CORPORATE COMMUNITY

Standard historical accounts sometimes suggest that the first American businesses were owned by individual families and only slowly evolved into large corporations with common ownership and many hired managers. In fact, the corporate community had its origins in jointly owned companies in the textile industry in New England in the late eighteenth and early nineteenth centuries. At that time the common directors reflected the fact that a small group of wealthy Boston merchants were joining together in varying combinations to invest in new companies. By 1845 a group of eighty men, known to historians as the "Boston Associates," controlled thirty-one textile companies that accounted for 20 percent of the nationwide textile industry. They also had a large role in financing the early railroads. Seventeen of these men served as directors of Boston banks that owned 40 percent of the city's banking capital, twenty were directors of six insurance companies, and eleven sat on the boards of five railroad companies (Dalzell 1987).

Meanwhile, wealthy investors in other major cities were creating commonly owned and directed companies as well. In New York, for example, the ten largest banks and ten largest insurance companies in 1816 were linked into one network; ten of the companies had from 11 to 26 interlocks, six had 6 to 10 interlocks, and four had 1 to 5 interlocks. In 1836, all but two of the twenty largest banks, ten largest insurance companies, and ten largest railroads were linked into one common network, with twelve of the thirty-eight companies having an amazing 11 to 26 interlocks, ten having 6 to 10 interlocks, and sixteen having 1 to 5 interlocks. Even at that time, which is often romanticized as one of small businesses, the ten largest banks had 70 percent of the bank assets in New York City and 40 percent of the bank assets in the entire state (Bunting 1983).

These big-city networks of financial companies and railroads persisted in roughly their mid-century form until they were transformed between 1895 and 1904 by a massive merger movement, which created a national corporate network that included huge industrial corporations for the first time (Roy 1983). Until that point, industrial companies had been organized as partnerships among a few men or families. They tended to stand apart from the financial institutions and the stock market. Detailed historical and sociological studies of the creation of this enlarged corporate community reveal no economic efficiencies that might explain the relatively sudden incorporation of industrial companies. Instead, it seems more likely that industrial companies adopted the corporate form of organization for a combination of economic, legal, and sociological reasons. The most important of these reasons seem to be a need to (1) regulate the competition among them that was driving down profits and (2) gain better legal protection against the middle-class reformers, populist farmers, and socialists who had mounted an unrelenting critique of "the trusts," meaning agreements among industrialists to fix prices, divide up markets, and/or share profits (Roy 1997). When trusts were outlawed by the Sherman Antitrust Act of 1890, which was coincidentally followed by a major depression and many strikes by angry workers, the stage was set for industrialists to resort to the legal device called a corporation.

Several studies show that the corporate community remained remarkably stable after the merger movement ended. Since then it always has included the largest corporations of the era, and until very recently financial companies tended to be at the center. Three changes in the patterns of corporate interlocks between 1904 and the present seem to reflect gradual economic and financial changes. First, railroads became more peripheral as they gradually declined in economic importance. Second, manufacturing firms became more central as they increased in economic importance. Third, as corporations became more independent of banks, the banks became less likely to place their top officers on non-bank boards and more likely to receive officers of non-bank corporations on their own boards; this reversal of flow may reflect the gradual transformation of commercial banks from major power centers to places of coordination and communication (Mizruchi 1982; Mizruchi and Bunting 1981).

In short, large American businesses always have been owned and controlled by groups of well-to-do people who share common economic interests and social ties even more than kinship ties. Moreover, the deposits and premiums held by banks and insurance companies for ordinary people were used for investment purposes and the expansion of corporations from the beginning. Then too, control of corporations by directors and high-level executives is an early feature of the American business system, not a change that occurred when stockholders allegedly lost control of companies to bankers or managers in the first half of the twentieth century (Bunting 1987). Contrary to the traditional claim by many social scientists that corporate growth and restructuring are sensible and efficient responses to changing technology and markets, a claim that leaves no room for any concern with power, historical and sociological research suggests that big corporations are a response to legal changes and class conflict even though it is also true that improvements in transportation and communication made such changes possible (Roy 1997).

Before taking a detailed look at the corporate community of today, it is necessary to say a few words about the board of directors.

THE BOARD OF DIRECTORS

The board of directors is the official governing body of the corporation. Usually composed of 10 to 15 members, it meets for a day or two at a time about ten times a year and receives reports and other information between meetings. Various board committees meet periodically with top managers as well. A smaller executive committee of the board often meets more frequently and the most important individual members are sometimes in daily contact with the management that handles the day-to-day affairs of the corporation. The major duty of the board of directors is to hire and fire high-level executives, but it also is responsible for accepting or rejecting significant policy changes. Boards seem to play their most critical role when there is conflict within management, when the corporation is in economic distress, or when there is the possibility of a merger or acquisition.

The board is the official governing body, but the company executives on the board, who are called *inside directors*, sometimes play the main role in shaping the board's decisions. These inside directors, perhaps in conjunction with two or three of the non-management directors (called *outside directors*), are able to set the agenda for meetings, shape board thinking on policy decisions, and select new outside directors. In those situations, the board may become little more than a rubber stamp for management, with the top managers having great influence in naming their successors in running the company.

Although the exact role of the board varies from corporation to corporation, boards of directors in general embody the complex power relations within the corporate community. In addition to their role in selecting high-level management and dealing with crises, their importance manifests itself in a number of ways. They speak for the corporation to the rest of the corporate community and to the public at large. New owners demand seats on boards to consolidate their positions and to have a "listening post." Electing the top officers of rival corporations to each other's boards may signal the end of conflicts over hostile merger attempts. Commercial bankers may seek seats on boards to keep track of their loans and to ensure that future business will be directed their way. The chief executives of leading companies take time from their busy schedules to be on two or three other boards because it is a visible sign that their advice is respected outside their home company. Their board memberships also provide them with general intelligence on the state of the business world. Then, too, the presence of investment bankers, corporate lawyers, and academic experts on a board is a sign that the corporations respect their expertise. The presence of a university president, former government official, well-known woman, or highly visible minority group leader is a sign that their high status and respectability are regarded as valuable to the image of the corporation, especially when it is being criticized for racial or gender discrimination (Zweigenhaft and Domhoff 2006, chapters 2–4; Zweigenhaft and Domhoff 1982, chapter 2).

Boards of directors are important for another reason. In the broadest sense, they are the institutionalized interface between corporations and the upper class in the United States, a crucial point that is overlooked or denied by pluralists and other theorists who claim that class power has been displaced by organizational power. Because of this role, boards of directors are one of the means by which the book attempts to synthesize a class-based theory and insights from organizational theory. From the standpoint of organizational theory, boards are important because they allocate scarce resources, deal with situations where there is uncertainty, and link with other organizations that are important to the organization's future success. The organizational perspective is represented on the board of directors by the inside directors, who are full-time employees of the corporation. They are concerned with organizational survival and therefore make sure that any new initiatives have a minimal effect on routine functioning. They see outside directors as the "ambassadors" of the organization, who help to reduce uncertainty in the organization's environment (DiTomaso 1980).

Outside directors, who are also members of other large-scale profit-making enterprises or wealthy members of the upper class, represent the class perspective on the board. They want to ensure that any given corporation's new policy proposals fit well with their other profit-making opportunities and do not jeopardize general public acceptance in the political realm. Outside directors have a number of "resources" that make it possible for them to represent a class perspective: their own wealth, their connections to other corporations and nonprofit organizations, their general understanding of business and investment, and their many connections to other wealthy people, fundraisers, and politicians. Such resources make it possible for them to have a very real impact when new leadership must be selected or new policy directions must be undertaken (Ostrander 1987).

THE CORPORATE COMMUNITY TODAY

The American economy is large and grew larger every year until 2008. According to a comprehensive survey for the year 2000, there were an estimated 5.5 million corporations, 2.0 million partnerships, and 17.7 million non-farm proprietorships, almost double the number of businesses in 1980. However, the ownership and control of these economic assets was highly concentrated, as first of all demonstrated by the fact that only 8,300 companies, constituting a mere 0.015 percent of the total number of businesses, had 1,000 or more employees; this handful of companies accounted for 44 percent of all private-sector employees. Even more striking, 500 companies, the heart of the corporate community, earned 57 percent of all profits while employing 16.3 percent of the private-sector workforce (White 2002).

The extent of economic concentration in the United States can be seen in the extreme case of commercial banks, which are at the epicenter of the economic crisis that erupted in 2008. As of the end of that year, just four of the approximately 1,700 commercial banks with

$300 million or more in assets controlled 49 percent of the $11.4 trillion in that sector. Topping the list were two Wall Street banks with long and storied histories, JPMorgan Chase, with $2.1 trillion, and Citigroup, which had $2.0 trillion. They were followed by the Bank of America, headquartered in Charlotte, North Carolina, with $1.8 trillion, and Wells Fargo Bank, located in San Francisco, with $1.3 trillion. Citigroup is now best known for the fact that it is at the center of the banking crisis due to the many risky investments made by its management, which led to government bailouts and guarantees of several hundred billion dollars by the spring of 2009. It may be bankrupt and in the hands of the federal government when this book is being read. As this and the following chapters show, Citigroup is also close to the center of the American power structure.

Several different studies, stretching from the 1970s to 2004, all of which are focused on the largest corporations, provide a detailed overview of interlocking directorates in the modern-day corporate community. It is first of all an extensive community in terms of corporate interlocks, encompassing 90 percent of the 800 largest publicly owned corporations studied for the 1970s, 89 percent of the largest 255 for 1995, and 84 percent of the 930 largest corporations for 2001 (Barnes and Ritter 2001; Davis, Yoo and Baker 2002; Mariolis 1975). Furthermore, most corporations are within three or four "steps" or "links" of any other, but for practical purposes only the first two links are usually apparent because most directors, like people in any setting, cannot see beyond the "friends of friends" level.

The most detailed study of corporate interlocks, based on 1,029 of the largest corporations in 1996, was carried out for the third edition of this book. The study was made possible by a unique resource, *Who Knows Who*, which is no longer compiled, so the study cannot be updated. *Who Knows Who* was a labor of love carried out by a retired Bank of America librarian who wanted to help nonprofit organizations find their way to corporate leaders who might support their efforts. It listed every interlock connection for each corporation and had a section presenting the corporate directorships held by each individual. It was in effect an inadvertent membership network matrix that was ideal for research purposes even though it was compiled for other reasons. Although the names and numbers have changed over time, past studies and smaller studies since that time suggest that it provides an enduring snapshot of the structure of the corporate community.

The study first of all showed that most corporations had 1 to 9 connections to the rest of the network, but over 100 of the smaller corporations had none. On the other hand, the largest corporations usually had 10 or more connections and some had as many as 28 to 45. The exact figures for the number of connections among the top

Table 2.1 Number of Network Connections for 1,029 Large
Corporations in 1996

Number of Connections	Number of Companies	Cumulative Percent
28–45	28	2.7
20–27	65	9.0
15–19	102	19.0
10–14	146	33.1
5–9	226	55.1
2–4	241	78.5
1	93	87.6
0	128	100.0

Source: Constructed from information in *Who Knows Who* (Detroit: Gale Research
Inc., 1997), chapter 4.

1,029 corporations are presented in Table 2.1. These findings suggest
that the network is extensive in that it includes 88 percent of the corporations in the database, but it is not dense because corporations
have relatively few ties with each other.

In general, the corporations with the most connections are also
the corporations that are in the center of a network (Bonacich 1972;
Bonacich and Domhoff 1981). This point is first of all demonstrated in
this study by studying the number of connections that the most highly
connected firms have with each other. Table 2.2 presents the intercon-
nections for the twenty-eight companies with 28 or more interlocks.
Twenty-four of the twenty-eight have 3 or more connections with each
other: American Express and Sara Lee head the list with 9 ties each in
the top group; Chase Manhattan Bank (now part of JPMorgan Chase
Bank), General Motors, and Procter & Gamble have 8; and Prudential
Insurance, 3M (formerly Minnesota Mining and Manufacturing), and
Mobil Oil (now merged with Exxon to create ExxonMobil) have 7.
Of the four highly interlocked companies with 2 or less connections
within the top twenty-eight, two are banks in San Francisco that have
most of their many connections to corporations located on the West
Coast. The other two are railroad companies.

The centrality of the twenty-eight firms with the most connections also is shown by their connections to other highly connected
corporations. Of the 313 firms with between 10 and 27 connections,
72.2 percent had at least one connection to the top 28. In addition,
every one of the 81 corporations without a connection to the top 28

Table 2.2 The Twenty-Eight Most Connected Corporations for 1996 and Their Connections to Each Other (Financial Companies Marked by Asterisks)

Company	Total Number of Connections	Connections among the Top 28
Chase Manhattan Bank*	45	8
Wells Fargo Bank*	41	2
American Express*	40	9
Prudential Insurance*	39	7
Sara Lee Foods	39	9
3M	37	7
General Motors	33	8
Kroger Stores	33	5
Ashland Oil	32	3
Bank of America*	32	1
CSX (railroad)	32	2
Verizon	31	6
Coca-Cola	31	3
Procter & Gamble	31	8
Spring Industries	31	6
AMR	30	4
Mobil Oil	30	7
TRW	30	3
Xerox	30	4
Ameritech	29	5
Bell South	29	3
Union Pacific	29	6
Westinghouse Electric	29	4
Burlington Northern	28	2
Cummins Engine	28	4
Kellogg	28	6
Kmart	28	4
AOL Time Warner	28	6

Source: Constructed from information in *Who Knows Who* (Detroit: Gale Research, Inc., 1997), p. 749.

Table 2.3 Examples of How Corporations with One Connection Link to the Top Twenty-Eight

Company	Linking Corporation	Linking Corporation's Connection to the Top 28
A. G. Edwards	Helig-Meyers	CSX
Ascend	Silicon Graphics	Mobil, Prudential, Sara Lee
Bally Co.	First Union Bank	Verizon
Dimm Co.	First Union Bank	Verizon
Big Flowers Press	Host Marriott	AMR
First Federal Savings	Teledyne	Wells Fargo Bank
Glendale Federal Savings	Teledyne	Wells Fargo Bank
Unitrin	Teledyne	Wells Fargo Bank

Source: Constructed from *Who Knows Who* (Detroit: Gale Research, Inc., 1997).

had at least 1 connection (and most had 3 or more) to the other 226. To provide a more general picture, a representative sample of 400 companies in the overall network showed that 39 percent of them had at least one direct link to the central group of 28. This means that the network tends to radiate out in concentric circles from its central core, but even that image does not capture the full picture because even some corporations with only two or three connections are linked directly to the top 28. Still more are only one step removed from it. Examples of this two-step relationship for eight corporations with only one network tie are shown in Table 2.3.

These findings are similar to results I compiled from the Corporate Library at www.thecorporatelibrary.com for the year 2004. For example, the average number of connections among 1,996 companies in their database was 6.1. On the other hand, the largest corporations usually had 10 or more connections and some had as many as 20 to 25. ExxonMobil, by then the largest corporation in the country, had links to 17 companies, Ford Motors had 14, and General Electric had 24. Citigroup, the largest bank in 2004, had 25 links with other corporations. Despite gradual turnover on boards, the number of connections to other corporations tended to remain stable: ExxonMobil had 21 in 2007, which was 4 more than three years before, and Citigroup had exactly the same number in 2007 as it had in 2004, which includes 2 director interlocks with Alcoa, Cummings, and Johnson & Johnson.

(In 2007, ExxonMobil also had 3 directors who were directors of the Business Roundtable and Citigroup had 2.)

Aside from some tendency to regional concentrations, there are no subgroups or cliques within the corporate community, at least as measured by director interlocks (Mintz and Schwartz 1983). Instead, as the findings in the previous paragraphs reveal, there tends to be a very general core, with smaller corporations around the periphery. One further piece of evidence for this conclusion can be found in the fact that corporate connections "broken" by the death or retirement of a director are not very often "restored" by a new director from closely related companies (Koenig and Gogel 1981; Palmer 1983). This is not what would be expected if the companies were part of distinctive sub-groups, as was the case 100 years ago when a few large commercial and investment banks controlled many industrial corporations. Now new directors are usually recruited from a small general pool of people who are highly visible in the corporate community, which suggests that most corporate directors now have an oversight and advice type of function rather than a control function (Davis, Yoo and Baker 2002). Thus, the main constants in the network are its large size, the centrality of large firms, and slight shifts in the degree of a corporation's centrality when directors are replaced. (For further information on corporate interlocks, see the document "Interlocking Directorates and the Corporate Community" at www.whorulesamerca.net.)

Readers who want to trace corporate networks for themselves, and to see how specific corporations relate to several of the think tanks and policy-discussion groups discussed in Chapter 4, can make use of the constantly updated information and software on *LittleSis: Profiles of the Powers That Be* at http://littlesis.org/. *LittleSis* also contains information on campaign finance contributions and connections to government.

THE DIRECTOR NETWORK AS AN "INNER CIRCLE"

Who are the directors who create a corporate community through their presence on boards of directors? They are 90–95 percent men, 95 percent white, 3–4 percent African-American, and 1–2 percent Latino and Asian-American. Most are business executives, commercial bankers, investment bankers, and corporate lawyers, but there are also a significant minority of university administrators, foundation presidents, former elected officials, and representatives of ethnic and racial minorities.

Compared to three or four decades ago, there is greater diversity in the corporate community in terms of the number of women and minorities, a response to the social movements that emerged in the 1960s. There is irony in this diversity, however, because the social class and educational backgrounds of the women and minorities tend to be similar to those of their white male counterparts. They also share the Christian religion and Republican politics with most of the white males. In the case of African-American and Latino corporate directors, they tend to have lighter skin color than leaders within their own communities. Based on this and other information, there is reason to believe that white male directors select new women and minority directors who are similar to them in class, education, and skin color. There is also evidence that women and minority directors usually share the same perspectives on business and government with other directors (Zweigenhaft and Domhoff 2006).

The most extensive study of the social backgrounds of corporate directors ever conducted used parental occupation, listing in the *Social Register*, and attendance at one of the prestigious private schools listed in Appendix A to estimate that 30 percent of several thousand directors in the early 1970s came from the upper class (the top 1 percent). This percentage is 30 times what might be expected if it is assumed for statistical purposes that people from all classes have an equal chance to serve on boards of directors, a clear example of overrepresentation on the *Who governs?* power indicator. Fifty-nine percent came from the middle class, which comprises about 21 percent of the population by this researcher's estimate, and only 3 percent from the remaining 78 percent of the population (Dye 1995).

Approximately 15–20 percent of all present-day directors sit on two or more corporate boards, thereby creating the corporate community as it is defined for the purposes of this book. This percentage has proven to be very stable over time. The figure was 24 percent for New York banks and insurance companies in 1816, and 18 percent in 1836. For 55 companies studied for 1891 and 1912, the figures were 13 percent and 17 percent. A larger sample of companies for the period 1898 to 1905 found that 12 percent of the directors were on two or more boards (Bunting 1983; Roy 1983). These people are called the *inner circle* of the corporate community. They do not differ demographically from other directors, but they do sit on more nonprofit boards and are appointed more frequently to government positions (Useem 1978; Useem 1980b). Thus, the inner circle contributes disproportionately to the general leadership group that represents the corporate community as a whole.

The extensive corporate network created by interlocking directors provides a general framework within which common business and political perspectives can gradually develop. It is one building block toward a more general class awareness that is reinforced in settings that are discussed in the next several chapters. The understanding gained by studying interlocking directors and the corporate network is therefore a useful starting point in understanding corporate power. But it is no substitute for showing how policy views are formed and how government is influenced on specific issues for which there is conflict.

STRATEGIC ALLIANCES/PRODUCER NETWORKS

Firms in the corporate community not only have numerous complex ties to each other, but also to multinational firms in other countries and smaller firms in both the United States and abroad. The relations to the multinationals are called *strategic alliances*; the relations with smaller companies create *producer networks*. Both types of ties developed more rapidly in the late twentieth century than they had in the past, in part due to increasing international economic competition, including competition within the United States from Japanese and Western European companies. This new competition forced American corporations to seek greater flexibility through internal reorganizations, changes in labor relations, and new relations with other companies.

Strategic alliances with foreign multinationals usually focus on a very specific issue, such as research and development, or the creation of one particular product. Thus, IBM, Toshiba (Japan), and Siemens (Germany) entered into an alliance for research and development on a new kind of microchip. General Motors and Toyota developed a joint venture to produce small cars in a plant in Fremont, California, using advanced technology and different labor relations. Such alliances make it possible for large corporations to (1) bypass political barriers blocking their entry into new foreign markets; (2) create new products more quickly by pooling technical know-how; and (3) avoid the expense of start-up costs and head-on competition (Harrison 1994).

Producer networks, on the other hand, provide supplies and services to big corporations. These networks give large companies the flexibility to rearrange their internal bureaucracies and cut back on employees. In particular, they allow corporations to subcontract, or outsource, for many of the parts and services they need. The corporations are thereby able to outflank unions, which often have difficulty in organizing workers when there are many small companies tied to a few large corporations. Thanks to outsourcing, the large corporations continue to maintain or enlarge their share of sales and profits while decreasing the size of their workforces. Nor does outsourcing reduce the power of the big corporations. Based on a detailed investigation of all new corporate strategies, one economist concluded: "Production may be decentralized into a wider and more geographically far-flung number of work sites, but power, finance, and control remain concentrated in the hands of the managers of the largest companies in the global economy" (Harrison 1994).

Outsourcing first seemed to be a feasible option for reducing union power as far back as 1961, but it took a decade for corporations to make use of its potential in the face of liberal-labor opposition. A brief discussion of this issue provides a preview of the importance of class conflict in shaping the strategies of the corporate community. The conflict began when the federal government's National Labor Relation Board, controlled at the time by Republican appointees, ruled that outsourcing did not violate union contracts. However, liberals and union leaders vigorously opposed the ruling because they saw it as a ploy to undercut unions. The decision was overturned one year later by the liberal appointees to the board by the new president, Democrat John F. Kennedy. The corporate community, convinced that this new ruling was the opening round in a liberal-labor attack on "management prerogatives," began to mobilize against any further growth in union power; this mobilization included companies that had maintained formally positive relations with unions for over a decade (Gross 1995). In retrospect, it is clear that this effort was one key factor in the corporate community's right turn in the 1970s, but it wasn't obvious to members of trade unions in the general turmoil of that era, as discussed further in the final chapter.

Top executives from these companies claimed they were willing to bargain with unions over wages, hours, and working conditions, but not over an issue that involved their rights as managers, including their right to weaken unions. Their successful battle, won through court cases and influence on appointments to the National Labor Relations Board, culminated in 1971 with a series of rulings against any need for collective bargaining over management decisions. These decisions opened the way for greater outsourcing, plant relocations, and plant closings. The organization that has coordinated the corporate community on policy issues since the 1970s, the Business Roundtable, had its origins in the committees and study groups set up to overturn the original pro-union ruling on outsourcing.

IS THERE A SEPARATE MILITARY-INDUSTRIAL COMPLEX?

Unlike the countries of Europe, which had to have big armies from the fifteenth century onwards to defend themselves against each other, the United States did not have a large military establishment until World

War II, only sixty-five to seventy years ago. This fact goes a long way toward explaining the relatively small size of the federal government historically and the major role of the corporate community within it. However, the large amount of defense spending since World War II has led a few social scientists to argue that there now exists a separate military-industrial complex which is able to win the budgetary allocations it needs to maintain at least some degree of independence from the corporate community. There are three major findings that contradict this notion.

First, several of the largest defense contractors, such as Boeing, General Electric, and United Technologies, are also among the largest corporations in the country irrespective of their military contracts. Second, research on the handful of companies that specialized in weapons manufacturing in the years following World War II demonstrated that they were completely integrated into the corporate community through their bank connections and interlocking directors; in addition, their directors went to the same universities and belonged to the same social clubs as other corporate directors (Johnson 1976). Third, the claim of a separate military-industrial complex is contradicted by the fact that the defense budget rises and falls in terms of foreign policy crises and military threats. This does not fit with the idea that defense contractors and their Pentagon allies have the power to allocate themselves all the money they would like to have. Budgetary decline was significant after World War II, the Korean War, and the Vietnam War (Goertzel 1985). The drop in defense spending in the decade after the end of the Cold War was substantial as well, although the defense budget continued to be a major part of the overall federal budget.

The case for a separate and independent military-industrial complex became even weaker in the 1990s when the Clinton Administration decided to adopt new contracting policies that in effect eliminated most defense companies because of declining defense needs at the time. These policies placed a greater emphasis on competition in the marketplace among a few large corporations as the means to ensure the continued development of sophisticated weapons systems. The result was a merger movement that downsized the defense industry by hundreds of thousands of employees and left just under 40 percent of the defense contracts in the hands of 10 corporations, several of which have large nondefense business operations as well (Sterngold 1996; Sterngold 1997). Even Lockheed Martin, the largest defense contractor, does a large amount of non-defense business through contracts with the U.S. Postal Service, the Census Bureau, the Social Security Administration, and other important agencies of government at the federal and state levels. Table 2.4 lists the ten largest defense contractors for 2003, along with their ranking among the largest 500 corporations ("the *Fortune* 500") and the number of interlocks they had with nondefense companies.

The remaining 60 percent of defense contracts were spread out among a large number of well-known corporations in all sectors of the economy in 2003. For example, HealthNet was the fourteenth largest defense contractor, FedEx the twentieth, ExxonMobil the twenty-ninth, Dell Computers the thirty-fifth, General Motors the thirty-sixth, and IBM the fiftieth. Based on these overall findings, it can be seen that there is no separate military-industrial complex. Instead, it is more accurate to say that the corporate community is a military-industrial complex in and of itself, as well as the producer of most of the goods and services purchased by American consumers (Pilisuk and Hayden 1965). Those who believe that a separate military-industrial complex shapes foreign and military policy for its own narrow economic ends often overlook this important point. The major influences behind American foreign policy are discussed in Chapter 4.

THE INCORPORATION OF HIGH-TECH COMPANIES

In the 1990s the combination of computers, the Internet, faxes, and cell phones made information storage, data analysis, and information transmittal far faster and cheaper, thereby improving productivity, warehousing, shipping, and customer service. The result was a new group of semiconductor, telecommunication, and dot-com companies that seemed for a brief instant to be on the way to forming a separate corporate cluster. However, it soon became apparent that these companies were actually becoming part of the ongoing corporate community in terms of their financing, organizational structure, business dealings, and policy orientations. Most of the start-ups were bought out by larger corporations or pushed aside by established companies in retail sales, which quickly developed their own Internet sites and marketing plans. Many of their high-level executives turned out to be from the same elite social and educational backgrounds as other corporate executives. Finally, the largest of these companies have numerous interlocks with the corporate community. The most integrated as of 2004 were Dell, with 19 interlocks to giants such as General Electric, Chevron-Texaco, and Coca-Cola; Microsoft, with 16 connections to the likes of General Electric, General Mills, Merck, and Northrop Grumman; Intel, with 14 links to companies such as American Express, Goldman Sachs, and Ford Motors; and Automatic Data Processing, with 12 ties to such firms as Citigroup, Johnson & Johnson, and CIT Financial.

Table 2.4 The Ten Largest U.S. Defense Contractors, 2003

Contractor	Size of Contracts (billions of dollars)	Percent of All Contracts	*Fortune* 500 Ranking	Links to Nonmilitary Corporations	Examples of Links to Nonmilitary Corporations
Lockheed Martin	$20.4	10.49%	48	21	Procter & Gamble, Bristol-Myers, Continental Airlines
Boeing	$17.3	8.30%	21	16	JPMorgan Chase, Walt Disney, 7-Eleven
Northrop Grumman	$11.1	5.32%	55	19	Microsoft, Comcast, IBM
General Dynamics	$8.2	3.94%	121	8	JPMorgan Chase, MetLife, Sara Lee
Raytheon	$7.9	3.79%	107	14	Citigroup, Sprint, Allied Waste
United Technologies	$4.5	2.18%	51	19	Citigroup, McGraw-Hill, DirecTV
Halliburton	$3.9	1.88%	122	20	Citigroup, ExxonMobil, Walt Disney
General Electric	$2.8	1.36%	5	24	Microsoft, General Motors, ChevronTexaco
Science Applications	$2.6	1.25%	289	10	Procter & Gamble, Baxter, Quantum
Computer Sciences	$2.5	1.21%	175	13	Commerce Bankshares, Tenet Healthcare, FirstFed
TOTALS	$81.2	39.72%			

Source: Department of Defense and Interlock Information on www.CorporateLibrary.com.

Nor do the owners of the biggest high-tech companies act any differently than empire builders in the past. For example, Microsoft claims to be a highly innovative company built on sheer brainpower, but it began as a quick and timely assemblage of newly developed ideas and techniques taken from others before software was patentable. Windows® and Word® came from the Xerox Research Center, Excel® from a little company named Software Arts, and Internet Explorer® from Netscape. As the retired founder of the Xerox Research Center concluded, the head of Microsoft, Bill Gates, was "immensely successful in positioning himself between the innovators and the users, taking from one and selling to the others" (e.g., Goldman 2000). His company then benefited enormously from violating antitrust laws by giving computer manufacturers a discount price on its software, thereby discouraging manufacturers from considering any other operating system. The Department of Justice investigated and forced Microsoft to stop these practices in 1993, but by then it had already captured 90 percent of the market for operating systems. Later the company lost an antitrust suit concerning its anticompetitive practices in relation to its Internet browser (Baker 2008).

Although many high-tech executives claim they have no need for government, they are in fact as dependent upon it as the rest of the corporate community. The Internet itself was created by the Pentagon's Defense Advanced Research Project Agency in the late 1960s. Other projects financed by the defense agency "helped create many of the nation's most impressive computers, the chips used in cellular phones, and vital networking technologies like the ability to send simultaneous signals of many wavelengths down a single optic cable" (Abbate 1999). Nor would companies have been able to benefit from the Internet if the Telecommunications Act of 1996 and rulings by the Federal Communications Commission had not freed telephone lines from the telephone company's monopoly grip (Hundt 2000).

High-tech companies also benefit handsomely from tax breaks that their lobbyists worked very hard to obtain through the special-interest process. Due to strong pressure in 1994, backed up by a Senate resolution sponsored by Senator Joseph I. Lieberman, later to be the Democratic Party's vice presidential nominee in 2000, companies can take a tax deduction for money their employees receive when they exercise their option to sell stock that the company allowed them to purchase.* This practice kept earnings artificially high for many years.

---

*A stock option is an arrangement by which an employee is allowed to buy company stock at any point within a future time period at the price of the stock when the option is granted. If the price of the stock rises, the employee purchases it at the original low price, often with the help of a low-interest or interest-free loan from the corporation. He or she then may sell the stock at the market value, realizing a large capital gain that is taxed at a far lower rate than ordinary income.

Giving employees stock options also encouraged them to work for lower wages, which also raised profits. Thanks to this tax break, some of these companies had years when they did not pay any taxes. When the market for high-tech stocks crashed in 2000, many employees were left with worthless stocks or stock options, which meant they had worked for far less money than they imagined.

Another important piece of special-interest legislation allows high-tech companies to bring several hundred thousand foreign software specialists a year into the country for six-year periods. Not only do these employees have to leave the country at the end of six years, but also they cannot easily change jobs without losing their visas. This arrangement comes close to indentured servitude, giving companies access to skilled employees without any risk that they might quit the company or join in unionization efforts.

The final old-fashioned secret to the high-tech companies' economic success is massive resistance to any attempts at unionization. Great success in this regard is critical in maintaining low-wage assembly plants. The absence of a unionized labor force also allows for a steady stream of low-income immigrant workers, which means there is no challenge to the right to move assembly plants to Third World countries. To provide further workforce flexibility, the firms in Silicon Valley use as many temporary software designers as possible and contract with employment agencies to hire janitors at very low wages.

THE CORPORATE LAWYERS

Lawyers specializing in corporate law go back to the beginnings of American corporations. Comprising only a few percent of all lawyers, they generally practice as partners in large firms that have hundreds of partners and even more "associates"—that is, recent law school graduates who work for a salary and aspire to an eventual partnership. Partners routinely earn several hundred thousand dollars each year and top partners may make several million.

Corporate law firms grew in size and importance in tandem with the large corporations that developed in the second half of the nineteenth century. Their partners played the central role in creating the state-level laws in New Jersey and Delaware that made the corporate form an attractive and safe haven for companies under pressure from reformers and socialists, who were trying to pass laws at the national level that would break up or socialize large businesses (Parker-Gwin and Roy 1996).

In more recent times, corporate lawyers prepare briefs for key legal cases, but rarely appear in court. They advise corporations on how widely or narrowly to interpret requests for information when facing lawsuits over the dangers of their products. They are central to mergers and acquisitions by corporate executives. They also serve as important go-betweens with government, sometimes as heads of major departments of the executive branch, sometimes as White House counsel. After government service, they return to their private practices with new knowledge and contacts that make them even more valuable to their corporate clients. Some of them become the heads of corporations at later points in their careers.

Despite these close ties with corporations, some social scientists have argued that corporate lawyers are "professionals" with a code of ethics and concern over the public at large that set them apart from the corporate community. However, a detailed analysis of four large corporate law firms in Chicago provides convincing evidence that these lawyers are an integral part of the corporate community. They have a strong loyalty to their clients, not to their profession or code of ethics. The sociologist who did this study concludes:

> My central thesis is that lawyers in large firms adhere to an ideology of autonomy, both in their perception of the role of legal institutions in society and the role of lawyers vis-à-vis clients, but that this ideology has little bearing in practice. In the realm of practice these lawyers enthusiastically attempt to maximize the interests of clients and rarely experience serious disagreements with clients over the broader implications of a proposed course of conduct. The dominance of client interests in the practical activities of lawyers contradicts the view that large-firm lawyers serve a mediating function in the legal system (Nelson 1988, p. 232).

Although closely tied to their clients, and in that sense not independently powerful, corporate lawyers are nonetheless important in shaping law schools, the American Bar Association, courts, and political institutions. The same author of the preceding quote concludes that corporate lawyers "maintain and make legitimate the current system for the allocation of rights and benefits," and that they do so for the benefit of their clients: "The influence of these organizations in the legal system derives from and can only serve the interests of corporate clients" (Nelson 1988, pp. 264, 269).

The socialization that creates the business-oriented mentality shared by corporate lawyers has been studied in great detail at Harvard Law School, the law school that trained both President Obama and the First Lady, Michelle Robinson Obama. Based on interviews and classroom observations, the sociological investigator reports that students end up actively participating in building "collective identities" within law school that all but ensure they will become members of the corporate community as a result of a grueling socialization process (Granfield 1992). As a key part of this socialization, students are taught that there is no such thing as right or wrong, only differing shades of gray. Summer internships provide the students with a taste of the corporate world. They come to feel that they must be special to be attending a high-status law school and to be sought after by powerful law firms that offer starting salaries of $100,000 a year or more. Thus, even though some students enter prestigious law schools with an interest in public interest law, all but a few percent end up in corporate law firms. First Lady Michelle Obama was one of those young corporate lawyers for a year or two after she graduated, working for the most prestigious firm in Chicago. She found the work tedious and left for a career in government and university employment, but not before she met her future husband when he did a summer internship at the firm and she was his mentor (Mendell 2007).

Not all young lawyers follow the corporate path, of course, and those from lower-status schools are very unlikely to do so. Some become trial lawyers who represent aggrieved or injured individuals or groups in cases against corporations. They are often viewed as the major enemies of corporate lawyers. They have been so successful that corporate and Republican leaders call for various changes that end up putting limits on liability. Many trial lawyers have become major donors to the Democratic Party in the face of this counterattack by the corporate community. Other young lawyers go to work for the government as prosecutors and public defenders. Still others focus on environmental, civil rights, or labor law, in effect joining the liberal-labor coalition in many instances.

Given this diversity of interests and viewpoints among lawyers, it makes little sense in terms of a power analysis to talk about lawyers in general as part of a profession that is separate from business and other groups in society. Although lawyers share some qualities that make them useful mediators and politicians, it is important to ascertain what kind of law a person practices for purposes of power studies, and to realize that corporate lawyers are the hired guns of the corporate community.

FROM SMALL FARMS TO GIANT AGRIBUSINESSES

In the last half of the nineteenth century, when the farm vote was a critical one in state and national elections, farmers often provided major opposition for the rising national corporations. Many angry farmers were part of an anticorporate populist movement that started in the 1870s and formed its own political party, the Populist Party, in the 1880s to challenge both Democrats and Republicans. Several of the reforms advocated by the populists—such as a government commission to set railroad rates, the direct election of senators, and the federal income tax—were eventually adopted.

But the day of farmers as challengers to the corporate community ended over 100 years ago. The populists were defeated at the turn of the twentieth century by a coalition of prosperous farmers and local business leaders. As the farm population declined and the average size of farms increased, farm owners became an interest group rather than a large popular movement. Moreover, the large-scale family farmers of the Midwest and Great Plains increasingly joined with the plantation owners of the South and the ranchers of California as employers of wage labor, especially part-time migrant labor, and identified themselves as business owners. The periodic attempts since the 1930s by farm workers to organize labor unions, often aided and encouraged by liberals and leftists, intensified the farm owners' sense of opposition to the liberal-labor coalition.

Although most of the approximately one million farms in existence today are still family owned, with less than one percent owned by large corporations in other business sectors, the overwhelming majority of them are extremely small. Roughly 55 percent of farms have less than $10,000 a year in sales, and 66 percent have less than $40,000 in sales. The people on these farms earn over 90 percent of their income in off-farm jobs, many in manufacturing and service firms that relocated to rural areas to take advantage of lower wages. Moreover, one-third of farm sales are made to large corporations under fixed-price contracts, moving many farmers closer to the status of corporate wage-workers (Barboza 1999; Lobao and Meyer 2001). At the high end of the farm ladder, the less than 3 percent of farmers with over $500,000 in sales provide half of all farm sales and the 7 percent with sales of $250,000 or above account for 74 percent. Many of the largest farms are part of agribusiness complexes, particularly for farm commodities where a few companies control most of the market (Lobao and Meyer 2004).

The small numbers of farmers with over $250,000 in yearly sales are organized into a wide variety of associations that look out for their interests. Some of these organizations are "commodity groups," made up of those who produce a particular crop (Browne, Skees, Swanson, Thompson and Unnevehr 1992). There are also two or three general farm groups, the most important of which is the American Farm Bureau Federation. The Farm Bureau, as it is known, and most other farm groups usually align with business trade associations in the political arena. The Farm Bureau in particular is an important part of the corporate community.

As this brief overview shows, farmers do not account for an independent power base in the United States. They are few in number and most of those few do not have enough income from their farms to have any political impact. As for middle-income farmers, they are becoming contract producers, working for a set price for the handful of giant corporations that have gained control of food production. The small percentage of large-scale farmers who produce most of the cash crops are integrated into the agribusiness complex within the corporate community through commodity groups and the Farm Bureau.

SMALL BUSINESS: NOT A COUNTERWEIGHT

It is sometimes claimed that small businesses, defined as businesses with less than 500 employees, are a significant counterweight to the corporate community because there are approximately 22 million such businesses in the United States compared to only 14,000 companies with 500 or more employees. They make about half of all consumer sales and employ approximately the same percentage of the private labor force; they have an important place in the American belief system because they are thought to embody the independence and initiative of all Americans.

But the owners of small businesses are too large in number, too diverse in size, too lacking in financial assets, and too divided in their political opinions to have any collective power that could challenge the corporate community. One-third of American businesses are part-time operations run from the home or as a sideline from a regular job, and another one-third are solo efforts. Others exist in immigrant ethnic enclaves and have no contacts with businesspeople outside their community. As a result of these problems, small businesspeople have not formed their own associations to lobby for them.

Nonetheless, there is one organization, the National Federation of Independent Business, which claims to represent the small-business viewpoint. Created in 1943 by a political entrepreneur as a way to make profits on dues and at the same time have a basis for lobbying for his conservative policy preferences, it now has 600,000 current members, which is less than 3 percent of small businesses. Members are recruited by traveling sales representatives who receive a commission for each new member they recruit, leading to a 20 percent turnover in membership each year. In recent decades the organization became a nonprofit organization and has been controlled by a small board of directors made up of wealthy business owners who pay the top officers several hundred thousand dollars a year to manage 700 employees and a $170 million budget. (The new president selected in 2005 is worth tens of millions after the sale of the company he helped start to a larger corporation [Birnbaum and McCarthy 2005].) The organization conducts periodic surveys of its members to determine their policy preferences on key issues, only 20 percent of which are returned each time. The opinions that are then put forth as representative of small business are far more conservative than what is known to be the case from more general surveys of the opinions of small-business owners, who often share the political views of their community or ethnic group (Hamilton 1975, chapter 7; Kazee, Lipsky and Martin 2008).

In fact, the National Federation of Independent Business is actually a very potent ultraconservative lobbying organization that draws most of its leadership and staff from the Republican Party. It works closely with other ultraconservative organizations in financing conservative Republican candidates at the state and congressional levels (Olson 2006; Shaiko and Wallace 1999). However, when the Democrats unexpectedly gained control of Congress in the 2006 elections, the organization began to reach out to business-oriented Democrats (Birnbaum 2007).

Contrary to the image projected by the National Federation of Independent Business, the small businesses that go beyond the part-time and one-person levels are most often part of trade associations that receive most of their funding and direction from large corporations. They are also part of the two largest general business organizations in the country, the U.S. Chamber of Commerce, which claims 180,000 companies and 2,800 state and local chambers as members, and the National Association of Manufacturers, which claims 12,500 companies and subsidiaries as members. These are figures that go well beyond the several hundred companies in the corporate community and the 14,000 companies with 500 or more employees.

Moreover, many small businesses are part of economic networks that have large corporations at the center. The most visible and long-standing examples of small businesses that are part of large corporations are the 900,000 franchise businesses that sell products and services to the general public—convenience stores, fast-food outlets, mall shops, automobile repair shops, and many more (see www.franchise.org for details). As for the small manufacturing companies sometimes said to be the sources of innovation and new jobs, they are often dependent upon their sales of parts and services to large corporations, making them unlikely counterweights to the corporate community. The fact that many of these firms start with 100 or more employees suggests the importance of their subcontracts for their existence and survival; they are often spin-offs from larger corporations attempting to shed unionized workers or obtain a tax break. Not all small manufacturing firms are directly tied to large corporations, however. Many are part of what one author calls "the minor industrial revolution" that brought small firms into southern states in search of low-wage, non-unionized labor (Browne et al. 1992, p. 24). Still others owe their origins to discoveries and patents that were developed in large universities, especially in the electronic and biotechnology industries.

When all is said and done, then, there is no "small business community" in the United States to provide any opposition to the corporate community. The relatively few small businesses that are full-time operations and have more than a handful of employees are incorporated into the power networks of the corporate community (1) by belonging to trade associations dominated by larger businesses; (2) as franchise outlets for larger businesses; and (3) as suppliers and service providers for big corporations. These ties place severe market and political constraints on most small businesses in relation to the large corporations. Small business is too fragmented to be a counterweight to the several thousand businesses that control a little over 50 percent of total business assets.

LOCAL BUSINESSES FORM GROWTH COALITIONS

The most important small businesses in the United States are organized into local growth coalitions whose members share a common interest in intensifying land use in their geographical locale, starting with landowners, developers, and contractors. Executives from local banks, gas and electric companies, and department stores are part of the growth coalitions as well because they have a strong stake in the growth of the local community. These land-based businesses are not directly involved in the main topic of this book, power at the national level, except in their quest for subsidies in the special-interest process. Nevertheless, it is important to consider them briefly to understand the complexities of the ownership class and to see the power openings that are created by the occasional conflicts between the corporate community and the growth coalitions, especially on environmental issues. They are also of interest because real estate developers pushing into low-income black neighborhoods on the South Side of Chicago were supporters of President Barack Obama at an early stage of his political career.

In economic terms, the *place entrepreneurs* at the heart of local growth coalitions are trying to maximize *rents* from land and buildings, which is a little different than the goal of the corporate community, namely, maximizing profits from the sale of goods and services. To emphasize this difference, the concept of rents includes purchases of land and buildings as well as payments that tenants or home buyers make to landlords, realtors, mortgage lenders, and title companies (Logan and Molotch 2007). More generally, local growth coalitions and the corporate community are different *segments* of the ownership class, meaning that as owners of property and employers of wage labor they are in the same economic class and therefore share more in common with each other than they do with non-owners. The main basis for their cooperation is the fact that the best way for a local growth coalition to intensify land use is to attract corporate investments to its area. The place entrepreneurs are therefore very much attuned to the needs of corporations, working hard to provide them with the physical infrastructure, municipal services, labor markets, and political climate they find attractive. The growth caused by corporate investments, along with investments by universities and government agencies, then leads to housing developments, increased financial activity, and increased consumer spending, all of which make land and buildings even more valuable.

Still, the relationship between the growth coalitions and the corporate community is not without its conflicts. This is first of all because corporations have the ability to move if they think that regulations are becoming too stringent or taxes and wages too high. The departure of a major corporation can have a devastating impact on a local growth coalition. Moreover, this ability to move contributes to the constant competition among rival cities for new capital investments, creating tensions between growth coalitions as well as between individual growth coalitions and the corporate community. The net result is often a "race to the bottom" as cities offer tax breaks, less environmental regulation, and other benefits to corporations in order to tempt them to relocate. Ironically, most studies of plant location suggest that environmental laws and local taxes are of minor importance in corporate decisions concerning the location or relocation of production facilities. A union-free environment and low-cost raw materials are the major factors (Bluestone and Harrison 1982; Dreier, Mollenkopf and Swanstrom 2004).

The most longstanding conflict between the corporate community and local growth coalitions concerns the environment, especially clean air. From as early as the 1890s local growth coalitions in major cities like Chicago tried to force railroads and manufacturers to control the air pollution problems that developed due to steam engines and smokestacks, but their efforts usually failed in the face of the corporate community's superior power. It was not until Pittsburgh and Los Angeles began to suffer serious blackouts and smog in the 1940s and 1950s that the growth coalitions were able to experience some success in these battles, leading to statewide organizations and legislation in California that began to mitigate some of the worst conditions. These conflicts between the corporate community and the growth coalitions are especially notable because they are one basis for the environmental movement that emerged in the late 1960s, which capitalized on this disagreement within the ownership class (Gonzalez 2005).

Local growth coalitions face still another source of potential tension and conflict: disagreements with neighborhoods about expansion and development. Neighborhoods are something to be used and enjoyed in the eyes of those who live in them, but they are often seen as sites for further development by growth coalitions, who justify new developments with the doctrine of "the highest and best use for land." Thus, neighborhoods often end up fighting against freeways, wider streets, high-rises, and commercial buildings. This conflict is the axis of local politics when the downtown interests try to expand the central business district, often at the expense of established low-income and minority neighborhoods. This expansionist land-clearing strategy contributed greatly to inner-city tensions from the 1960s onward because the African-Americans who are most frequently displaced by it cannot readily find housing in white neighborhoods, forcing them into crowded tenements with high rents and few amenities. The expansion of elite private universities located in urban areas, including the University of Chicago and Yale University, contributed to these tensions and continue to do so today (Domhoff 2005; Rossi and Dentler 1961).

The success rate of neighborhoods in conflicts with the growth coalitions is very low. Since the primary focus of residents is on their everyday lives, they usually do not persist in their protests and seldom join larger coalitions with other neighborhoods in the city. There are, however, a few exceptions, such as Santa Cruz, California, where a coalition of neighborhood leaders, environmental activists, and student voters on the University of California, Santa Cruz, campus have stopped every development proposal since 1969. They have controlled city government since 1981 with a coalition of socialist-feminists, environmentalists, and neighborhood leaders (Gendron and Domhoff 2009). (For further information on Santa Cruz and other cities where neighborhood-based coalitions have had an impact, see the documents "Power at the Local Level: Growth Coalition Theory" and "Santa Cruz: The Leftmost City" at www.whorulesamerica.net.)

STRUCTURAL POWER AND ITS LIMITS

What does all this mean in terms of corporate power? First, the major businesses in the United States are closely intertwined in enough ways to be called a corporate community. Despite the constant competition and deal-making among them, which can lead to intense and long-lasting disagreements and personal animosities, the corporate community is able to maintain cohesion on its common interests through the main organizations that bring it together—the National Association of Manufactures, the Conference Board, the U.S. Chamber of Commerce, the Business Council, and the Business Roundtable. Second, none of the other economic interests studied in this chapter—small farmers, small businesses, and local growth coalitions—provide the organizational base for any significant opposition to the corporate community at the national level. To the degree that the corporate community faces any direct challenges, they come from the union movement and the liberals and leftists in universities, religious communities, and literary/artistic communities. The liberals in this coalition are often highly visible and vocal through their writing and media appearances, giving an initial impression of considerable strength. This image is reinforced by repeated ultraconservative claims in the media about the great power of liberals. But this image is not accurate, as explained at different points in later chapters.

The economic power exercised by corporate leaders through their companies is considerable. For example, they can invest their money when and where they choose. If they feel threatened by new laws or labor unions, they can move or close their factories and offices. Unless restrained by union contracts, which now cover only 7.5 percent of employees in the private sector, they can hire, promote, and replace workers as they see fit, often laying off employees on a moment's notice. These economic powers give them a direct influence over the great majority of Americans, who are dependent upon wages and salaries for their incomes, and therefore hesitant to challenge corporations directly. Economic power also gives the corporate community indirect influence over elected and appointed officials because the growth and stability of a city, state, or the country as a whole can be jeopardized by a lack of business confidence in government.

In short, the sheer economic power of the corporate community usually can influence government without any effort on the part of corporate leaders. Because businesspeople have the legal right to spend their money when and as they wish, and government officials are hesitant to take over the function of investing funds to create jobs unless it is a time of economic crisis, the government generally has to cater to business. If government officials do not give corporate leaders what they want, there are likely to be economic difficulties that would lead people to desire new political leadership. Since most government officials do not want to lose their positions, they do what is necessary to satisfy business leaders and maintain a healthy economy (Lindblom 1977).

Private control over the investment function provides leaders within the corporate community with a *structural* power that is independent of any attempts by them to influence government officials directly. While such power is very great, it is not sufficient in and of itself to allow the corporate community to dominate government, especially in times of economic or political crisis. First, it does not preclude the possibility that government officials might turn to non-business constituencies to support new economic arrangements. Contrary to claims by conservative economists, there is no necessary relationship between private ownership and markets. Improbable though it may seem to most readers, it would be possible for government to create firms to compete in the market system and thereby revive a depressed economy, or to hire unemployed workers in order to increase their ability to spend. In fact, the liberal-labor coalition mounted a legislative effort of roughly this sort shortly after World War II, only to be defeated by the conservative congressional voting bloc made up of Southern Democrats and Northern Republicans (Bailey 1950; Domhoff 1990, chapter 7). Today, one of the sticking points in current debates over health insurance is the unwillingness of corporate leaders to have the government offer insurance plans that would compete with private insurance companies. Since most Americans have very positive attitudes toward Medicare, insurance companies worry that a campaign for "Medicare for all" (which is in effect what a "single-payer" system would be) would eliminate their highly profitable health insurance business.

Second, structural power does not guarantee that employees will accept an ongoing economic depression without taking over factories or destroying private property. In such situations, the corporate leaders need government to protect their private property. They have to be able to call on the government to keep unauthorized persons from entering their factories or to eject workers who refuse to vacate the premises. Just such a situation developed seemingly out of the blue in Chicago in December 2008, when workers refused to leave the Republic Windows and Doors factory (which had been shut down without any notice so that it could be moved to a low-wage location in another state) until they were given the severance and vacation pay the company owed them. They also decided not to allow the company to remove the windows they had built over the previous weeks because keeping possession of the windows gave them a bargaining chip. Chicago city officials expressed sympathy for the workers, as did President-elect Obama, and the police did not force the workers to vacate the premises. Bank of America, which had refused to loan the company the money to make these final payments, quickly changed its mind (Luo and Cullotta 2008). It turned out that JPMorgan Chase owned 40 percent of Republic Windows and Doors and agreed to help with the loan; its Midwest chairman, William M. Daley, an early backer of President Obama, is the brother of the mayor of Chicago.

In short, structural economic power primarily concerns the relationship between the corporate community and government officials. It is not always able to contain the volatile power conflict between owners and workers that is built into the economy, as the sit-down at Republic Windows and Doors shows once again. Nor do the confrontations always remain nonviolent. When angry railroad workers went on strike in 1877 in the face of a sudden and unannounced wage cut, the clash that soon followed left over 100 people dead, mostly at the hands of 3,000 federal troops who moved from city to city via train trying to quell the disturbances. Twenty people died in Pittsburgh alone, where angry mobs retaliated by looting and burning thirty-nine buildings, 104 locomotives, forty-six passenger cars, and 1,200 freight cars owned by the Pennsylvania Railroad (Bruce 1959; Foner 1977). The deaths and property destruction were not as extensive during the upheavals of the 1930s, but fourteen people were killed in the textile strikes in New England and the South in September 1934 and there were 477 sit-down strikes in 1937 in demand of union recognition (Bernstein 1969; Fine 1969). Significantly, many of those sit-down strikes were carried out by the United Electrical, Radio, and Machine Workers, the same union that decades later represented the workers at Republic Windows and Doors in Chicago, which shows that traditions and organizational memories from the turbulent 1930s still endure.

As these examples make clear, there is uncertainty in the relationship between the corporate community and government because there is no guarantee that the underlying population or government officials will accept the viewpoint of corporate owners under all economic circumstances, which is what makes the present time so volatile. It is risky for corporate officials to refuse to invest or to remain passive in the face of an economic depression. They know from past history and from sudden actions such as the one by workers at Republic Windows and Doors that they have to do something. They have to decide if they want to encourage the government to make reforms or to call for the use of police force to put down unrest: reform or repression. They therefore need ways to have an influence on both public opinion and government officials, and they have developed a number of organizations to realize those objectives. During a research interview, a sociologist suggested to a top corporate leader that his company probably had enough structural economic power to dispense with its efforts to influence elected officials, and the corporate leader replied: "I'm not sure, but I'm not willing to find out" (Clawson, Neustadtl and Scott 1992, p. 121).

To fully explain how corporate owners and top-level managers are able to organize themselves in an effort to create new policies, shape public opinion, elect politicians they trust, and influence government officials, it is first necessary to examine the relationship between the corporate community and the social upper class.

3

The Corporate Community and the Upper Class

This chapter demonstrates that the corporate community and the upper class are closely intertwined. They are not quite two sides of the same coin, but almost. Such a demonstration is important for three reasons. First, it refutes the widely accepted idea that there has been a separation between corporate ownership and control in the United States. According to this view, there is on the one hand a wealthy but powerless upper class that is more or less window dressing, consisting of playboys and fashion plates, and on the other a "managerial class" that has power independent of wealthy owners by virtue of its role in running corporations. Due to this division between high-society owners and well-trained independent managers, the argument continues, there is no longer a dominant social class whose general interest in profits transcends the fate of any one corporation or business sector. Instead, corporate managers are reduced to an "interest group," albeit a very potent one.

Contrary to this view, the evidence presented in the final third of this chapter shows that (1) many super-wealthy stockholding families in the upper class continue to be involved in the direction of major corporations through family offices, investment partnerships, and holding companies; and (2) the professional managers of middle-level origins are assimilated into the upper class both socially and economically, and share the values of upper-class owners.

Evidence for the intertwining of the corporate community and the upper class is important for a second reason in building the case for the class-dominance perspective: Research in social psychology

55

shows that the most socially cohesive groups are the ones that do best in arriving at consensus when dealing with a problem. The members are proud of their identification with the group and come to trust each other through their friendly interactions, so they are more likely to listen to each other and seek common ground. As a classic study of the upper class in New York in the 1930s concluded: "The elaborate private life of the plutocracy serves in considerable measure to separate them out in their own consciousness as a superior, more refined element" (Almond 1998, p. 108).

Social cohesion develops through the two types of relationships found in a membership network: common membership in specific social institutions, and friendships based on social interactions within those institutions. Research on small groups in laboratory settings suggests that social cohesion is greatest when (1) the social groups are seen to be exclusive and of high status; and (2) when the interactions take place in relaxed and informal settings (Cartwright and Zander 1968; Hogg 1992). This chapter shows that many of the social institutions of the upper class provide settings and occasions that fit these specifications very well. From the viewpoint of social psychology, the people who make up the upper class can be seen as members of numerous small groups that meet at private schools, social clubs, retreats, resorts, and social gatherings.

Finally, the fact that the corporate community is closely linked to the upper class makes it possible to convert economic power into *status power*. It operates by creating respect, envy, and deference in others, making them more likely to accept what members of the upper class tell them. Although the more extravagant social activities of the upper class—the expensive parties, the jet-setting to spas and vacation spots all over the world, the involvement with exotic entertainers—are in most ways superfluous trivialities, these activities nonetheless can play a role in reinforcing the class structure. They make clear that there is a gulf between members of the upper class and ordinary citizens, reminding everyone of the hierarchical nature of the society. They reinforce the point that there are great rewards for business success, helping to stir up the personal envy that can be a goad to competitive striving. For example, in a pamphlet meant for students as part of an economics education initiative, the Federal Reserve Board in Minneapolis specifically wrote that large income differentials in the United States have "possible external benefits" because they provide "incentives for those who are at low- to middle-income levels to work hard, attain more education, and advance to better-paying jobs" (Morris 2004).

So, to the degree that the rest of the population tries to emulate the upper class or defers to it, economic power has been transformed into status power. However, the importance of status power must not be overstated. In times of social upheaval, respect and deference are often replaced by angry outbursts and mass action, especially if the social upheaval is blamed on members of the upper class.

PREPPING FOR POWER

From infancy through young adulthood, members of the upper class receive a distinctive education. This education begins early in life in preschools that sometimes are attached to a neighborhood church of high social status. Schooling continues during the elementary years at a local private school called a day school. The adolescent years may see the student remain at day school, but there is a strong chance that at least one or two years will be spent away from home at a boarding school in a quiet rural setting. Higher education is obtained at one of a small number of prestigious private universities. Although some upper-class children may attend public high school if they live in a secluded suburban setting, or go to a state university if there is one of great esteem and tradition in their home state, the system of formal schooling is so insulated that many upper-class students never see the inside of a public school in all their years of education. This separate educational system is important evidence for the distinctiveness of the mentality and lifestyle that exists within the upper class, because schools play a large role in transmitting the class structure to their students (Cookson and Persell 1985).

The linchpins in the upper-class educational system are the dozens of boarding schools developed in the last half of the nineteenth and the early part of the twentieth centuries, coincident with the rise of a nationwide upper class whose members desired to insulate themselves from an inner city that was becoming populated by lower-class immigrants. They become surrogate families that play a major role in creating an upper-class subculture on a national scale in America. The role of boarding schools in providing connections to other upper-class social institutions is also important. As one informant explained to a sociologist doing an interview study of upper-class women: "Where I went to boarding school, there were girls from all over the country, so I know people from all over. It's helpful when you move to a new city and want to get invited into the local social club" (Ostrander 1984, p. 85).

It is within these several hundred schools that a unique style of life is inculcated through such traditions as the initiatory hazing of beginning students, the wearing of school blazers or ties, and participation in esoteric sports such as lacrosse, squash, and crew. Even a different language is adopted to distinguish these schools from public schools. The principal is a headmaster or rector, the teachers are sometimes called masters, and the students are in forms, not grades. Great emphasis is placed upon the building of character. The role of the school in preparing the future leaders of America is emphasized through the speeches of the headmaster and the frequent mention of successful alumni. Thus, boarding schools are in many ways the kind of highly effective socializing agent called *total institutions*, isolating their members from the outside world and providing them with a set of routines and traditions that encompass most of their waking hours. The end result is a feeling of separateness and superiority that comes from having survived a rigorous education.

Virtually all graduates of private secondary schools go on to college, and most do so at prestigious universities. Graduates of the New England boarding schools, for example, historically found themselves at three or four large Ivy League universities: Harvard, Yale, Princeton, and Columbia. However, that situation changed somewhat after World War II as the universities grew and provided more scholarships. An analysis of admission patterns for graduates of fourteen prestigious boarding schools between 1953 and 1967 demonstrated this shift by showing that the percentage of their graduates attending Harvard, Yale, or Princeton gradually declined over those years from 52 to 25 percent. Information on the same fourteen schools for the years 1969 to 1979 showed that the figure had bottomed out at 13 percent in 1973, 1975, and 1979 (Cookson and Persell 1985; Gordon 1969). Since that time, private schools have more than held their own in sending their graduates to Harvard, Yale, and Princeton, as revealed by an enterprising journalist who ferreted out the 100 high schools that sent the highest percentage of their students to one of those three Ivy League schools between 1998 and 2001. He found that 94 of the 100 were private schools, with 10 that sent more than 15 percent of their students to Harvard, Yale, or Princeton (Yaqub 2002). The difference from the past is that more of them are day schools and are located in New York City. Table 3.1 presents information on the top ten schools.

Graduates of private schools outside of New England most frequently attend a prominent state university in their area, but a significant minority go to eastern Ivy League and top private universities in other parts of the country. For example, the Cate School, a boarding school near Santa Barbara, California, is modeled after its New England counterparts and draws most of its students from California and other western states. In the four years between 1993 and 1996, 35 percent of the 245 graduates went to one of fifteen prestigious Ivy League schools, with Middlebury (12), Harvard (10), and Brown (7) topping the list. The other leading destinations for Cate graduates

Table 3.1 The Ten Private High Schools That Sent the Highest Percentage of Their Graduates to Harvard, Yale, or Princeton, 1998–2001

School	Type	Location	HYP%[1]	Tuition	Avg. Grad. Class Size
Roxbury Latin School	boys	West Roxbury, MA	21.1	$14,000	50
Brearley School	girls	New York, NY	20.9	$22,850	44
Collegiate School	boys	New York, NY	20.0	$22,300	53
Groton School	coed	Groton, MA	17.9	$24,115	84
Dalton School	coed	New York, NY	17.6	$23,200	110
Spence School	girls	New York, NY	17.2	$20,700	42
Horace Mann School	coed	Bronx, NY	16.8	$22,980	158
Winsor School	girls	Boston, MA	16.7	$22,600	54
Milton Academy	coed	Milton, MA	15.8	$22,950	172
Phillips Andover	coed	Andover, MA	15.7	$22,160	266

[1]HYP percent is the percentage of students who went to Harvard, Yale, or Princeton.

Source: Compiled from *Worth Magazine*, September 2002.

were the University of California (27), Stanford (9), the University of Colorado (9), Georgetown (8), Duke (7), Vanderbilt (6), and the University of Chicago (5). Or, to take another example, St. John's in Houston is a lavishly endowed day school built in the Gothic architecture typical of many universities. From 1992 through 1996, 22 percent of its 585 graduates went to the fifteen Ivy League schools used in the Cate analysis, with Princeton (27), the University of Pennsylvania (15), Cornell (13), Harvard (12), and Yale (12) the most frequent destinations. As might be expected, 105 graduates went to the University of Texas (18 percent), but Rice (49), Vanderbilt (33), and Stanford (15) were high on the list. Only a few graduates of either Cate or St. John's went to less prestigious state schools.

Most private school graduates pursue careers in business, finance, or corporate law, which is evidence for the intertwining of the upper class and the corporate community. Their business-oriented preoccupations are demonstrated in the greatest detail in a study of all those who graduated from Hotchkiss between 1940 and 1950. Using the school's alumni files, the researcher followed the careers of 228 graduates from their date of graduation until 1970. Fifty-six percent of the sample became either bankers or business executives, with eighty of the ninety-one businessmen serving as president, vice president, or partner in their firms. Another 10 percent of the sample were lawyers, mostly as partners in large firms closely affiliated with the corporate community (Armstrong 1974).

The involvement of private school graduates on boards of directors is demonstrated in a study for this book of all alumni over the age of 45 from one of the most prestigious eastern boarding schools, St. Paul's. Using *Poor's Register of Corporations, Directors and Executives*, and *Who's Who in America* for 1980, it shows that 303 of these several thousand men were working as officers or directors in corporations in general, and that 102 were directors of 97 corporations in the *Fortune* 800. Their involvement was especially great in the financial sector. Most striking of all, twenty-one graduates of St. Paul's were either officers or directors at J. P. Morgan Bank, (now JPMorgan Chase after its merger in 2000 with another large bank). This finding suggests that the alumni of particular schools may tend to cluster at specific banks or corporations.

Due to special recruitment programs financed by wealthy individuals and corporations, private schools have become a major educational launching pad for a small percentage of low-income African-American and Latino students who graduate from elite universities and go to work in the corporate world. The oldest of these programs, A Better Chance, founded in the 1960s in response to the upheavals of the Civil Rights Movement, has graduated over 11,000 students. As of 2004 it had 1,600 students enrolled in 714 boarding schools and 699 independent day schools. The Prep for Prep program in New York City and the Steppingstone Foundation in Boston and Philadelphia, both of more recent vintage, have developed programs that identify high-achieving children of color in grade school and help prepare them for private schools with after-school, weekend, and summer instruction. Of the 609 Prep for Prep graduates in college in 2001, 113 were at Wesleyan, 96 at Harvard, 91 at Yale, 80 at Penn, 79 at Columbia, and 63 at Brown (Zweigenhaft and Domhoff 2003, pp. 167–170).

Today, the most visible graduate of one of these programs is Deval Patrick, elected as the first African-American governor of Massachusetts in 2006 after a long career in corporate law and corporate management. Raised by his mother in a low-income neighborhood in Chicago, he went to Milton Academy in Milton, Massachusetts, in 1970 on an A Better Chance scholarship and then graduated from Harvard University and Harvard Law School. He worked for the NAACP's Legal and Educational Defense Fund for three years and went on to join a prestigious corporate law firm in Boston. From 1994 until 1997 he served in the Clinton Administration as the assistant attorney general in charge of the Civil Rights Division of the Department of Justice, then chaired a task force created to ensure fairness and equal opportunity for employees at Texaco after the settlement of a racial discrimination suit. From 2001 to 2004, he served as an executive vice president at Coca-Cola, and he has also served as a corporate director for United Airlines and Reebok. He was an early supporter of Barack Obama's presidential campaign.

SOCIAL CLUBS

Private social clubs are a major point of orientation in the lives of upper-class adults. These clubs also have a role in differentiating members of the upper class from other members of society. The clubs of the upper class are many and varied, ranging from family-oriented country clubs and downtown men's and women's clubs to highly specialized clubs for yachtsmen, sportsmen, gardening enthusiasts, and fox hunters. Downtown men's clubs originally were places to have lunch and dinner, and occasionally to attend an evening performance or a weekend party. As upper-class families deserted the city for large suburban estates, a new kind of club, the country club, gradually took over some of these functions. The downtown club became almost entirely a luncheon club, a site for holding meetings, or a place to relax on a free afternoon. The country club, by contrast, became a haven for all members of the family. It offered social and sporting activities ranging from dances, parties, and banquets to golf, swimming, and tennis. Special group dinners were often arranged for all members on Thursday night, the traditional maid's night off across the United States.

Initiation fees, annual dues, and expenses vary from a few thousand dollars in downtown clubs to $100,000 to $150,00 in some country clubs, but money is not the only barrier in gaining membership to a club. Each club has a very rigorous screening process before accepting new members. Most require nomination by one or more active members, letters of recommendation from three to six members, and interviews with at least some members of the membership committee (Kendall 2008). Negative votes by two or three members of what is typically a ten- to twenty-person committee often are enough to deny admission to the candidate.

Men and women of the upper class often belong to clubs in several cities, creating a nationwide pattern of overlapping memberships. These overlaps provide evidence for social cohesion within the upper class. An indication of the nature and extent of this overlapping is revealed in a study of membership lists for twenty clubs in several major cities across the country in the late 1960s, including the Links Club in New York, the Chicago Club in Chicago, the Pacific Union Club in San Francisco, and the California Club in Los Angeles. There is sufficient overlap among eighteen of the twenty clubs to form three regional groupings and a fourth group that provides a bridge between the two largest regional groups. The several dozen men who are in three or more of the clubs, most of them very wealthy people who also sit on several corporate boards, are especially important in creating the overall pattern. The fact that these clubs often have from 1,000 to 2,000 members makes the percentage of overlap within this small number of clubs relatively small, ranging from a high of 20 to 30 percent between clubs in the same city to as low as 1 or 2 percent in clubs at opposite ends of the country (Bonacich and Domhoff 1981).

The overlap of this club network with corporate boards of directors provides further evidence for the intertwining of the upper class and corporate community. In a study in the 1960s for an earlier edition of this book, the club memberships of the chairpersons and outside directors of the 20 largest industrial corporations were counted. The overlaps with upper-class clubs in general were ubiquitous, but the concentration of directors in a few clubs was especially notable. At least one director from twelve of the twenty corporations was a member of the Links Club, which is the New York meeting ground of the national corporate establishment. Seven of General Electric's directors at the time were members, as were four from Chrysler, four from Westinghouse, and three from IBM. In addition to the Links, several other clubs had directors from four or more corporations. Another study, using membership lists from eleven prestigious clubs in different parts of the country, confirmed and extended these findings. A majority of the top twenty-five corporations in every major sector of the economy had directors in at least one of these clubs, and several had many more. For example, all of the twenty-five largest industrials had one or more directors in these eleven clubs. The Links in New York, with 79 connections to twenty-one industrial corporations, had the most (Domhoff 1975).

These clubs came under extreme criticism as bastions of Christian white male privilege in the 1970s, first by wealthy Jewish members of the corporate community who were incensed by their exclusion, then by civil rights activists who decried the lack of any African-American members, and then by feminist groups, which pointed out that the exclusion of women deprived women executives of opportunities to attend business luncheons and develop connections with executives from outside their own workplace (Baltzell

1964; Driscoll and Goldberg 1993; Zweigenhaft and Domhoff 1982). These criticisms made it more difficult to obtain membership lists for updated studies. They also led to a decline in the listing of club membership in publicly available sources, such as *Who's Who in America*, because the information was being used to raise questions about the men's fairness at confirmation hearings for government appointments. But one detailed study using *Who's Who in America* for the years 1962, 1973, 1983, and 1995 showed that corporate executives listed the same few clubs over the decades even though they were mentioned by a declining number of executives in each decade (Barnes and Sweezea 2006).

However, a lack of good membership information has not precluded studies based on other sources of information. For example, a recent study of social clubs in several Texas cities based on 100 interviews and newspaper articles shows that little if anything has changed in the club world over the decades, except for the huge increase in membership fees and monthly dues for country clubs. The members are still overwhelmingly white Christian men of wealth. Wealthy Jews have a parallel club structure, and women are generally excluded from membership, except in country clubs, where they are prohibited from using the golf course at certain times and excluded from some of the club rooms. The members attach great personal significance to belonging to these clubs and believe they are of value as a source of information, contacts, and support; that is, they remain places to renew social capital. Some of them have weekend arts shows or lecture series that add to the members' cultural capital as well, such as an exhibition of paintings by an upcoming artist or a mini-course on fine wines (Kendall 2008).

An interview study with forty-seven members of five elite country clubs in a Northeastern state showed many of the same patterns while focusing on the rationales members used for various forms of exclusionary practices. They endorsed greater ethnic and racial diversity, although they were vague about the fact that their clubs had very few minority-group members. Women for the most part accepted their secondary status in country clubs as being due to forces beyond club members' control, such as less wealth and more domestic duties, but some of the women in one of the clubs sued the club because of restrictions on when they could play golf (Sherwood 2004). As if to confirm these sociological studies, a male member of the Phoenix Country Club in Arizona was expelled from membership in July 2008 for "multiple violations of club etiquette" because he spoke to a *New York Times* reporter about a lawsuit that he and other members had filed against the club for excluding women from the men's grill (Steinhauer 2008).

The Bohemian Grove as a Place of Affirmation and Renewal

One of the central men-only clubs in the club network, the Bohemian Club of San Francisco, is also the most unusual and frequently studied. Its annual two-week retreat in its 2,700-acre Bohemian Grove, seventy-five miles north of San Francisco, brings together members of the upper class, corporate leaders, celebrities, and government officials for relaxation and entertainment. Several hundred "associate" members who pay lower dues in exchange for producing plays, skits, artwork, and other forms of entertainment are also members. There are 50 to 100 professors and university administrators, most of them from Stanford University and campuses of the University of California. This encampment provides a good view of the role of clubs in uniting the corporate community and the upper class. It is a microcosm of the world of the upper class.

Leaders of the Bohemian Club purchased the pristine forest setting called the Bohemian Grove in the 1890s after twenty years of holding the retreat in rented woodland quarters. Bohemians and their guests number anywhere from 1,500 to 2,500 for the three weekends in the encampment, which is always held during the last two weeks in July. However, there may be as few as 400 men in residence in the middle of the week because most return to their homes and jobs after the weekends. During their stay the campers are treated to plays, symphonies, concerts, lectures, and commentaries by entertainers, scholars, corporate executives, and government officials. They also trapshoot, canoe, swim, drop by the art gallery, and take guided tours into the outer fringe of the mountain forest. But a stay at the Bohemian Grove is mostly a time for relaxation in the modest lodges, bunkhouses, and even teepees that fit unobtrusively into the landscape along the two or three dirt roads that join the few "developed" acres within the Grove. It is like a summer camp for corporate leaders and their entertainers. Pranks, storytelling, off-color jokes, bragging, and the massive consumption of expensive alcoholic beverages are the order of the day.

The men gather in small camps comprised of ten to thirty members during their stay, although the camps for associate members are often larger, a telling reminder of the status differentials that are maintained even during the encampment. Each of the approximately 120 camps has its own pet name, such as Sons of Toil, Cave Man, Mandalay, Toyland, Owl's Nest, Hill Billies, and Parsonage. Some camps are noted for special drinking parties, brunches, or luncheons to which they invite members from other camps. One advertises its soft-core pornography collection as an attraction which guests can look at while having a drink. The camps are a fraternity system within the larger fraternity.

There are many traditional events during the encampment, including plays called the High Jinx and the Low Jinx, which sometimes include men playing the parts women would play if they were not excluded from the club. The most memorable event, however, is an elaborate ceremonial ritual called the Cremation of Care, which is held on the first Saturday night. It takes place at the base of a forty-foot owl shrine, constructed out of poured concrete and made even more resplendent by the mottled forest mosses that cover much of it. According to the club's librarian, who is also a historian at a large university, the event "incorporates druidical ceremonies, elements of medieval Christian liturgy, sequences directly inspired by the Book of Common Prayer, traces of Shakespearean drama and the seventeenth century masque, and late nineteenth century American lodge rites" (Vaughn 2006). Bohemians are proud that the ceremony has been carried out for 136 consecutive years as of 2008.

The opening ceremony is called the Cremation of Care because it involves the burning of an effigy named Dull Care, who embodies the burdens and responsibilities that these busy Bohemians now wish to shed temporarily. More than 250 Bohemians take part in the ceremony as priests, elders, boatmen, and woodland voices. After many flowery speeches and a long conversation with Dull Care, the high priest lights the fire with the flame from the Lamp of Fellowship, located on the "Altar of Bohemia" at the base of the shrine. The ceremony ends with fireworks, shouting, and a band playing tunes such as "There'll Be a Hot Time in the Old Town Tonight." The attempt to create a sense of cohesion and in-group solidarity among the assembled is complete. (For a detailed account of the Bohemian Grove, along with photographs and posters, see the document "Social Cohesion and the Bohemian Grove" at www.whorulesamerica.net.)

The retreat sometimes provides an occasion for more than fun and merriment. Although business is rarely discussed, except in an informal way in groups of two or three, the retreat provides members with an opportunity to introduce their friends to politicians and to hear formal noontime speeches called Lakeside Talks from political candidates and a wide range of experts. In 2008 a former secretary of state, a retired admiral, a retired university president, and the current Librarian of Congress were among the speakers for this occasion.

Every Republican president since the early twentieth century has been a member of the Bohemian Club or a guest at the Bohemian Grove, with Herbert Hoover, Richard Nixon, Gerald Ford, Ronald Reagan, and George H. W. Bush as members. Hoover was sitting in the Grove in the summer of 1927 when Calvin Coolidge announced from Washington that he would not run again, and soon dozens of Hoover's club mates dropped by his camp to urge him to run and offer their support. Future president Dwight D. Eisenhower made his first prenomination political speech in a Lakeside Talk at the Grove in 1951, which was positively received by the previously skeptical West Coast elites around Hoover, including Nixon, who was soon to become Ike's running mate.

Nixon himself wrote in his memoirs that he made his most important speech on his path to the presidency at the Grove in 1967, calling it "the speech that gave me the most pleasure and satisfaction of my political career," and one that "in many ways marked the first milestone on my road to the presidency" because it was "an unparalleled opportunity to reach some of the most important and influential men, not just from California, but from across the country" (Nixon 1978, p. 284). During that same week he and Reagan had a chat in which Reagan agreed he would not challenge Nixon in the early Republican primaries, coming into the fray only if Nixon faltered. More recently, George H. W. Bush used a Lakeside Talk in 1995 to introduce his son George W. Bush to the members as a potential future president (Vaughn 2006). In 1999 he brought George W. to the Grove to meet more of his friends:

> In early August, father took son to a private gathering at the secretive and exclusive Bohemian Grove in California. George H. W. Bush had gone to a meeting there prior to his run, in 1979. He figured it would also benefit George W. to meet his circle of friends there, including corporate heads. The former president was a member of Hill Billies camp, which included William F. Buckley and Donald Rumsfeld as members (Schweizer and Schweizer 2004, p. 460).

Perhaps the most striking change in the Lakeside Talks in the 1990s was the absence of any leading Democrats. No Democratic president has ever been a member of the Bohemian Club, but cabinet members from the Kennedy, Johnson, and Carter administrations were prominent guests and Lakeside speakers in the past. In 1990 Jimmy Carter gave a Lakeside Talk, 10 years after his presidency. Nor are there many Democrats remaining among the regular members (Wehr 1994).

Three studies demonstrate the way in which this one club intertwines the upper class with the corporate community. The first uses the years 1970 and 1980, the second compares 1970 and 1993, and the third focuses on 2008. In 1970, according to the first study, 29 percent of the top 800 corporations had at least one officer or director at the Bohemian Grove festivities; in 1980 the figure was 30 percent. As might be expected, the overlap was especially great among the largest corporations, with twenty-three of the top twenty-five industrials represented in 1970 and fifteen of twenty-five in 1980. Twenty of the twenty-five largest banks had at least one officer or director in attendance in both 1970 and 1980. Other business sectors had somewhat less representation.

An even more intensive study, which included participant-observation and interviews, along with a membership network analysis, extended the sociological understanding of the Bohemian Grove into the 1990s. Using a list of 1,144 corporations, well beyond the 800 used in the studies for 1970 and 1980, the study found that 24 percent of these companies had at least one director who was a member or guest in 1993. For the top 100 corporations outside of California, the figure was 42 percent, compared to 64 percent in 1970 (Phillips 1994). In terms of what goes on during the encampment, little or nothing had changed since the 1970s. An even more recent study based on several summers of participant-observation supports this conclusion about the continuity of the club's culture (Vaughn 2006).

In 2008, there were 101 directors of 116 companies among the 2,259 members. This percentage is lower than in the previous studies because it does not include guests at the Grove; guest lists are now kept under lock and key, if they are printed at all. In addition, the members in 2008 included many stock brokers and investment advisers, dozens of retired corporate officials, several appointees from past Republican administrations, the owner of the country's largest privately held company (Koch Industries), the husband of the Speaker of the House of Representatives (Paul F. Pelosi), singer Jimmy Buffett, actor Clint Eastwood, and author Herman Wouk.

As the case of the Bohemian Grove and its theatrical performances rather dramatically illustrates, clubs seem to have the same function within the upper class that secret societies and brotherhoods have in tribal societies. With their restrictive membership policies, initiatory rituals, and great emphasis on tradition, clubs carry on the heritage of primitive secret societies. They create an attitude of prideful exclusiveness within their members that contributes to an in-group feeling and a sense of fraternity within the upper class.

Sociologically speaking, retreats such as the Bohemian Grove also reaffirm the shared values needed to reinforce class solidarity. There is first of all a ritual separation from the mundane everyday world through the Cremation of Care ceremony, which brings people into the realm of a make-believe time and space that reaffirms a whole range of beliefs that the men hold about themselves and the nature of American society (Vaughn 2006). The encampment also reaffirms another allegedly timeless aspect of the moral universe that the Bohemians want to sustain: male dominance. The very exclusion of women from the Bohemian Grove makes this point, but it is underlined by sexual jokes, dressing up as women for some of the plays and skits, the pornography collection, and frequent verbal put-downs of women. However, the exclusion of women also relates to the larger issue of male bonding: The men are reaffirming that they trust each other by sharing in activities that would be frowned upon if they were carried out in public spaces. They are learning to keep secrets from outsiders, which is also a good part of what is going on when college fraternities force their new initiates to learn a considerable amount of worthless information and undergo endless amounts of hazing.

There is a final but futile attempt at reaffirmation that is part of the retreat: Members and guests can escape from the reality of being aging alpha males coming face to face with their own mortality and imagine themselves as the same youthful and vigorous collegians they were when they joined fraternities and carried out pranks decades earlier. It is the good old days all over again. In their heart of hearts, they still feel like they are somewhere between 18 and 23 years old, at least after a drink or two, so they enjoy being part of this timeless and unchanging world for a few days.

In concluding this discussion of the Bohemian Club and its retreat as one small example of the intersection of the upper class and corporate community, it needs to be stressed that the Bohemian Grove is not a place of power. As the foregoing account makes clear, no business deals, policy plans, or conspiracies are hatched there. Instead, it is a place where people of power relax, make new acquaintances, and enjoy visiting with old friends. It is primarily a place for social bonding and the renewal of traditional values.

THE FEMININE HALF OF THE UPPER CLASS

During the late nineteenth and early twentieth centuries, women of the upper class carved out their own distinct roles within the context of male domination in business, finance, and law. They went to separate private schools, founded their own social clubs, and belonged to their own voluntary associations. As young women and party goers, they set the fashions for society. As older women and activists, they took charge of the nonprofit welfare and cultural institutions of the society, serving as fundraisers, philanthropists, and directors in a manner parallel to their male counterparts in business and politics. To prepare themselves for their leadership roles, they created the Junior League in 1901 to provide internships, role models, mutual support, and training in the management of meetings.

Due to the general social changes of the 1960s, and in particular the revival of the feminist movement, the socialization of wealthy young women has changed somewhat in recent decades. Most private schools are now coeducational and their women graduates are encouraged to go to major four-year colleges, where they join one of the four or five sororities with nationwide social prestige (e.g., Kappa Kappa Gamma, Kappa Alpha Theta, Pi Beta Phi, and Delta Delta Delta). Women of the upper class are more likely to have careers; there are already two or three examples of women who have risen to the top of their family's business. During the 1980s, women became more likely to serve on corporate boards (Ghiloni 1986). Still, due to the emphasis on tradition, there may be even less gender equality in the upper class than there is in the professional stratum. The extent to which further equality can be attained remains an open question.

The most informative and intimate look at the adult lives of traditional upper-class women is provided in four different interview and observation studies from four different regions of the country: the East Coast, the Midwest, the Southwest, and the West Coast (Daniels 1988; Kendall 2002; MacLeod 1984; Ostrander 1984). They reveal the similarities in upper-class lifestyles throughout the United States. They show that the women exercise power in numerous cultural and civic organizations, but also take traditional roles at home vis-à-vis their husbands and children. By asking the women to describe a typical day and to explain which activities are most important to them, these sociologists found that the role of community volunteer is a central preoccupation for upper-class women. It has significance as a family tradition and as an opportunity to fulfill an obligation to the community. One elderly woman involved for several decades in both the arts and human services said: "If you're privileged, you have a certain responsibility. This was part of my upbringing; it's a tradition, a pattern of life that my brothers and sisters [follow] too" (Ostrander 1984, pp. 128–129).

The volunteer role is institutionalized in the training programs and activities of a variety of service organizations. This is especially the case with the Junior League, which is meant for women between 20 and 40 years of age, including some upwardly mobile professional women. "Voluntarism is crucial and the Junior League is the quintessence of volunteer work," explained one woman. "Everything the League does improves the situation but doesn't rock the boat. It fits into existing institutions" (Ostrander 1984, p. 113). Quite unexpectedly, many of the women serving as volunteers, fundraisers, and board members for charitable and civic organizations view their work as a protection of the American way of life against the further encroachment of government into areas of social welfare. Some even see themselves as bulwarks against socialism. "There must always be people to do volunteer work," one commented. "If you have a society where no one is willing, then you may as well have communism, where it's all done by the government." Another stated: "It would mean that the government would take over, and it would all be regimented. If there are no volunteers, we would live in a completely managed society which is quite the opposite to our history of freedom." Another equated government support with socialism: "You'd have to go into government funds. That's socialism. The more we can keep independent and under private control, the better it is" (Ostrander 1984, pp. 132–137).

Despite this emphasis on volunteer work, the women placed high value on family life. They arranged their schedules to be home when children came home from school and they stressed that their primary concern was to provide a good home for their husbands. Several of them wanted to have greater decision-making power over their inherited wealth, but almost all of them preferred to be in the traditional roles of wife and mother, at least until their children were grown.

Although it comes as a surprise to many people, the debutante season—a series of parties, teas, and dances that culminates in one or more grand balls—remains an important part of the social life of upper-class women. These highly expensive rituals, in which great attention is lavished on every detail of the food, decorations, and entertainment, are a central focus of the Christmas social season, but in some cities debutante balls are held in the spring as well. Parents, with the help of upper-class women who work as social secretaries and social consultants, spend extensive time planning the details with dress designers, caterers, champagne importers, florists, decorators, and band leaders.

Despite the great importance placed upon the debut tradition by upper-class parents, debutante events came into considerable disfavor among young women as the social upheavals of the late 1960s and early 1970s reached their climax. This decline reveals that the reproduction of the upper class as a social class is an effort that must be made with each new generation. Although enough young women participated to keep the tradition alive, the refusal to take part by a significant minority led to the cancellation of some balls and the curtailment of many others. Stories appeared in newspapers across the country telling of debutantes who thought the whole process was "silly" or that the money should be given to a good cause. By 1973, however, the situation began to change again, and by the mid-1970s things were back to normal. As a wealthy young Texas woman told a sociologist in the late 1990s:

> I was very busy while I was in college. On top of my studies, I was presented [as a debutante] in Dallas, Austin, Tyler, and New Orleans. I went to teas and dinners and parties. It was really fun because some of my sorority sisters were also presented, representing other cities, and we could all be together at these activities away from school. When my parents had my deb party, there were dozens of my [sorority] sisters there. One December my family and I were in New York for my International Debutante Ball presentation (Kendall 2002, p. 100).

Following graduation, this debutante attended graduate school for a short time and then moved to Washington to take a job in the Bush Administration that she obtained through family connections.

The decline of the debutante season and its subsequent resurgence in times of domestic tranquility shows very clearly that one of its latent functions is to help perpetuate the upper class from generation to generation. When the underlying values of the class were questioned by a few of its younger members, the institution went into decline. Attitudes toward such social institutions as the debutante ball are one indicator of whether or not adult members of the upper class have succeeded in insulating their children from the rest of society.

In the light of all the changes of recent decades, women of the upper class remain in a paradoxical position. They are subordinate to male members of their class, but they nonetheless exercise important power in some institutional arenas. They may or may not be fully satisfied with their ambiguous power status, but they recognize that they have considerable class power and social standing nonetheless. Both they and their male counterparts realize that they bring an upper-class, antigovernment perspective to their exercise of power. There is thus class solidarity between men and women toward the rest of society. Commenting on the complex role of upper-class women, a feminist scholar drew the following stark picture: "First they must do to class what gender has done to their work—render it invisible; next, they must maintain the same class structure they have struggled to veil" (Daniels 1988, p. x).

DROPOUTS, FAILURES, AND CHANGE AGENTS

Not all men and women of the upper class fit the usual molds. A few are dropouts, jet-setters, failures, or even critics of the upper class. Except for a few long-standing exceptions, however, the evidence also suggests that many of the young jet-setters and dropouts return to more familiar pathways. Numerous anecdotal examples show that some members of the upper class even lead lives of failure, despite all the opportunities available to them. Although members of the upper class are trained for leadership and given every opportunity to develop feelings of self-confidence, there are some who fail in school, become involved with drugs and alcohol, or become mentally disturbed. Once again, however, this cannot be seen as evidence for a lack of cohesion in the upper class, for there are bound to be some problems for individuals in any group.

There are even a few members of the upper class who abandon its institutions and values to become part of the liberal-labor coalition or leftists. They participate actively in liberal or leftist causes as well as lending financial support. Such people have supported several of the leading liberal and socialist magazines of the past and present, including *The Nation* and *Mother Jones*. Some of the most visible recent examples of this tendency work through a national network of 15 change-oriented foundations called the Funding Exchange. These foundations gave away over $50 million between the time they were founded in the 1970s and the 1990s. They receive money from wealthy individuals and then donate it to feminist, environmentalist, low-income, and minority-group activists. They also set up discussion groups for college-age members of the upper class who are working through issues relating to their class backgrounds and thinking about providing money for liberal causes. In the case of the Haymarket Foundation, the committee that makes the donations (about $400,000 per year) is composed primarily of activists from groups that have been supported by the foundation. This approach provides a way to overcome the usual power relations between donors and recipients (Ostrander 1995).

CONTINUITY AND UPWARD MOBILITY

Americans always have believed that anyone can rise from rags to riches if they try hard enough, but in fact a rise from the bottom to the top is very rare and often a matter of luck or being in the right place at the right time. In the late nineteenth century, a wealthy upper class Bostonian with a Harvard education, Horatio Alger, became a best-selling author by writing short fictional books about young boys who had gone from penniless adversity to great wealth. In real life, the commentators of his day pointed to three or four actual examples. Subsequent research showed that most of the business leaders of that era did not fit the Horatio Alger myth. As one historian put it, Horatio Alger stories appeared more frequently in magazines and textbooks than they did in reality (Miller 1949).

Since 1982 the Horatio Alger story line has been taken up by *Forbes*, a business magazine that publishes an annual list of the 400 allegedly richest Americans. "Forget old money," says the article that introduces the 1996 list. "Forget silver spoons. Great fortunes are being created almost monthly in the U.S. today by young entrepreneurs who hadn't a dime when we created this list 14 years ago" (Marsh 1996). But the Horatio Alger story is no less rare today than it was in the 1890s. A study of all those on the *Forbes* lists for 1995 and 1996 showed that at least 56 percent of them came from millionaire families and that another 14 percent came from the top 10 percent of the income ladder (Collins 1997). These figures are probably an underestimate because it is difficult to obtain accurate information on family origins from those who want to obscure their pasts. Even those in the upwardly mobile 30 percent often have excellent educations or other advantages. As for the immigrants on the *Forbes* list, they too sometimes come from wealthy families; contrary to the stereotype, not all immigrants to the United States arrive poor, at least not anymore (Zweigenhaft and Domhoff 2006; Zweigenhaft and Domhoff 1982).

To take one example, consider the social background of Wayne Huizenga, estimated to be worth $1.4 billion in 1996 through the creation of, first, Waste Management Company, and then Blockbuster Video. Huizenga is often depicted as starting out as a mere garbage collector. As *Current Biography* puts it: "The hero of a real-life Horatio Alger story, in his early twenties, Huizenga worked as a garbage-truck driver." But he was born in a Chicago suburb, graduated from a private high school, and had a grandfather who owned a garbage-collection business in Chicago. His father was a real estate investor. True, Huizenga did start his own garbage company in southern Florida after not showing much aptitude for college, but he also merged it with companies in Chicago that were successors to his grandfather's firm, one of which was headed by a cousin by marriage. This is enterprising behavior, but it is not a Horatio Alger saga.

Forbes also talks about several people on its list as "college dropouts," but people who leave a prestigious institution like Harvard or Stanford to pursue a new opportunity where timing is everything hardly fit the image of a "college dropout." For example, Bill Gates, the richest person in the United States in 2008, is often described as a college dropout because he left Harvard early to found Microsoft before someone could beat him to what was the next logical step in the marketing of computer software. However, he is also the son of a prominent corporate lawyer in Seattle and a graduate of the top private school in that city, and he did go to Harvard.

According to research studies, most upward social mobility in the United States involves relatively small changes for those above the lowest 20 percent and below the top 5 percent. The grandfather is a blue-collar worker, the father has a good white-collar job based on a B.A. degree, and one or two of the father's children are lawyers or physicians, but most of the father's grandchildren are back to being white-collar workers and middle-level executives. Upward social mobility of this type may be even less frequent for non-whites. In addition, the best recent studies suggest that upward social mobility may be declining in recent years (Kerbo 2000; Mishel, Bernstein and Allegretto 2007, chapter 2).

As the findings on the rarity of great upward mobility suggest, the continuity of the upper class from generation to generation is very great. This finding conflicts with the oft-repeated folk wisdom that there is a large turnover at the top of the American social ladder. Once in the upper class, families tend to stay there even though middle-class brides and grooms who marry into their families join them in each generation. One study demonstrating this point began with a list of twelve families who were among the top wealth-holders in Detroit for 1860, 1892, and 1902. After documenting their high social standing as well as their wealth, it traced their Detroit-based descendants into the late twentieth century. Nine of the twelve families still had members in the Detroit upper class; members from six families were directors of top corporations in the city as of the early 1970s. The study casts light on some of the reasons why the continuity is not even greater. One of the top wealth holders of 1860 had only one child, who in turn had no children. Another family persisted into a fourth generation of four great-granddaughters, all of whom married outside of Detroit (Schuby 1975).

A study of listings in the *Social Register* for 1940, 1977, and 1995 reveals the continuing presence of families descended from the largest fortunes of the nineteenth and early twentieth centuries. Using a list of eighty-seven families from one history of great American fortunes and sixty-six families from another such book, a sociologist found that 92 percent of the families in the first book were still represented in 1977, with the figure falling slightly to 87 percent in 1995. In similar fashion, 88 percent of the families in the second book were represented in 1977 and 83 percent in 1995. Over half of these families signaled their connection to the founder of the fortune by putting "the Fourth," "the Fifth," or "the Sixth" after their names. Almost half were given the last name of their wealthy mothers as their first name, once again demonstrating the concern with continuity (Broad 1996).

The American upper class, then, is a mixture of old and new members. There is both continuity and social mobility, with the newer members being assimilated into the lifestyle of the class through participation in the schools, clubs, and other social institutions described earlier in this chapter. There may be some tensions between those who are newly arrived and those of established status, as novelists and journalists love to point out, but what they have in common soon outweighs their differences.

THE UPPER CLASS AND CORPORATE CONTROL

So far this chapter has demonstrated the overlap between upper-class social institutions and top leadership in the corporate community. It is now possible to show how members of the upper class involve themselves in the ownership and control of specific corporations through family ownership, family offices, holding companies, and investment partnerships.

Family Ownership

As shown by the early history of the corporate community discussed in the previous chapter, it has never been the case that American corporations were primarily owned by separate families, but by groups of investors, banks, and other types of financial companies. However, there are nonetheless many such firms in the United States today that are often overlooked when talking about the separation of ownership and control. They include 305 privately owned firms that have $1 billion or more in sales, many of which would be in the *Fortune* 1000 if they were publicly owned. The way in which these companies can be part of larger family empires is seen in the case of the Pritzker family in Chicago, who provide a useful example because several members of the family became strong financial backers of future president Barack Obama when he first ran for the U.S. Senate representing Illinois in 2004, as discussed in Chapter 6. Building on their core property, Hyatt Hotels, which has been in the family for three generations and is now called Global Hyatt because it has over 200 hotels around the world, the Pritzkers also own an industrial conglomerate that was the 36th largest privately held company in 2007, as well as Galaxy Aerospace, a joint venture with Israel Aircraft Industries to build a new business jet; Encore Senior Living, a network of assisted living centers; and Royal Caribbean Cruises, where it has a 25 percent ownership stake.

In addition, the family has a real estate arm, Pritzker Realty, and owns a majority interest in the Parking Spot, which operates parking lots near airports. Very recently, the family leaders had to sell a major share of their industrial conglomerate to Warren Buffett, the second-richest person in America in 2008, and a minority share of Global Hyatt to Goldman Sachs in order to settle a lawsuit filed by two young members of the family who felt their father, uncles, and older cousins had misused their trust funds. The suit revealed the family was worth $15–20 billion that was wrapped up in over 1,000 trust funds, some of which were held in offshore locations (Andrews 2003; Savage 2008a).

Even in the case of publicly controlled corporations, three different studies provide detailed evidence on the extent of family involvement in the largest American corporations. The first used both official documents and the informal—but often more informative—findings of the business press as its source of information. It concluded that 40 percent of the top 300 industrials were probably under family control in the 1960s, using the usual cut-off point of 5 percent of the stock as the criterion (Burch 1972). Analyzing the official records that became available in the 1970s, a team of researchers at Corporate Data Exchange provided detailed information on the major owners of most of the top 500 industrials for 1980, showing that significant individual and family ownership continued to exist for all but the very largest of corporations. In 44 percent of the 423 profiled corporations that were not controlled by other corporations or foreign interests, one individual or family was a top stockholder, with at least 5 percent of the stock. The figures were much lower among the fifty largest, however, where only 17 percent of the forty-seven companies included in the study showed evidence of major family involvement (Albrecht and Locker 1981). The small percentage of the very largest industrials under individual or family control concurs with findings in a third study, which focused on the 200 largest nonfinancial corporations for 1974–1975 (Herman 1981). For the 104 companies common to the two studies, there were only four disagreements in classifying the nature of their control structure, and some of those may be due to changes in ownership patterns between 1974 and 1980.

The Family Office

A family office is an informal organization through which members of a family or group of families agree to pool some of their resources in order to hire people to provide them with advice on investments, estate planning, charitable giving, and even political donations in some cases. Family offices often handle all financial transactions and legal matters as well as personal needs such as theater tickets and car rentals. Their relevance here is in terms of their potential for maintaining control of corporations founded by an earlier generation of the family. Such offices contradict the belief that corporate control is necessarily lost due to the inheritance of stock by a large number of descendants. They often serve as a unifying source for the family as well. They sometimes have employees who sit on boards of directors to represent the family.

In 2008 there were an estimated 4,000 family offices that were each responsible for $100 million or more. One office has kept track of $840 million for four families for three generations (Konigsberg 2008). During the past few decades, multifamily offices began to appear, usually serving an average of fifty families with $10 million or more in assets. One survey concluded that there were eighty such offices handling $305 billion in assets in 2006 (Hawthorne 2008).

The most detailed account of a family office was provided by a sociologist as part of a study in the 1970s of the Weyerhaeuser family of Saint Paul, Minnesota, and Tacoma, Washington, whose great wealth is concentrated in the lumber industry. By assembling a family genealogy chart that covered five generations and then interviewing several members of the family, he determined that a family office, called Fiduciary Counselors, Inc. (FCI), aided the family in maintaining a central role in two major corporations. He demonstrated that there are members of the family on the boards of these companies whose last names are not Weyerhaeuser and that the stock holdings managed by the family office were large enough to maintain control.

Fiduciary Counselors, Inc., also housed the offices of two Weyerhaeuser holding companies (meaning companies created only to own stock in operating companies). These holding companies were used to make investments for family members as a group and to own shares in new companies created by family members. Although the primary focus of the Weyerhaeuser family office was economic matters, the office served other functions as well. It kept the books for fifteen different charitable foundations of varying sizes and purposes through which family members gave money and it coordinated political donations by family members all over the country.

Holding Companies and Investment Partnerships

Holding companies, briefly defined in the previous paragraph, can serve the economic functions of a family office if the family is still small and tight-knit. They have the added advantage of being incorporated entities that can buy and sell stock in their own names. Because they are privately held, they need report only to tax authorities on their activities.

Warren Buffett, the scion of third-generation wealth, operates through a holding company, Berkshire Hathaway. Along with his partners, he sat on the boards of several of the companies in which he invested until he recently began to ease into retirement (Lowenstein 1995). Some wealthy individuals and families operate through a slightly different financial arrangement, an investment partnership, which gives them more flexibility than the corporate form. Kohlberg, Kravis, Roberts, usually known as KKR, is the most visible example since the 1980s because it has been involved in many corporate takeovers. The lead partner, Henry Kravis, who is sometimes listed as a self-made person because it is not generally known that his father was worth tens of millions of dollars, sat on eight corporate boards at one point, including those of Safeway Stores and Gillette, companies that he and his partners acquired after 1986. His cousin and partner, George Roberts, joined him on seven of those boards, and was on one other board as well. There can be little doubt about who controls these companies, or about the control of any other companies where investment partnerships or holding companies have representatives on the board of directors. The takeovers by KKR and similar firms show that firms allegedly controlled by their managers can be acquired by groups of rich investors whenever they so desire, unless of course they are resisted by a rival group of owners (Bruck 1988; Stewart 1991).

Successful Wall Street investment bankers who raise money from super-wealthy families also start investment trusts. Such was the case with a stock trader at Goldman Sachs in the 1980s who went on to found ESL Investments, which in 2004 owned 52.6 percent of Kmart (67th on the *Fortune* 500 list in 2004), 28.5 percent of AutoNation, a chain of car dealerships (97th on the *Fortune* list), and 26.8 percent of AutoZone, a parts retailer (331st on the *Fortune* list). The former stock trader was worth an estimated $1.7 billion before the stock market decline (the stock market fell by 33 percent in 2008).

People with Washington experience put other successful investment trusts together. A former White House aide to Jimmy Carter started the Carlyle Group in 1987 with money from the billionaire Mellon family of Pittsburgh and began making deals that soon involved defense companies. He added several prominent Washington insiders, including a former secretary of defense from the George H. W. Bush Administration, and the company was off and running. The company gained greater visibility in 1995 when former president George H. W. Bush became a senior adviser on its Asia Advisory Board, traveling to South Korea, China, Kuwait, and Saudi Arabia to open doors for the people who made the actual business deals. It became even better known after 2002 because an estranged half-brother of Osama Bin Laden, one of his 52 siblings, had invested in the company in the late 1990s, along with other Saudis (Schweizer and Schweizer 2004). Carlyle was the 15th largest defense contractor in 2004 with $1.7 billion in contracts, 1.7 percent of the total defense contract budget.

The Crown family of Chicago, worth an estimated $4.1 billion in 2007, operates through a combined holding and investment company, Henry A. Crown and Company, that manages investments in banking, transportation, oil and gas, cellular phones, home furnishings, and resort properties. The company is worth using as an example because several family members became financial supporters of President Obama's political career in the early 2000s, as discussed in Chapter 6. Starting with a company that sold building supplies, the two brothers who founded the dynasty in 1921 used that company to take control of General Dynamics, one of the country's largest defense contractors, in 1959 (Zweigenhaft and Domhoff 1982, pp. 27–29). In addition, the family owns parts of JPMorgan Chase, Hilton Hotels, Rockefeller Center, and the New York Yankees. Its private holdings include Crown Golf Properties, which operates golf courses in seven states.

The current patriarch of the family, Lester Crown, a son of one of the founding brothers, sits on the boards of General Dynamics and Maytag. One of his sons, James S. Crown, who raised large amounts of money for Barack Obama's presidential campaign, is on the boards of General Dynamics, JP Morgan Chase, and Sara Lee; he is also the chair of the board of trustees of the University of Chicago. Another of Lester

Crown's sons is on the boards of Hilton Hotels and Caesars Entertainment, and a third was on the board of Alltel, a wireless communication company, until it was purchased by Verizon in early 2009. One of Lester Crown's daughters, who manages the family's charitable foundation, is a director of Northern Trust Bank and Illinois Tool Works and a trustee of Yale. The family's top employee at Henry Crown & Company is on the board of General Dynamics.

The cumulative findings on the involvement of family ownership, family offices, holding companies, and investment partnerships in large corporations suggest that a significant number of corporations continue to be controlled by major owners. However, the very largest corporations in several sectors of the economy show no large ownership stake by individuals or families, whether through family offices, holding companies, or other devices. Their largest owners, in blocks of a few percent, are bank trust departments, investment companies, mutual funds, and pension funds. Moreover, interview studies suggest that bank trust departments and investment companies do not take any role in influencing the management of the corporations in which they invest (Herman 1975; Herman 1981).

As for the pension funds, the corporate and other private pension funds have taken a hands-off role as well, especially during the bonanza decades on Wall Street that ended in 2008. During the late 1980s and early 1990s, however, several public employee and union pension funds, whose assets account for less than 15 percent of all pension assets, seemed to be flexing their muscles in corporate board rooms, attempting to force policy changes and even changes in management. Their actions raised the possibility of an investor capitalism in which government employees and unions could challenge the prerogatives and power of the traditional owners and executives inside the corporate community, but this fledgling challenge to corporate managers met with little or no success. It all but died after a high point in the early 1990s because the public pension fund activists drew criticism from elected officials and some of the officials appointed to the pension funds' boards of directors (Dobrzynski 1996a; Dobrzynski 1996b).

Reflecting on their efforts in September 2000, many of the leading pension-fund activists expressed disappointment with the cautious approach adopted by most institutional investors. The executive director of the Council of Institutional Investors, an organization of pension fund mangers, said that they had "won the easy battles," such as being able to have nonbinding shareholder proposals sent out along with company proxies, but that they were in danger of ending up merely writing letters asking executives why they ignore the reformer's proposals. She saw the movement at a turning point and talked about "closing up shop" (Day 2000). By 2003 *The New York Times* called the movement a

"Revolution That Wasn't" based on interviews with its disheartened leaders; in 2004 the executive director of the Council of Institutional Investors resigned after growing weary of the conflicts between representatives from corporate and union pension funds, each of which thwarted reform efforts in their own self-serving ways (Deutsch 2003; Walsh 2004).

As this account makes clear, public pension funds are best seen from a power point of view as large pools of money that Wall Street financial firms try to make use of in their merger deals and other profit-making activities. In fact, many pubic pension funds have been hurt because of their purchase of risky financial assets between 2005 and 2008 that were backed by mortgages sold to people who could not make the payments. Many ended up with egg on their faces because they had been conned by the Wall Street advisers who enticed them into these investments with promises of extremely high returns. (For a detailed history of the rise and fall of the pension fund movement, see the document "Pension Fund Capitalism" at www.whorulesamerica.net.)

Contrary to the hopes of the public pension fund activists, the largest corporations in the United States are still controlled by a combination of their high-level executives, the for-profit financial institutions that are concerned with the value of their stockholdings, and top individual stockholders, all of which are usually represented on the board of directors. However, the power to run such corporations on a day-to-day basis belongs to the CEO and his or her handful of supporters on the board. The CEOs and other top corporate executives are the topic of the next two sections.

WHERE DO CORPORATE EXECUTIVES COME FROM?

There have been many studies of the class origins of the top executives in very large corporations. They most frequently focus on the occupation of the executive's father. These studies show that "between 40 percent and 70 percent of all large corporation directors and managers were raised in business families, which comprised only a tiny fraction of families of that era" (Useem 1980a; Useem and Karabel 1986). One study compared business leaders at thirty-year intervals over the century and found that the percentage whose fathers were businesspeople remained constant at 65 percent (Useem 1980a).

However, even though many corporate executives at large corporations come from business backgrounds, the fact remains that there are a significant number of high-level managers who come from middle-level origins and work their way up the corporate ladder. The number of such people may be exaggerated somewhat because relevant information on schools and clubs is not always available, but their role within the corporate community is a large one even by conservative estimates.

Today, few if any chief executive officers at the largest corporations were born into the upper class. This raises the possibility, often expressed by pluralists, that professional managers are distinct from upper-class owners and directors, which suggests there might be some degree of separation between the corporate community and the upper class.

Before turning to this issue, the relative lack of members of the upper class in top-level executive positions in large corporations can be addressed briefly. While it may seem surprising at first glance that members of the upper class have their least involvement at the executive level in the very largest corporations, the reasons have nothing to do with lack of education, ability, or expertise. Simply put, members of the upper class usually are not interested in a career that requires years of experience climbing the corporate ladder in a large bureaucratic organization when there is no incentive for them to do so. They prefer to work in finance, corporate law, or their own family businesses, or they spend their time managing their own large fortunes and following the stock market. All of these pursuits give them greater personal autonomy and more opportunities to exercise power. In recent decades, they have been especially attracted to Wall Street, where the real money has been. In a word, members of the upper class are capitalists who strive to make a profit by investing their funds, not corporate managers who have to deal with the day-to-day problems of keeping an organization together.

THE ASSIMILATION OF RISING CORPORATE EXECUTIVES

The evidence presented in this section shows how rising corporate executives are assimilated into the upper class and come to share its values, thereby cementing the relationship between the upper class and the corporate community rather than severing it. The aspirations of professional managers for themselves and for their offspring lead them into the upper class in behavior, values, and style of life.

Whatever the social origins of top managers, most of them are educated and trained in a small number of private universities and business schools. The results from several different studies reveal that about one-third of those who manage the largest companies graduated from Harvard, Yale, or Princeton, and two-thirds went to one of the dozen most heavily endowed universities (Useem 1980a). It is in these schools that people of middle-class origins receive their introduction to the values of the upper class and the corporate community, mingling for the first time with men and women of the upper class, and sometimes with upper-class teachers and administrators who serve as role models. This modeling continues in the graduate schools of business that many of them attend before joining the corporation. Minority group members who are not from wealthy families show the same educational patterns as upwardly mobile white corporate executives in terms of attendance at these same schools (Zweigenhaft and Domhoff 2006; Zweigenhaft and Domhoff 2003).

The conformist atmosphere within the corporations intensifies the rising executives' socialization into upper-class styles and values. The great uncertainty and latitude for decision-making in positions at the top of complex organizations creates a situation in which trust among leaders is absolutely essential. That need for trust is what creates a pressure toward social conformity:

> It is the uncertainty quotient in managerial work, as it has come to be defined in the large modern corporations, that causes management to become so socially restricting; to develop tight inner circles excluding social strangers; to keep control in the hands of socially homogeneous peers; to stress conformity and insist upon a diffuse, unbounded loyalty; and to prefer ease of communication and thus social certainty over the strains of dealing with people who are "different" (Kanter 1993, p. 49).

In this kind of an atmosphere, it quickly becomes apparent to new managers that they must demonstrate their loyalty to the senior management by working extra hours, tailoring their appearance to that of their superiors, and attempting to conform in their attitudes and behavior. Rightly or wrongly, they come to believe that they have to be part of the "old-boy network" in order to succeed in the company. Although there are competence criteria for the promotion of managers, they are vague enough or hard enough to apply that most managers become convinced that social factors are critical as well.

Executives who are successful in winning acceptance into the inner circle of their home corporations are invited by their superiors to join social institutions that assimilate them into the upper class. The first invitations are often to charitable and cultural organizations, where they serve as fundraisers and as organizers of special events. The wives of rising executives, whose social acceptability is thought to be a factor in managers' careers, experience their first extensive involvement with members of the upper class through these same organizations. Then, too, the social clubs discussed earlier in the chapter are important socializing agents for the rising executive.

Upwardly mobile executives also become intertwined with members of the upper class through the educational careers of their children. As their children go to day schools and boarding schools, the executives take part in evening and weekend events for parents, participate in fund-raising activities, and sometimes become directors or trustees in their own right. The fact that the children of successful managers become involved in upper-class institutions also can be seen in their patterns of college attendance. This is demonstrated very clearly in a classic study of upwardly mobile corporate presidents. Whereas only 29 percent of the presidents went to an Ivy League college, 70 percent of their sons and daughters did so (Hacker 1961).

Rising executives are assimilated economically at the same time as they are assimilated socially. One of the most important of these assimilatory mechanisms is the stock option, explained in a footnote in Chapter 2. Stock-option plans, in conjunction with salaries and bonuses in the millions to tens of millions of dollars, allow some top executives to earn hundreds of times more than the average wage earner each year. These high levels of remuneration enable upwardly mobile corporate leaders to become multimillionaires in their own right and important leaders within the corporate community.

The assimilation of professional executives into the upper class also can be seen in the emphasis they put on profits, the most important of ownership objectives. This manifests itself most directly in the performance of the corporations they manage. Several past studies that compared owner-controlled companies with companies that have professional managers at the top showed no differences in their profitability. Corporations differ in their profitability, but this fact does not seem to be due to a difference in values between upper-class owners and rising corporate executives (Useem 1980a).

By any indication, then, the presence of upwardly mobile executives does not contradict the notion that the upper class and the corporate community are closely related. In terms of their wealth, their social contacts, their values, and their aspirations for their children, successful managers become part of the upper class as they advance in the corporate hierarchy.

CLASS AWARENESS: A CAPITALIST MENTALITY

The institutions that establish the owners and high-level executives of corporations as a national upper class transcend the presence or absence of any given person or family. Families can rise and fall in the class structure, but the institutions of the upper class persist. Not everyone in this nationwide upper class knows everyone else, but everybody knows somebody who knows someone in other areas of the country, thanks to a common school experience, a summer at the same resort, membership in the same social club, or membership on the same board of directors. The upper class at any given historical moment consists of a complex network of overlapping social circles knit together by the members they have in common and by the numerous signs of common cultural styles and values that emerge from a similar upbringing, education, and lifestyle. Viewed from the standpoint of social psychology, the upper class is made up of innumerable face-to-face small groups that are constantly changing in their composition as people move from one social setting to another.

Involvement in these institutions usually instills a class awareness that includes feelings of superiority, pride, and justified privilege. Deep down, most members of the upper class think they are better than other people and therefore fully deserving of their station in life. This class awareness is based in corporate ownership, but it is reinforced by the shared social identities and interpersonal ties created through participation in the social institutions of the upper class. More important, the fact that the upper class is based in the ownership and control of profit-producing investments in stocks, bonds, and real estate shows that it is a capitalist class as well as a social class. Its members are not concerned simply with the interests of one corporation or business sector, but with such matters as the "investment climate," the "rate of profit," and the overall "political climate." That is, they have a capitalist mentality.

With the exception of those few who join the liberal-labor coalition or a leftist movement, members of the upper class also have a conservative outlook on issues that relate to the well-being of the corporate community as a whole. As noted in the introductory chapter, they may be liberal or conservative on social issues, and they vary somewhat on the degree to which they are wary of government, but they are nearly unanimous in their opposition to labor unions, which they see as the major potential challengers to their wealth and power. This tendency toward a general class perspective is utilized and reinforced within the policy-planning network discussed in the next chapter. The organizations in that network build upon the structural economic power explained in the previous chapter and the social cohesion demonstrated in this chapter in reaching consensus on policy matters, where the potential for misunderstanding and disagreement are great. Human beings are often distrustful or egotistical, and there can be differences in needs between corporations in different industries and of different sizes.

In other words, developing a common policy outlook is not automatic even for the corporate community and upper class. Their leaders have to create plans that satisfy as many different sectors of the corporate community as possible, or at least minimize the damage to those that cannot be fully accommodated. Then they have to develop access to government. At the same time, they have to contend with the possible objections of everyday working people who have little or nothing except a job, a house, and the opportunity to obtain educational credentials that might help them move up the occupational ladder.

4

The Policy-Planning Network

Shared economic interests and social cohesion provide the foundation for the development of policy consensus, but they are not enough in and of themselves to lead to agreed-upon policies without research, consultation, and deliberation. The issues facing the corporate community are too complex and the economy is too large for new policies to arise naturally from common interests and social cohesion alone. That is why a set of nonprofit, ostensibly nonpartisan organizations is a necessary feature of the corporate landscape. They take the form of charitable foundations, think tanks, and policy-discussion groups, which are defined shortly. These organizations are the basis of a policy-planning process through which the corporate community articulates its general policy preferences and then conveys them to the two major political parties, the White House, and Congress.

Members of the corporate community and upper class involve themselves in the policy-planning process in four basic ways. First, they finance the organizations at the center of these efforts. Second, they provide a variety of free services such as legal and accounting help for some of these organizations. Third, they serve as the trustees of these organizations, setting their general direction and selecting the people who will manage the day-to-day operations. Finally, they take part in the daily activities of some of the groups in the network or send their assistants to keep them abreast of new developments.

The policy-planning network explains how seemingly independent experts, who often provide new policy ideas, fit into the power equation. They do their work as employees of or consultants to key organizations in the network. These organizations give them financial support, confer legitimacy on their efforts, and provide the occasions for them to present their ideas to decision-makers. Although the corporate community has a near monopoly on what is considered respectable or legitimate expertise by the mass media and government, this expertise does not go unchallenged. There also exists a small group of think tanks and advocacy groups financed by liberal foundations, wealthy liberals, unions, and direct mail appeals. Some of these liberal policy organizations also receive part of their funding from major foundations controlled by moderate conservatives, to the great annoyance of ultraconservatives. Standing between the two sets of partisan experts there is a small number of academic experts at university research institutes who try to remain above the fray; most of them are more marginal than historical institutionalists believe to be the case.

Moreover, as the annoyances expressed by the ultraconservatives reveal, the policy network is not totally homogeneous. Reflecting differences of opinion within the corporate community, the moderate and ultraconservative subgroups have longstanding disagreements. The ultraconservative organizations are the ones most often identified with "big business" in the eyes of social scientists and the general public. In the past they opposed the expansion of trade with Europe and Asia, and still oppose any type of government regulation or occasional increases in the minimum wage. The fact that they are generally naysayers who lost on several highly visible issues in the turmoil of the late 1960s and early 1970s is one reason pluralists and media commentators doubt that the corporate community is the dominant influence in shaping government policy. However, most of these differences were smoothed over between 1975 and 2008 as the ultraconservatives accepted the need for an expansion of trade and the moderate conservatives decided that lower taxes and cutbacks in government spending on social programs were necessary.

More recently, since the late 1990s, the two groups have developed serious differences over foreign policy. The internationally oriented moderate conservatives, who long held sway in this issue-area, are *multilateralists* when it comes to foreign policy; they favor working closely with allies and making use of the United Nations whenever possible. They think they won the Cold War by patiently containing the Soviet Union and waiting for its non-market economy to fail, all the while working with Soviet leaders on arms control and other issues. The ultraconservatives, who have tendencies to ignore what is happening in other countries and shun foreign aid, are *assertive nationalists* when they do engage one or another part of the world, as seen in the unilateralism and the disdain for the United Nations that were visible in the Bush Administration. Assertive nationalists, ignoring the fact that Soviet premier Mikhail Gorbachev knew full well that the country's economy needed major adjustments, believe they won the Cold War by increasing defense spending in the early 1980s and arming the Mujahedeen to fight the Soviets in Afghanistan, thereby forcing the Soviets into an unwinnable arms race that ruined their economy and contributing to their defeat in Afghanistan. They thought that the kind of bold initiatives allegedly taken during the Reagan Administration would work in Iraq, Iran, and North Korea, but all of them backfired (Daalder and Lindsay 2003).

No one factor has been shown by systematic studies to be the sole basis for the division into moderates and ultraconservatives within the corporate community. There is a tendency for the moderate organizations to be directed by executives from the very largest and most internationally oriented of corporations, but there are numerous exceptions to that generalization. Moreover, there are corporations that support policy organizations within both policy subgroups. Then, too, there are instances where some top officers from a corporation will be in the moderate camp and others will be in the ultraconservative camp. There is therefore a need for much more research on this issue while avoiding any attempts to reduce the divisions to simple differences in economic interests. For all their disagreements, however, leaders within the two clusters of policy organizations have a tendency to search for compromise policies due to their common membership in the corporate community, their social bonds, and the numerous interlocks among all policy groups. When compromise is not possible, the final resolution of policy conflicts often takes place in legislative struggles in Congress, discussed in Chapter 7.

In considering the information that follows, it is important not to be overly impressed with the outcome of these efforts. For all their education, financial backing, and media attention, the experts who are involved in this network—and thereby legitimated for government service and sought out by the media for comments—are wrong far more than they are right. They are as likely to screen out information that does not fit with their biases and sense of self-importance as anyone else. They are also as susceptible to subtle social pressures to arrive at a consensus as any other group of people. There is no better evidence for these points than the certitudes that were expressed by most foreign policy experts within the policy-planning network about the ease with which Iraq could be transformed and the certainty with which most economists in the network said that the economy could prosper without much government oversight because of the self-regulating nature of markets.

AN OVERVIEW OF THE POLICY-PLANNING NETWORK

The policy-planning process begins in corporate boardrooms, social clubs, and informal discussions, where problems are identified as "issues" to be solved by new policies. It ends in government, where policies are enacted and implemented. In between, however, there is a complex network of people and institutions that plays an important role in sharpening the issues and weighing the alternatives. This network has four main components—foundations, think tanks, university research institutes, and policy-discussion groups.

Foundations are tax-free institutions created to give grants to both individuals and nonprofit organizations for activities that range from education, research, and the arts to support for the poor and the upkeep of exotic gardens and old mansions. They are an upper-class adaptation to inheritance and income taxes. They provide a means by which wealthy people and corporations can in effect decide how their tax payments will be spent. From a small beginning at the turn of the twentieth century, they have become a very important factor in shaping developments in higher education and the arts, and they play a significant role in policy formation as well. Although the grants of several hundred thousand to a few million dollars that they give to think tanks and policy-discussion groups each year are essential to the functioning of those organizations, the amount of money involved is small compared to what foundations give to education, research, charity, and cultural organizations. "To a Wall Streeter, intellectuals are pretty cheap," a senior fellow at one policy-discussion group told a *New York Times* reporter. "There are wedding rings that cost more than I do" (Bumiller 2008, p. A12).

Historically, the Rockefeller, Carnegie, Ford, and Sloan foundations were the most influential. Since the 1980s they have been joined by a new set of heavily endowed liberal and moderate-conservative foundations as well as by several somewhat smaller, but highly coordinated ultraconservative foundations. Beyond these several dozen large foundations, there are tens of thousands of small family foundations that allow wealthy individuals to provide charitable support and high culture at the local and state levels.

Think tanks are nonprofit organizations that provide settings for experts in various academic disciplines to devote their time to the study of policy alternatives free from the teaching, committee meetings, and departmental duties that are part of the daily routine for most members of the academic community. Supported by foundation grants, corporate donations, and government contracts, think tanks are a major source of the new ideas discussed in the policy-planning network. The policy-discussion organizations are nonpartisan groups that bring together corporate executives, lawyers, academic experts, university administrators, government officials, and media specialists to talk about general problems such as foreign aid, international trade, and environmental policies. Using discussion groups of varying sizes, these organizations provide informal and off-the-record meeting grounds in which differences of opinion on various issues can be aired and the arguments of specialists can be heard. In addition to their numerous small-group discussions, they encourage general dialogue by means of luncheon speeches, written reports, and position statements in journals and books. Taken as a whole, the several think tanks and policy-discussion groups are akin to an open forum in which there is a constant debate concerning the major problems of the day.

The organizations in the policy-planning network are interlocked with each other and the corporate community in terms of both common trustees and funding. The evidence for this conclusion is presented throughout the chapter. Figure 4.1 presents an overview of the network

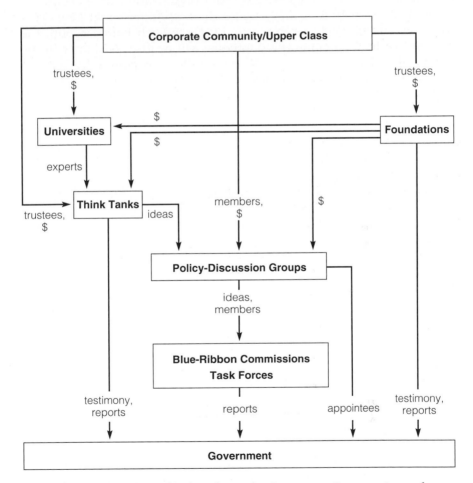

Figure 4.1   The Flow of Policy from the Corporate Community and Upper Class to Government through the Policy-Planning Network.

with linkages expressed in terms of (1) trustee interlocks; (2) money flows; and (3) the flow of ideas and plans. Anticipating the discussion of how the corporate community shapes government policy, which is presented in Chapter 7, the diagram shows some of the ways the "output" of the policy network reaches government.

No one type of organization is more important than the others. It is the network as a whole that shapes policy alternatives, with different organizations playing different roles on different issues. There is, however, one organization in the network, the Business Roundtable, discussed in Chapter 2, that tends to have the final say in attempting to influence government on the most important issues relating to economic policy. It is also the case that organizations can decline in importance over time if they outlive their usefulness and new organizations are created to replace them. Once such fading group, the Committee for Economic Development, will be discussed later in the chapter because its decline sheds light on the more conservative direction that many moderate conservatives took in the 1970s.

FOUNDATIONS

Among the 65,000 to 70,000 foundations that exist in the United States, with some going out of business each year and new ones being added, only a few hundred have the money and interest to involve themselves in funding programs that have a bearing on public policy. Foundations are of four basic types:

1. According to the authoritative *Guide to U.S. Foundations*, published by the Foundation Center in New York, there are about 65,000 *independent* foundations, all of which were created by families to serve a wide variety of purposes. Most are relatively small and local. About 10 percent of them donate over $500,000 a year, led by the Gates Foundation ($2.8 billion in 2007), the Ford Foundation ($580.7 million), and the Robert Wood Johnson Foundation ($367.6 million). The 731 foundations with $100 million or more in assets gave 51.6 percent of all donations in 2007.

2. There are over 2,000 *corporate* foundations that are funded on a year-by-year basis by major corporations. Their number and importance has increased greatly since the 1980s, but many may reduce donations or stop giving altogether due to the decline in their profits in 2008. The top twelve gave a total of $914 million in 2007, which is almost as much as the Ford Foundation and the Robert Wood Johnson Foundation combined. The Wal-Mart Foundation headed the list with

$155.1 in donations, followed by the Bank of America Foundation ($123.3 million) and JPMorgan Chase Foundation ($79.9 million).

3. There are approximately 660 *community* foundations at the local level that are designed to aid charities, voluntary associations, and special projects in their home cities. They receive funds from a variety of sources, including independent foundations, corporate foundations, and wealthy families. Boards that include both corporate executives and community leaders direct them. In some cities, such as Cleveland, the community foundation is an integral part of the local power structure (Tittle 1992). A few of the larger ones give money outside of their local area, usually at the direction of a wealthy donor who has set up a separate fund within the foundation, thereby saving administrative costs.

4. Finally, there are nearly 4,000 foundations that use their money to finance a particular museum, garden project, or artistic exhibit. They are called *operating* foundations and are not of concern in terms of the policy-planning process. The women of the upper class discussed in the previous chapter are often the directors of operating foundations. Operating foundations contribute to the cultural domination of the country by the corporate rich.

Upper class and corporate representation on the boards of the large general-purpose foundations most involved in policy-oriented grants has been documented in several past studies. In a study of the twelve largest foundations in the 1960s, for example, it was found that half the trustees were members of the upper class (Domhoff 1967). A study of corporate connections into the policy network in the 1970s showed that 10 of these 12 foundations had at least one connection to the 201 largest corporations; most had many more than that (Salzman and Domhoff 1983). More recently, due to a combination of factors—smaller boards, an effort to diversify on the basis of gender and color, and the addition of a few directors from other countries—the connection between the largest foundations and the corporate community is less tight than it used to be. At the Ford Foundation, the only corporate executives on the fourteen-person board of trustees are the vice chairman of Goldman Sachs, who also sits on the board of directors of Bed, Bath, and Beyond; the CEO of the Sonic Corporation; and the CEO of Infosys Technologies in India. At the Rockefeller Foundation, seven of the fifteen trustees are also the directors of thirteen corporations, which include two directors each at Citigroup and Aetna Insurance; there are also two South

African businessmen on the board of trustees. Four of the thirteen trustees of the Carnegie Corporation are on eight corporate boards and there are business executives from Mexico and Spain on the Carnegie Corporation board of trustees as well.

Foundations often become much more than sources of money when they set up special programs that are thought to be necessary by their trustees or staff. Then they search out appropriate organizations to undertake the project or create special commissions within the foundation itself. A few foundations have become so committed to a specific issue that they function as a policy-discussion organization. The Ford Foundation provides the best example of this point because it became involved in two of the main issues that arose in the 1960s and have persisted ever since.

First, it played a major role in creating and sustaining the main-stream organizations that have been the leaders of the environmental movement for many decades. Its conference on resource management in 1953 and subsequent start-up funding led to the founding of the first and most prominent environmental think tank, Resources for the Future. This organization broke new ground by incorporating market economics into thinking about conservation work. Economists at Resources for the Future and other think tanks showed that resource substitution could be managed through the price system and that it was a myth to claim there is a trade-off between jobs and environmental regulation. They also pointed out that there was money to be made in cleaning up the air and water. Their work reassured moderate conservatives that most environmental initiatives were completely compatible with corporate capitalism, contrary to the angry outcries of ultraconservatives and the hopes of leftists (Alpert and Markusen 1980; Goodstein 1999).

In the early1960s, the Ford Foundation spent $7 million over a three-year period developing ecology programs at seventeen universities around the country, thereby providing the informational base and personnel infrastructure for efforts to control pesticides and industrial waste. At the same time, the foundation put large sums into the land-purchase programs of the Nature Conservancy and the National Audubon Society. It also encouraged environmental education and citizen action through grants to municipal conservation commissions and the nationwide Conservation Foundation, the latter founded by the Rockefeller family as a combined think tank and policy-discussion group (Robinson 1993). The new militant wing of the environmental movement soon moved beyond the purview envisioned by the moderate conservatives, but the fact remains that much of the early grassroots movement was encouraged and legitimated by major foundations.

In the 1970s the Ford Foundation aided environmentalists in another way by backing several new environmental law firms that used the legal system to force corporations and municipal governments to clean up the water, air, and soil. Leaders at the foundation actually created one of these organizations, the Natural Resources Defense Council, by bringing together several Wall Street corporate lawyers with a group of young Yale Law School graduates who wanted to devote their careers to environmental law. Ford then gave the new organization $2.6 million between 1970 and 1977. Between 1971 and 1977, it also gave $1.6 million to the Center for Law in the Public Interest in Los Angeles, $994,000 to the Environmental Defense Fund, and $603,000 to the Sierra Club Legal Defense Fund. Many of the young leaders in these organizations are now senior spokespersons for the environmental movement (Mitchell 1991; NRDC 1990).

Appointees to the Nixon Administration from the mainstream environmental groups helped secure tax-exempt status for the environmental law firms. They then presided over the creation of the federal government's Council on Environmental Quality and the Environmental Protection Agency. Indeed, the origins of these agencies provides an ideal example of how moderate conservatives create policies that are later seen as setbacks for the corporate community. At the same time, these organizations are often criticized by strong environmentalists as being too cautious and for "selling out" via compromises on key issues (Dowie 1995). Although the Ford Foundation still gives environmental grants, mostly to organizations in other nations, its support for American environmental groups has been more modest now that these organizations are firmly established. However, several dozen major foundations, including corporate foundations, have picked up the slack. Table 4.1 on page 94 lists the largest of hundreds of foundation grants to the Natural Resources Defense Council in recent years.

Second, the Ford Foundation became the equivalent of a policy group on the issue of urban unrest, creating a wide range of programs to deal with the problems generated by urban renewal and racial tensions in cities. One of these programs, called the Gray Areas Project, became the basis for the War on Poverty declared by the Johnson Administration in 1964. Once the War on Poverty was launched, the Ford Foundation invested tens of millions of dollars in support for minority-group and community-action organizations. These investments were seen at the time as a way of encouraging insurgent groups to take a non-violent and electoral direction in addressing the obstacles they encountered. By the 1970s, when the social disruption had subsided, ultraconservatives began to criticize the Ford Foundation for its support of what they called liberal

Table 4.1 Contributions by Foundations to the National Resources Defense Council between 2003 and Early 2008

Name	NRDC
Hewlett Foundation	$6,565,000
Energy Foundation*	$5,780,000
Marisla Foundation	$3,000,000
Aria Foundation	$2,229,000
Google Foundation	$2,000,000
Bauman Foundation	$2,100,000
Joyce Foundation	$1,057,000
Park Foundation	$900,000
McKnight Foundation	$710,000
MacArthur Foundation	$600,000
Total	**$24,851,000**

*The Energy Foundation was created in 1991 on the basis of grants from the MacArthur, Packard, Joyce, Rockefeller, McKnight, and Pew foundations.

Source: Foundation Directory Online (New York: The Foundation Center, 2008).

experiments. However, the foundation has persisted in this support, which is seen by moderate conservatives in the corporate community as a sensible way to incorporate minority groups into the larger society. (For a detailed account of the Ford Foundation's leadership on urban issues, see the document "The Ford Foundation in the Inner City" at www.whorulesamerica.net.)

Foundation funding also has been essential for four Mexican-American advocacy organizations: the National Council of La Raza, the Southwest Voter Registration Education Project, the Mexican American Legal Defense and Educational Fund, and the Texas Industrial Areas Foundation network. All four developed during the turmoil of the 1960s and continue their work today. A study of their income statements to the Internal Revenue Service over the ten-year period from 1991 to 2000 showed that most of them receive virtually all of their money from a handful of foundations, led by the Ford Foundation, the Rockefeller Foundation, and the Mott Foundation. Furthermore, the Ford Foundation played a role in establishing the National Council of La Raza and the Mexican American Legal Defense Fund (Marquez 1993).

The absence of any local or membership fundraising in the case of the Texas Industrial Areas Foundation network in Texas cities is striking because the inspiration for its efforts, the radical urban activist Saul Alinsky, emphasized that outside funding should be used only at the outset of an organizing effort to ensure that the grassroots groups are controlled by their local volunteer leadership. With only two or three exceptions out of seven cities where the project operates, most of their monies came from large foundations and local business, and none had a majority of its funding from neighborhood members. The funding for these organizations increased greatly when they set up an Interfaith Education Fund that became a major conduit for foundations. In effect, organizers paid by foundations run the Industrial Areas Foundation affiliates in Texas even though they are nominally controlled by local volunteer leadership (Marquez 2003). Table 4.2 provides a summary of foundation grants

Table 4.2 Foundation Donations to Advocacy Organizations in 2003 and 2004

Category/Organization	Number of Granting Foundations	Number of Grants	Total $
African-American			
Urban League	134	282	$15,461,742
NAACP*	46	73	$6,840, 359
Children's Defense Fund	31	42	$4,935,297
National Council for Negro Women	5	5	$575,000
Latino			
National Council of La Raza	31	44	$12,179,694
MALDEF**	20	23	$1,970,700
Feminist			
Planned Parenthood	172	314	$35,106,492
Ms. Foundation	16	23	$2,230,000
Total Grants			**$79,299,284**

*NAACP = National Association for the Advancement of Colored People
**MALDEF = Mexican American Legal Defense and Education Fund

Source: Compiled from *Foundation Grants Index on CD Rom 6.0* (New York: The Foundation Center, 2006).

to a wider range of advocacy groups, including women's groups, for 2003 and 2004.

Ford's support for disadvantaged minority communities, women, and the environmental movement led to the claim that it became a liberal organization in the 1960s despite its corporate-dominated board of trustees, including the chairman of Ford Motor Company at the time, Henry Ford II. However, this conclusion confuses liberalism with a sophisticated conservatism that is supportive of changes that do not challenge the class structure. This is shown by the fact that the Ford Foundation took a different stance on issues that involve class conflict, as seen in the foundation's support for opposition to unionization efforts. In 1967, for example, it entered into an emerging conflict over public employee unions by financing a think-tank study that was very negative toward unions. Then, in 1970, it provided $450,000 to three associations of government managers—the U.S. Conference of Mayors, the National League of Cities, and the National Association of Counties—to establish the Labor-Management Relations Service, an organization intended to help government managers cope with efforts at union organizing. One year later this organization set up the National Public Employer Labor Relations Association with money from the Ford Foundation and other foundations (Miller and Canak 1995b). Publications from these two organizations provided advice on defeating organizing drives and surviving strikes. They suggested contracting out public services to private businesses to avoid unions and decrease wage costs. This opposition to public employee unions is consistent with the distance that all major foundations have kept from the labor movement (Magat 1999).

Systematic studies of the degree to which public employees are unionized in each state suggest that these efforts to help government managers were successful. Less than half of the 50 states allow full collective bargaining for all public employee groups and nearly all states forbid public employees to strike. The relative strength of organized business and the liberal-labor coalition in each state is the main factor in determining the degree to which state employees are successful in their efforts to unionize. Union density in the public sector, meaning the percent of public employees who are in unions, rose from 10.8 percent in 1960 to a peak of 40.2 percent in 1976, and has stabilized right around 36 percent since that time (Miller and Canak 1995a; Miller and Canak 1995b).

Foundations, as this range of examples shows, are an integral part of the policy-planning process both as sources of funds and as program initiators. Contrary to the usual perceptions, they are not merely donors of money for charity and value-free academic research. They are extensions of the corporate community in their origins, leadership, and goals.

THINK TANKS

The most sustained research and brainstorming within the policy-planning network usually takes place in various think tanks. Any new initiatives that survive criticism by other experts are then brought to the policy-discussion groups for modification and assimilation by the corporate leaders. Among the relative handful of major think tanks, some highly specialized in one or two topics, the most important are the Brookings Institution, the American Enterprise Institute, the Urban Institute, the National Bureau of Economic Research, and the Rand Corporation. Their efforts are sometimes augmented by institutes and centers connected to universities, especially in the area of foreign relations, but these university institutes are one step removed from the policy-planning network, as explained in the next section.

Three highly visible think tanks—the Brookings Institution, the American Enterprise Institute, and the Heritage Foundation—vie for attention and influence in Washington. The Brookings Institution, the oldest and generally most respected of the three, was founded in 1927 from three institutes that go back as far as 1916. Virtually all of its early money came from foundations, although by the 1930s it was earning income from a small endowment provided by the Rockefeller Foundation and other sources. The Brookings Institution is sometimes said to be a liberal think tank, but that is a misperception generated in good part by ultraconservatives. The fact that Keynesian economists from Brookings advised the Kennedy and Johnson administrations also contributed to this stereotype. In fact, the Brookings Institution always has been in the mainstream or on the right wing. Although some of its economists were important advisers to the Democrats in the 1960s, by 1975 these same economists were criticizing government initiatives in ways that later were attributed to the employees of their main rival, the American Enterprise Institute (Peschek 1987).

The Brookings Institution's most noteworthy recent effort, the Hamilton Project, named after the first secretary of treasury, Alexander Hamilton, brought together Wall Street bankers and academic economists starting in 2006 to write reports on such topics as economic growth, the federal budget, and international trade. Sponsored by one of the Brookings Institution's most prominent trustees, Robert E. Rubin, a director of Citigroup and a former Secretary of the Treasury in the Clinton Administration, it was meant to have an impact on a future Democratic administration. Rubin and some of the other participants did end up working on President Obama's economic transition team and two economists in the group were appointed to the new president's White House staff. It did not hurt the visibility of the project that the current president of the Brookings Institution, Strobe Talbott, a member of a wealthy Cleveland family and a graduate of Yale, served as Deputy Secretary of State in the Clinton Administration.

The American Enterprise Institute (AEI), formed in 1943 as an adjunct to the U.S. Chamber of Commerce, had little money and no influence until the early 1970s when a former Chamber employee began selling the need for a new think tank to corporate executives by exaggerating the liberal inclinations of the Brookings Institution. His efforts received a large boost in 1972 when the Ford Foundation gave him a $300,000 grant (the equivalent of a grant of $1,500,000 in 2008). This gift was viewed as a turning point by the institute's staff because of the legitimacy a Ford grant conferred for future fundraising. The institute went from a budget of $1.1 million in 1971 to over $10 million in the 1980s. It now has a budget of about $25 million a year, well below the Brookings Institution's budget of $60 million for 2007 (Bumiller 2008).

The Heritage Foundation, created in 1974, is the most recent and famous of the Washington think tanks. It is wrongly thought to reflect current wisdom in the corporate community when it is actually the product of a few highly conservative men of inherited wealth. The most important of these ultraconservatives are members of the Coors family, then the sole owners of the beer company that bears their name (Bellant 1991). Close behind them is Richard Mellon Scaife, who is discussed in a later section of this chapter.

Unlike the AEI, the Heritage Foundation makes no effort to hire established experts or build a record of respectability within the academic or policy communities. Instead, it hires young ultraconservatives who are willing to attack all government programs and impugn the motives of all government officials as bureaucratic empire builders. While this approach doesn't endear the Heritage Foundation to its counterparts in Washington, it did lead to staff positions in the Reagan, George H. W. Bush, and George W. Bush administrations, which needed people to carry out their antigovernment objectives.

The relationship of these three think tanks to the corporate community can be seen through their boards of directors. Brookings and the AEI have fairly similar interlock patterns, with about 60 percent of their directors sitting on an average of 1.3 boards for companies of comparable size and stature. However, as will be shown shortly, the AEI's pattern of interlocks within the policy-planning network itself suggests that it is now somewhat more central than the Brookings Institution. The situation is very different at Heritage, where only one of twenty directors, a retired executive from Microsoft, sits on a corporate board. There are other businesspeople on the Heritage board, but they are retired middle-level executives or have small companies of their own. There are also some wealthy inheritors on the Heritage board. Its marginal nature to the corporate community will be shown again later in this chapter when network studies are discussed.

THE MIXED ROLE OF UNIVERSITIES IN AMERICAN POWER CONFLICTS

The thousands of research institutes at the top 100 or so American universities train many of the experts who become employees at think tanks. Some of the professors in these institutes advise think tanks or take part in policy-discussion groups. Thus, it may seem that universities should be considered a part of the policy-planning network, but that would not take into account the complex role that universities have in the American power structure. In a very general sense, universities are part of the power equation because they educate future leaders and train the experts who work for the think tanks discussed in the previous section. This is especially the case for the handful of prestigious private schools such as Harvard, Yale, Stanford, and the University of Chicago, which have very large endowments to support their students and programs. It is also true that the trustees of the top private universities, and many large state universities for that matter, are disproportionately from the corporate community and upper class, as demonstrated by numerous investigations stretching back to the early twentieth century (e.g., Barrow 1990, chapter 2, for one good summary; BondGraham 2007, for the best recent analysis and literature review).

Nevertheless, universities are not part of the policy-planning network because only specific institutes within them are directly involved in it in any way. Furthermore, both the faculty and student bodies at many universities are too diverse in their intellectual and political orientations to be considered part of the power structure unless corporations or organizations in the policy formation network employ them. Then, too, a significant minority of faculty in some departments supports the liberal-labor coalition or are leftists of various kinds. In addition, the institution of tenure, which protects senior faculty members from arbitrary dismissal in order to encourage academic freedom, gives the faculty some degree of independence from trustees and administrators. The nationwide American Association of University Professors and other faculty organizations zealously guard this tenure system and other faculty rights.

Nor are all students who graduate from high-status universities uniformly destined to join the corporate community or the policy-planning network. A small minority become leading activists in the liberal-labor coalition, sometimes immediately after graduation, sometimes after a career in business. Longtime consumer activist Ralph Nader is a graduate of Princeton University and Harvard Law School, for example. The person who provided much of the money in the early 1960s to start the

Institute of Policy Studies, a very liberal think tank in Washington, was a wealthy graduate of Harvard who worked as an investment banker on Wall Street before beginning his journey to liberalism (Warburg 1964). Pacifist David Dellinger, whose father was a corporate lawyer, led many major antiwar efforts from the 1950s through the 1980s and was arrested dozens of times. The title of his autobiography, *From Yale to Jail*, provides a useful reminder of the extent to which some graduates of Ivy League universities become leaders of the American left (Dellinger 1993).

Put another way, universities provide resources and recruits for both the corporate community and its critics. In recent decades corporations have come to fund or benefit from the research carried out on university campuses in the natural sciences, information sciences, and engineering to the point where "campus capitalism" and "University, Inc." are used in the titles of books examining the near takeover of many research areas (Greenberg 2007; Washburn 2005). However, even though liberals and leftists are in the minority on most campuses, universities are a far more important political base for them than they are for the corporate community. Indeed, the educational system in general, including public high schools and libraries, may be the most important institutional home for liberalism in the United States. The educational system also is the basis for two of the largest unions in the liberal-labor coalition, the National Education Association (3.2 million members) and the American Federation of Teachers (1.4 million members).

Based on these complexities, it seems more useful to see the universities as a training ground for people on both sides of class conflict in the United States. Thus, only those experts from universities who work for think tanks or consult for policy-discussion groups in the policy-planning networks are relevant to the corporate side of the power equation. Even then, many of them may have very temporary roles out of personal choice or because they are not seen as helpful. Only those who come to have major roles within the policy-planning network are part of the leadership group, the power elite, which is defined in the final section of this chapter.

THE POLICY-DISCUSSION GROUPS

The policy-discussion groups are in many ways the linchpins in the policy-planning network because they serve several important functions for the corporate community.

1. They provide a setting in which corporate leaders can familiarize themselves with general policy issues by listening to and questioning the experts from think tanks and university research institutes.

2. They provide a forum where conflicts between moderate conservatives and ultraconservatives can be discussed and compromised, usually by including experts of both persuasions within the discussion group, along with an occasional liberal or university professor on some issues.

3. They provide an informal training ground for new leadership. It is within these organizations that corporate leaders can determine in an informal fashion which of their peers are best suited for service in government and as spokespersons to other groups.

4. They provide an informal recruiting ground for determining which policy experts may be best suited for government service, either as faceless staff aides to the corporate leaders who take government positions or as high-level appointees in their own right.

In addition, the policy groups have three functions in relation to the rest of society:

1. These groups legitimate their members as serious and expert persons capable of government service. This image is created because group members are portrayed as giving of their own time to take part in highly selective organizations that are nonpartisan and nonprofit in nature.

2. They convey the concerns, goals, and expectations of the corporate community to those young experts and young professors who want to further their careers by receiving foundation grants, invitations to work at think tanks, and invitations to take part in policy discussion groups.

3. Through such avenues as books, journals, policy statements, press releases, and speakers, these groups try to influence the climate of opinion both in Washington and the country at large. This point is developed when the opinion-shaping network is discussed in the next chapter.

The most extensive study of the relationship of policy discussion groups to foundations and think tanks, carried out with information from the late 1970s, started with a sample of seventy-seven large foundations, which included twenty that had over $100 million in assets and gave over $200,000 in public policy grants. These twenty foundations led to a group of thirty-one think tanks and policy-planning groups that received grants from three or more of these foundations. Of the 225 trustees who served on the twenty foundations, 124 were

also trustees of another 120 foundations. Ten of the twenty foundations had interlocks with eighteen of the thirty-one policy-planning
organizations and think tanks. The Rockefeller Foundation had the
largest number of interlocks with other foundations (34), followed by
the Sloan Foundation, the Carnegie Corporation, and the Ford Foundation. The Rockefeller Foundation also had the largest number of
trustee connections to the policy groups it financed (14), followed once
again by the Sloan, Carnegie, and Ford foundations. Moreover, all
four of these foundations tended to be involved with the same policy
groups. Together, these foundations, think tanks, and policy-planning
groups form the moderate-conservative portion of the network, which
was even larger and more intertwined than any previous studies had
led social scientists to expect (Colwell 1980; Colwell 1993).

This analysis also discovered that a set of policy groups and think
tanks identified with ultraconservative programs, such as the American
Enterprise Institute, the Hoover Institution, and the Hudson Institute,
were linked to another set of foundations, including the Bradley, Sarah
Scaife, and Donner foundations. These findings on the ultraconservative foundations were confirmed in another study that used tax returns
to reveal that twelve foundations provided half the funding for the
American Enterprise Institute as well as 85 percent or more of the
funding for the other prominent ultraconservative think tanks (Allen
1992). Corporate foundations also supported some of these groups, but
they gave donations to the moderate-conservative groups as well. To
demonstrate the continuity of this pattern, Table 4.3 shows the donations that five ultraconservative foundations gave to five present-day
ultraconservative think tanks in the five years before the publication of
the sixth edition of this book.

The tremendous impact of a few extremely wealthy ultraconservatives can be seen in the funding career of the aforementioned
Richard Mellon Scaife, an adopted son and heir to a major portion
of an oil and banking fortune in Pittsburgh. Based on a computer-
ized record of all his donations from the early 1960s to late 1990s,
The Washington Post estimated that he and his foundations, including
the Sarah Scaife Foundation in Table 4.3, had given $790.5 million
in 2008 dollars to a wide range of ultraconservative causes, including the concerted attempt to find defamatory material on President
Bill Clinton's personal life from the outset of his presidency (Conason
1997; Kaiser and Chinoy 1999). He also gives large donations to conservative political candidates and the Republican Party. A similar picture of combined policy and advocacy donations could be drawn for
several other extremely wealthy ultraconservatives as well (Callahan
1999; Covington 1999; Krehely, House, and Kernan 2004).

Table 4.3 Core Ultraconservative Think Tanks and Their Main Funders, 2003–2008

Foundations[2]	Think Tanks[1]				
	AEI	Heritage	Hoover	Hudson	Manhattan
Bradley	$2,795,000	$1,762,500	$1,655,000	$3,510,200	$1,575,000
Donner	$0	$145,000	$305,000	$0	$293,000
Howard	$0	$10,000,000	$6,000,000	$0	$0
Kirby	$0	$680,000	$124,000	$119,000	$392,000
Sarah Scaife	$1,625,000	$4,000,000	$1,150,000	$1,015,000	$1,090,000
Total Donations from These Five Foundations	$4,420,000	$16,587,500	$9,234,000	$4,644,200	$3,350,000

[1]These groups receive donations from other ultraconservative foundations, but not as consistently. The AEI also receives grants from some moderate conservative foundations.
[2]These foundations give to many other ultraconservative projects, which are usually smaller in size, local in nature, or in academic settings.

Source: The Foundation Directory Online (New York: The Foundation Center, 2008).

The centrality of the moderate-conservative policy planning groups within both the corporate community and the policy-planning network is demonstrated by studies for the 1970s and 1990s that included corporations and foundations as well as think tanks and policy-discussion groups. These studies found the same few policy-discussion groups at the center of the combined network in both decades, along with the largest banks and corporations (Moore, Sobieraj, Whitt, Mayorova and Beaulieu 2002; Salzman and Domhoff 1983).

A network analysis focused exclusively on interlocking trustees among 12 moderate-conservative and ultraconservative think tanks and policy groups for the years 1973 to 2000 revealed that moderate-conservative groups remained at the center of the policy network, but that they now have more interlocks with some of the ultraconservative groups than earlier. Table 4.4 on page 104 presents the centrality scores for the 11 organizations in the study that have been mentioned in this book. It is notable that the Hoover Institution and the Heritage Foundation are only linked with each other and therefore are not part of the overall network of trustee interlocks.

Table 4.4 The Centrality Scores for Eleven Think Tanks and Policy-Discussion Groups in 2000

Organization	Centrality Score
Business Roundtable	2.51
Business Council	2.08
American Enterprise Institute	1.51
Council on Foreign Relations	1.31
U.S. Chamber of Commerce	1.17
Conference Board	.87
National Association of Manufacturers	.67
Committee for Economic Development	.65
Brookings Institution	.64
Hoover Institution	.00
Heritage Foundation	.00

Note: These centrality scores reflect the number of interlocks maintained by each organization, controlling for variation in the size of boards and weighting each link by the centrality of the organization to which it connects. The scores have been rescaled so that 1.0 represents the average centrality score for 2000. Adapted from Burris, 2008.

It is now time to look at some of the policy-discussion groups in more detail.

The Council on Foreign Relations

The Council on Foreign Relations (CFR) is the largest of the policy organizations. Established in 1921 by bankers, lawyers, and academicians interested in fostering the larger role the United States would play in world affairs as a result of World War I, the CFR's importance in the conduct of foreign affairs was well established by the 1930s. Before 1970, the members were primarily financiers, executives, and lawyers, with a strong minority of journalists, academic experts, and government officials. After that time there was an effort to respond to criticism by including a larger number of government officials, especially foreign-service officers, politicians, and aides to congressional committees concerned with foreign policy. By 2008, the council had approximately 4,500 members, most of whom do little more than receive reports and attend large banquets. Although originally strictly a discussion group, the CFR now has a Studies Department that makes it the largest think-tank in the area of foreign policy as well as the leading center for discussion groups.

Several past studies demonstrate the organization's connections to the upper class and corporate community. A sample of 210 New York members in the 1960s found that 39 percent were listed in the *Social Register*, and a random sampling of the full membership in the 1970s found 33 percent in that directory (Domhoff 1967; Shoup and Minter 1977). In both studies, trustees were even more likely than regular members to be members of the upper class. Overlaps with the corporate community are equally pervasive. Twenty-two percent of the 1969 members served on the board of at least one of *Fortune's* top 500 industrials, for example. In a study of the directors of 201 large corporations, it was found that 125 of these companies had 293 interlocks with the CFR. Twenty-three of the very largest banks and corporations had four or more directors who were members (Salzman and Domhoff 1983).

The 40-person board of directors in 2008 reflects the continuing ties of the Council on Foreign Relations to the corporate community. Nineteen of its forty members are on one or more boards, linking the council to twenty-nine companies across the country. The list begins with three links with AIG, an insurance company that had been given $150 billion in bailout money and another $30 billion in guarantees by the spring of 2009, and may be owned by the government when this book is being read. There are 2 links with IBM, and 1 each with American Express, ChevronTexaco, Citigroup, FedEx, Goldman Sachs, Intel, and Texas Instruments. The board also includes two former secretaries of state, Madeleine Albright and Colin Powell, along with scholars and a retired television reporter (Tom Brokaw).

The CFR receives its general funding from wealthy individuals, corporations, and subscriptions to its influential periodical, *Foreign Affairs*. For special projects it often relies upon major foundations for support. It conducts an active program of luncheon and dinner speeches at its New York clubhouse and a more recently established Washington, D.C., site, featuring government officials and national leaders from all over the world as the main speakers. It also encourages dialogue and disseminates information through books, pamphlets, and articles in *Foreign Affairs*. The most important aspects of the CFR program, however, are its discussion groups and study groups. These small gatherings of about fifteen to twenty-five people bring together business executives, government officials, scholars, and military officers for detailed consideration of specific topics in the area of foreign affairs. Discussion groups, which meet about once a month, are charged with exploring problems in a general way, trying to define issues and identify alternatives.

Discussion groups often lead to a study group as the next stage. Study groups revolve around the work of a visiting research fellow (financed by a foundation grant) or a regular staff member. The group leader and other experts present monthly papers that are discussed and criticized by the rest of the group. The goal of such study groups is a detailed statement of the problem by the scholar leading the discussion. Any book that eventuates from the group is understood to express the views of its academic author, not of the council or the members of the study group, but the books are nonetheless published with the sponsorship of the CFR. The names of the people participating in the study group are listed at the beginning of the book.

The organization itself is far too large for its members to issue policy proclamations as a group. Moreover, its usefulness as a neutral discussion ground would be diminished if it tried to do so. As things now stand, its leaders can help to mediate disputes that break out in the foreign policy establishment and also serve in both Republican and Democratic administrations.

The CFR's most successful set of study groups created the framework for the post–World War II international economy. Beginning in 1939 with financial support from the Rockefeller Foundation, its War-Peace Studies developed the postwar definition of the national interest through a comprehensive set of discussion groups. These groups brought together approximately 100 top bankers, lawyers, executives, economists, and military experts in 362 meetings over a five-year period. The academic experts within the study groups met regularly with officials of the State Department. In 1942, the experts became part of the department's new postwar planning process as twice-a-week consultants, while at the same time continuing work on the War-Peace project. As all accounts agree, the State Department had little or no planning capability of its own at the time.

Although the study groups sent hundreds of reports to the State Department, the most important one defined the minimum geographical area that was needed for the American economy to make full utilization of its resources and at the same time maintain harmony with Western Europe and Japan. This geographical area, which came to be known as the "Grand Area," included Latin America, Europe, the colonies of the British Empire, and all of Southeast Asia. Southeast Asia was necessary as a source of raw materials for Great Britain and Japan and as a consumer of Japanese products. The American national interest was then defined in terms of the integration and defense of the Grand Area, which led to plans for the United Nations, the International Monetary Fund, and the World Bank, and eventually to the decision to defend Vietnam from a communist takeover at all costs. The goal was to avoid both another Great Depression and increased government control of what was at the time a very sluggish economy. This work provided the framework within which American dominance of the world has unfolded over the past sixty-five years (Domhoff 1990, chapters 5, 6, and 8; Shoup and Minter 1977).

The Council came under intense scrutiny in 1979 when its president and several other Council leaders, including former Secretary of State Henry Kissinger, persuaded President Jimmy Carter to admit the recently deposed and ailing shah of Iran into the United States for medical treatments, despite warnings that this action might increase tensions with the insurgents who had just taken over the country. The direct result was the hostage crisis and the refusal of the American government to recognize the new Iranian government, which had replaced a dictator installed by the CIA after it overthrew the elected Iranian government in 1953. A 2004 report calling for a reassessment of the United States's relationship with Iran therefore stands out among more than three dozen CFR reports in recent years because it called for negotiations with Iran. The coleader of the study group, Robert M. Gates, a former CIA official then serving as the president of Texas A&M, went on to be a key member of the bipartisan Iraq Study Group that made a similar recommendation for negotiations to the Bush Administration in 2006. Gates was appointed Secretary of Defense shortly after the study group's report appeared and then was asked to continue in that position by President Obama.

THE COMMITTEE FOR ECONOMIC DEVELOPMENT: A POLICY GROUP IN DECLINE

The Committee for Economic Development (CED), established in the early 1940s to help plan for the postwar world, played a forward-looking role in the corporate community until the 1970s, when it took a right turn and declined in importance. Today it is still in the center of the corporate network in terms of its director interlocks, but most of those directors are retired or working in consultative types of roles. Nor has the organization received grants of any significance from corporate foundations in recent years. The story of the CED is important as a case study in the rise and fall of a policy group, but it is also a very good window into how and why the corporate community decided to take a more conservative direction in the 1970s.

In its early years the CED's membership consisted of 200 corporate leaders. Later it added a small number of university presidents. In addition, leading economists and public administration experts served as advisers and conducted research for it; many of them went on to serve in advisory roles in both Republican and Democratic administrations, especially with the Council of Economic Advisors housed within the White House (Domhoff 1987). Like the Council on Foreign Relations, the CED works through study groups that are aided by academic experts. Unlike the CFR, the results of committee study groups are released as official policy statements of the organization. They contain footnotes in which trustees register any disagreements they may have with the overall recommendations. These statements are of great value to social scientists for studying the range of policy orientations in the corporate community.

The corporate leaders instrumental in creating the CED had two major concerns: (1) There might be another depression after World War II ended; and (2) if they did not have a viable economic plan for the postwar era, the liberal-labor coalition might present plans that would not be acceptable to the corporate community. Its members were strong backers of General Dwight D. Eisenhower for president in 1952, to the great frustration of ultraconservatives in the Republican Party, and several of its most active trustees had a major role in convincing Congress to pass laws that would increase international trade (Domhoff 1990, chapters 6–7). In the 1960s the leadership became even more moderate on domestic issues in the face of turmoil and disruption in inner cities across the country and antiwar protests on campus, with the exception of a strong antiunion stance that is standard for all corporate policy groups. By 1970 CED reports were calling for campaign finance reforms to make the system more transparent and for many improvements in social benefit programs. But by 1976 the organization was in disarray because the majority of its members decided that it had gone too far in advocating government programs.

The leaders within the CED decided to change its orientation at this point as part of a general rightward shift in the corporate community in the face of large increases in oil prices, rapid inflation, rising unemployment, and calls for greater government control of the economy by the liberal-labor coalition. The story of how this right turn was accomplished, which is based on my unpublished research, provides an ideal example of how a new policy direction on the part of leading trustees can bring about shifts within a policy group and quickly end even a small role for liberal experts. Although the corporate community in general was reacting to a new set of challenges, the specific triggers to changes in the CED were internal to the organization. First, the economist serving as president at the time made the mistake of joining labor leaders and liberal economists in signing a public statement suggesting a small step toward greater government planning. Second, a CED study group on controlling inflation, advised in part by liberal economists, was moving in the direction of advocating wage and price controls by government.

CED trustees from several large companies were extremely upset by what they interpreted as a trend toward greater acceptance of government controls. They reacted on a number of levels. First, several of their companies lowered their financial contributions or threatened to withdraw support altogether. Since large companies make the biggest contribution to the organization's budget, these threats were of great concern to the president and his staff.

Second, the chairman of the trustees, a senior executive at what is now ExxonMobil, appointed the CEOs of three other large corporations as a three-person committee to make a study of the internal structure of the organization. One result of this study was the retirement of the president one year earlier than expected; a conservative monetary economist from the Federal Reserve Bank of Minneapolis replaced him. The new president immediately wrote to all trustees asking for their advice on future policy directions, pledging greater responsiveness to the trustees. He also brought in several new staff members; one of them told me in an interview in 1995 that it was their job to neutralize the somewhat more liberal staff members.

Third, many of the trustees on the Research and Policy Committee, which oversees all study groups, decided to oppose the report on inflation and price controls. In all, there were 15 pages of dissents attached to the report, most from a very conservative perspective, and seven trustees voted to reject publication altogether. Fourth, the three economists primarily responsible for drafting the report—a university president, a prominent think tank representative, and a CED staff member—were criticized in letters to the CED president for allegedly having too much influence in shaping the recommendations. The CED leader from ExxonMobil later characterized the ill-fated statement as a "poor compromise between the views of trustees and a stubborn chairman and project director," which was a way of smoothing over differences among corporate leaders by blaming staff members and outside advisers for the disagreement. Fifth, some trustees were personally hostile to the economists who were said to be too liberal. The think-tank economist told me he was accused in personal conversations with corporate executives of being a Communist even though he had worked with the organizations for several years as a liberal who enjoyed the give-and-take with conservatives.

The dramatic difference between the CED at the beginning and end of the 1970s is demonstrated by a comparison of policy statements issued in 1971 and 1979. In the first report, the emphasis was on the social responsibility of corporations and the need for corporations to work in partnership with government on social problems. The report at the end of the decade stressed the need to limit the role of government in a market system. The CED now ignored all the social issues it had addressed before 1974, which it could do because the ghetto uprisings had faded away and the Vietnam War was over. This change occurred even though almost half of the 40 members of the Research and Policy Committee in 1979 were on the committee in 1971 and endorsed the earlier policy statement (Frederick 1981). This is strong evidence that the moderate conservatives had come to agree with ultraconservatives on many issues under the new circumstances.

The organization's internal critics also claimed that it was ineffective in its attempts to influence the policy climate in Washington and that it overlapped with other policy groups in any case. Ironically, the CED's Washington liaison, Kenneth Duberstein, who was not supposed to lobby because of the organization's tax-exempt status, was one of the key links between business and the Republicans in Congress at the time. He went to work in the Reagan Administration in 1981, eventually ending up as the president's White House chief of staff. (By 2008 he was a director of Boeing, ConocoPhillips, and Travelers Insurance as well as a trustee of the Council on Foreign Relations and the Brookings Institution.) Although the outgoing CED president wrote a lengthy memo documenting the organization's behind-the-scenes effectiveness in lobbying for its policies, the new president was instructed to find a new niche for the organization in relation to other organizations, especially the Business Roundtable. The increasing importance of the Business Roundtable led to a repositioning of CED by corporate executives who were top officers in both organizations. As one of these officers wrote in a letter to several trustees in the summer of 1978 after a meeting with a small group of CEOs from leading corporations:

> The meeting was especially helpful in sharpening our sense of CED's special role within the spectrum of major national business-related organizations. The group was encouraged to learn of new efforts by CED to coordinate its work with that of the Business Roundtable, the Conference Board, the American Enterprise Institute, and others, thus minimizing duplication and overlap. CED can be especially effective, it was felt, in synthesizing the ideas of scholars and converting them into practical principles that can provide guidance for public policy on a selected number of key issues (CED memo in my personal files).

None of this upheaval was visible to outside observers at the time, which underscores the importance of historical studies in understanding how the policy-planning network functions. The only article mentioning the CED's problems appeared in *The Wall Street Journal* in December, 1976. It quoted one trustee, an oil company executive, claiming that "In the early days, the trustees were men who saw a need for some more government intervention, but now some of the trustees believe the intervention has gone far enough." An academic economist who once advised the CED said it had "lost its purpose" and "doesn't have the sense to go out of business" (*WSJ* 1976, p. 38). It would have been hard to know what to make of such charges at the time without extensive interviewing or access to the kind of internal files that only became available to me many years later. This is why it is necessary to take on-the-spot investigative studies with a grain of salt; they often reflect the attempt by those who are interviewed to shape the analysis in a self-serving way.

When the fate of the liberal experts in this example is coupled with the importance of foundation grants and appointments to think tanks for the careers of policy experts, there is little reason to believe that experts are free to say and recommend whatever they wish. To the contrary, the experts who want to leave the university realm and take a role in Washington have to learn to work within the constraints of what is acceptable to the corporate leaders who finance and direct the organizations of the policy-planning network. What is acceptable can vary from time to time, depending on changing circumstances, but that does not mean there are no constraints. In this case, the shift to the right by the moderate conservatives in the corporate community led to the removal of liberal experts and the decline in importance of the CED.

THE BUSINESS COUNCIL

The Business Council is a unique organization in the policy-planning network because of its close formal contact with government. It was created during the 1930s as a quasigovernmental advisory group. It still holds regular consultative meetings with government officials even though it became an independent organization in 1962. Since the 1960s, most of its private meetings with government officials have been held in the relaxed and friendly atmosphere of an expensive resort hotel sixty miles from Washington. During the meetings Business Council members hear speeches by government officials, conduct panels on issues of the day, receive reports from their staff, and talk informally with each other and the government officials in attendance. Business sessions are alternated with social events, including golf tournaments, tennis matches, and banquet-style dinners for members, guests, and spouses. Corporate leaders pay the expenses for the meetings, reports, and social events. With few exceptions, the members are the chairs or presidents of the largest corporations in the country (McQuaid 1982).

THE BUSINESS ROUNDTABLE

The Business Roundtable, composed of CEOs from a cross section of the corporate community, with most of the largest fifteen always represented, is at the center of the policy-planning network, as shown in Table 4.4. Its 161 members in 2004 not only ran major corporations, but they sat on an additional 140 corporate boards as well. These directorships are widely distributed among corporations, but ExxonMobil, IBM, AT&T, and Citigroup each had three directors on the Business Roundtable in addition to their own CEOs. Decisions on where the Roundtable will focus its efforts are determined by a policy committee that meets every two months to discuss current policy issues, create task forces to examine selected issues, and review position papers prepared by task forces. Task forces are asked to avoid focusing on problems in any one industry and to concentrate instead on issues that have a broad impact on business. With a staff of less than a dozen people, the Business Roundtable does not have the capability to develop its own information. However, this presents no problem because the organization has been designed so that task force members will utilize the resources of their own companies as well as the information developed in other parts of the policy network.

As explained briefly in Chapter 2, the Business Roundtable had its origins in the mid-1960s as the informal coordinating committee for the successful effort to overturn a decision by the National Labor Relations Board forbidding outsourcing unless a company bargained with unions about the change. Formally incorporated in 1972, it began its more public efforts by coordinating the successful lobbying campaign against a consumer-labor proposal for a new governmental Agency for Consumer Advocacy in the mid-1970s. It created a Clean Air Working Group that battled the environmental-labor coalition to a standstill from 1980 to 1990 on proposed tightening of the Clean Air Act, agreeing to amendments only after several standards were relaxed or delayed and a plan to trade pollution credits in market-like fashion was accepted by environmentalists (Gonzalez 2001). On a less conservative note, it helped reign in the ultraconservatives in the Reagan Administration by calling for tax increases in 1982 and 1983 that began to reduce the huge deficits the administration's earlier tax cuts had created. In 1985 it called for cuts in defense spending as well. Along with other business organizations, it quietly opposed the attack on affirmative action by the ultraconservatives in the Reagan Administration, pointing out that the policy had proven to be very useful for corporate America. It even supported a mild extension of the Civil Rights Act in 1991, putting it at odds with the U.S. Chamber of Commerce (Belz 1991; Vogel 1989).

During the Clinton Administration, the Business Roundtable joined with the U.S. Chamber of Commerce and the National Federation of Independent Business in defeating a proposal for national health care reform in 1994 (Mintz 1998). Then it organized the grassroots pressure and forceful lobbying for the corporate community's victories in 1994 on the North American Free Trade Agreement and in 2000 on permanent normal trading status for China (Dreiling 2001; Dreiling and Darves 2007). Both of these trade initiatives were strongly resisted by organized labor, environmentalists, and many of their liberal allies because "trade" in both instances meant that the corporations' production facilities would be moved to low-wage countries, thereby undercutting the union movement and the middle-class lifestyle it had brought to its members. Then the finished products would be brought back to the United States for sale.

THE LIBERAL-LABOR POLICY NETWORK

There is also a small liberal-labor policy network. It suggests new ideas and perspectives to liberal political organizations, unions, and the government in an attempt to challenge the corporate community. Because the organizations in it are small in comparison to the corporate-backed organizations, some of them also serve as advocacy groups as well as think tanks. Most of them are focused on domestic economic policy. Several organizations in the liberal-labor network receive some of their financial support from labor unions, but the sums are seldom more than a few hundred thousand dollars per year. It is difficult to know the exact figures because the donations come from different unions and the AFL-CIO is not enthusiastic about the idea of compiling the totals. The liberal policy groups also receive grants from a small number of liberal foundations and from a few mainstream foundations.

Even when they receive grants from the mainstream foundations and backing from labor unions, the liberal-labor policy organizations usually do not come close to matching the budgets of their moderately conservative and ultraconservative opponents. Table 4.5 on page 114 presents the major foundation support for four liberal groups in recent years.

The liberal-labor coalition also includes two think tanks, the Progressive Policy Institute and the Center for American Progress, that are in reality adjuncts of the Democratic Party. Until early 2009, the Progressive Policy Institute was the policy arm of the Democratic Leadership Council, an organization of centrist Democrats founded in the early 1980s in an attempt to counter the party's liberal wing and bring the party's image back into what its leaders defined as the mainstream. Many of these moderates were Southern Democrats, including future president Bill Clinton and future vice president Al Gore, both of whom had leadership roles in the group in the 1980s and developed strong connections with funding sources for their future campaigns through it (Baer 2000).

Table 4.5 Four Liberal Groups and Their Main Foundation Funders between 2003 and Early 2008

Foundations[2]	Think Tanks[1]			
	Center on Budget and Policy Priorities	Consumer Federation of America	Economic Policy Institute	New America Foundation
Casey Foundation	$3,710,800	$593,492	$535,100	$1,031,000
Ford Foundation	$10,420,000	$690,000	$4,475,000	$4,386,600
Mott Foundation	$3,075,000	$0	$900,000	$1,375,000
Open Society Institute	$1,375,000	$75,000	$2,210,000	$1,191,875
Rockefeller Foundation	$3,220,270	$0	$1,305,000	$1,935,000
Total donations from these five foundations	$21,801,070	$1,358,492	$9,425,100	$9,919,475

[1]These groups received funding from other sources as well.
[2]These foundations gave to many other groups as well.
Source: The Foundation Directory Online (New York: The Foundation Center, 2008).

The Center for American Progress was started in 2003 by a former chief of staff for President Clinton, John Podesta, after he grew restless working for trade groups such as the Nevada Resort Association and the American Insurance Association as part of a lobbying firm he cofounded with his brother. Major Democratic donors provide most of its funding (e.g., George Soros, chairman of Soros Investment Company, with personal income of $2.9 billion in 2007; Peter B. Lewis, chairman of Progressive Insurance; Herbert and Marion Sandler, owners of World Savings at the time; and Peter Bing, a Hollywood producer who inherited tens of millions). By late 2008 the center had a staff of 180 and a budget of $25 million a year. It also received $15 million in grants from several small liberal foundations. Positioned as a counterweight to the Heritage Foundation, most of its policy analysts had worked in the Clinton Administration. It was known in 2008 as a government-in-exile (Savage 2008b). President Obama put Podesta in charge of his transition team.

As briefly noted in the first chapter, the liberal-labor coalition has excellent media connections, in part because some of its members are prominent journalists. Although its reports are not featured as often as those of its conservative rivals, it nonetheless has the ability to obtain wide coverage for stories critical of corporate policy proposals. This media visibility is further enhanced by claims about the allegedly great power of the liberal-labor coalition in alarmist fund-raising letters sent out by ultraconservative organizations. However, as explained in Chapters 6 and 7, the visibility of these organizations translated into very few successes between 1975 and 2000.

THE POWER ELITE

In concert with the large banks and corporations in the corporate community, the foundations, think tanks, and policy-discussion groups in the policy-planning network provide the organizational basis for the exercise of power on behalf of the owners of all large income-producing properties. The leaders of these organizations are therefore the institutionalized leadership group for those who have an economic stake in preserving the governmental rules and regulations that maintain the current wealth and income distributions.

This leadership group is called *the power elite*. The power elite is made up of those people who serve as directors or trustees in profit and nonprofit institutions controlled by the corporate community through stock ownership, financial support, involvement on the board of trustees, or some combination of these factors. This precise definition of who is and who is not in the power elite includes the top-level employees who are asked to join the boards of the organizations that employ them. It is useful for research purposes in tracing corporate involvement in voluntary associations, the media, political parties, and government. Although the power elite is a leadership group, the phrase usually is used with a plural verb in this book to emphasize that the power elite is also a collection of individuals who have some internal policy disagreements as well as personal ambitions and rivalries that receive detailed media attention and often overshadow the general policy consensus. In other words, the power elite is not a monolithic leadership group.

The concept of a power elite makes it possible to integrate class and organizational insights in order to create a more complete theory of power in America. Once again, as in the case of corporations, the key point is that any differences between class and organizational perspectives on issues are worked out in meetings of the boards of trustees where wealthy owners and CEOs from major corporations meet with the top employees of the policy-network organizations. This intertwining of class and organizational theories is discussed further in Chapter 8 when the main alternative theories are compared with the one that is unfolding in this book.

The corporate community, the upper class, and the policy-planning network provide the organizational basis and social cohesion for the creation of a power elite. A person can be a member of one of the three, or two of the three, or all three of these networks, which

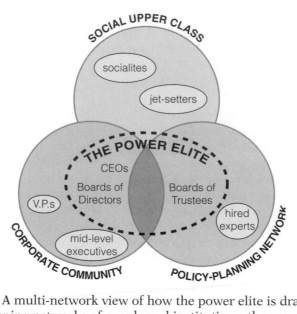

Figure 4.2   A multi-network view of how the power elite is drawn from three overlapping networks of people and institutions: the corporate community, the social upper class, and the policy-formation network. The power elite is made up of those members of these three overlapping circles who sit on the board of directors of a corporation in the corporate community or the board of trustees of a nonprofit organization in the policy-planning network.

can be pictured in terms of the three intersecting circles presented in Figure 4.2. But not all the people in these three overlapping networks are part of the power elite. First, there are upper-class people who are only socialites and sit on no boards of directors in the corporate community or the policy-planning network. Except for their campaign donations to political candidates, they play no part in the exercise of power. Second, there are corporate leaders just below the board level who are neither upper class nor involved in policy planning; they focus exclusively on their roles in the corporate community. Finally, there are policy experts who are neither members of the upper class nor on boards of directors of corporations; they are simply employees of the power elite who spend all their time doing research and writing reports. These distinctions clear up a point that can be confusing when first encountering a class-domination theory: Not all members of the dominant class are involved in governing and not all members of the power elite are part of the dominant class.

As a practical matter, the interrelations among these three sectors are closer than the image of three intersecting circles would indicate. A majority of the male members of the upper class between 45 and 65 are part of the corporate community as financiers, active investors, corporate lawyers, officers of privately held companies, or titled executives even when they do not serve on a board of directors. Then, too, some members of the policy network become involved in the corporate community as consultants and advisors even though they do not rise to the level of corporate directors. In other words, the corporate community becomes the common sector that encompasses many of the older males within the three overlapping circles, along with a small number of women.

Although this chapter provides evidence for the existence of a network of policy-planning organizations that is an extension of the corporate community in its financing and leadership, it does not claim there is a completely unified power elite policy outlook that is easily agreed upon. Instead, it shows that the upper class and corporate community have created a complex and only partially coordinated set of institutions and organizations that often disagree among themselves about what policies are most compatible with the primary objectives of the corporate community. Nonetheless, the emphasis has to be on the considerable similarity in viewpoint among institutions that range from moderately conservative to highly conservative in their policy suggestions. Moreover, even though they are not able to agree completely among themselves, they have accomplished an equally important task: They have been able to marginalize the few experts with a more liberal point of view. This point cannot be stressed enough, but there is not much more that can be said about it. Liberal experts appear on talk shows and publish books, but there is barely a sign of their existence even in the Obama Administration. As shown in Chapter 7, centrists have been appointed to carry out whatever liberal measures may be necessary to deal with the economic and foreign policy crisis inherited from the Bush Administration.

This chapter thus provides evidence for another form of power exercised by the corporate community and upper class through the power elite—expertise. *Expert power* is an important complement to the structural power and status power discussed in the previous two chapters. Since government officials with only small policy-planning staffs must often turn to foundations, policy groups, and think tanks for new ideas, it is once again a form of power that can be exercised without any direct involvement in government.

Structural power, status power, and expertise are formidable quite independent of any participation in politics and government, but they are not enough to make owners and top executives a dominant class because they do not ensure domination of government. It still could be possible for the liberal-labor coalition to use government legislation to bring about some redistribution of the country's wealth and income in a democratic way by electing a liberal Congress and president. In addition, government can pass laws that help or hinder profit making, and it can collect and utilize tax funds in such a way as to stimulate or discourage economic growth. It also can take on greater involvement in corporations when the economy is in crisis, as the hundreds of billions in bailout money in 2008 and 2009 stunningly reveal.

Given the great stakes involved, there is too much uncertainty in the relationship between the corporate community and the government for the power elite to rely solely on structural economic power, status power, and expertise to ensure that their interests are realized. They therefore work very hard to shape public opinion, influence elections, and determine government policy on the issues of concern to them.

5

The Role of Public Opinion

Due to the constitutional protections surrounding free speech and the right of assembly, there is the potential for public opinion to have an influence on government policies. Citizens also can organize into pressure groups to run newspaper ads and lobby Congress in order to communicate their preferences on specific policy issues, a fact given great weight in pluralist theory. Contrary to pluralist theory, many college students, especially those of a highly liberal or highly conservative persuasion, believe that the mass media shape public opinion. This chapter suggests that neither public influence on policy issues nor media dominance of public opinion is the case. People develop their own opinions based on their own lives and their interactions with people they know, as pluralist theory would also argue. Furthermore, their general opinions on both foreign policy and economic policy often differ from those of the power elite despite any media biases that might exist. But contrary to pluralism, public opinion usually has little or no influence on specific policies unless it takes the shape of a massive outcry or a social movement.

More specifically, the results of several decades of public opinion surveys present a seeming paradox. On the one hand, public opinion is rational and sensible within the context of people's lives and the quality of the information available to them. For example, more men came to accept the idea of women working outside the home as they saw more women in the workplace. More white people came to have positive opinions concerning African-Americans as they learned more about the Civil Rights Movement. The great majority favor more social support from government on health and employment issues and they advocate a foreign policy that is more cooperative with other nations and less militaristic (Page and Shapiro 1992; Page 2008; Page and Jacobs 2009). On the other hand, surveys asking about the stands taken by elected officials or the respondents' views on specific issues being considered in Congress suggest that most people pay little attention to politics, have a limited understanding of the options being considered, and do not develop specific opinions on impending legislation even when it has received much attention in the media. These findings suggest it is unlikely that public opinion is focused enough on any specific issue to have any direct effect (Zaller 1992).

Although public opinion rarely has any direct impact on policy debates, members of the power elite are nonetheless very fearful that it might lead to policies they do not like. Since they are well aware through opinion polls and past experience that a majority of citizens disagree with them on many issues, they therefore spend hundreds of millions of dollars each year trying to shape public opinion in order to guarantee the success of the policies they favor. They are not willing to take the chance that policy-making in Washington will remain insulated from the wishes of the majority. As a result, they have developed an opinion-shaping network that operates at many different levels and reaches into many middle-class voluntary and charity organizations that do not at first glance seem to be relevant to the issue of public opinion.

THE OPINION-SHAPING NETWORK

Many of the foundations, policy-discussion groups, and think tanks in the policy-planning network also operate as part of the opinion-shaping network. In this network, however, two other very weighty forces, large public relations firms and the public affairs departments of the major corporations, also play a role. Both have large staffs and the ability to complement their efforts with financial donations from the corporate foundations discussed in the previous chapter. These core organizations are connected to a widespread dissemination network that includes special committees to influence single issues, corporate-financed advertising councils, local advertising agencies, and the mass media. In contrast to the policy-planning process, where a relatively small number of organizations do most of the work, there are hundreds of small organizations within the opinion-shaping process that specialize in public relations or persuasion on virtually every issue. Thus, the opinion-shaping network is extremely diverse and diffuse at its point of direct contact with the general public. Figure 5.1 provides a general picture of the opinion-shaping network.

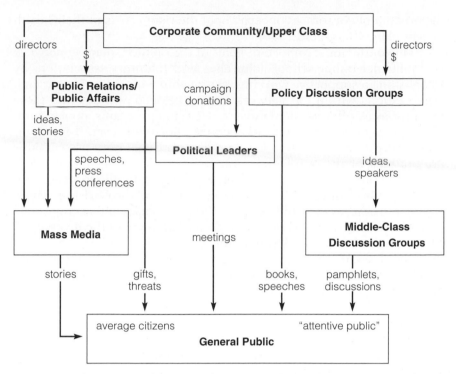

Figure 5.1   The General Network through Which the Power Elite Try to Shape Public Opinion

The policy discussion groups at the heart of this network do not enter into the opinion-shaping process directly except through releasing their reports to newspapers and magazines. Instead, their leaders set up special committees to work for changes in public opinion on specific issues. Sometimes it is not possible to illustrate this close connection until historical archives are available. For example, three of the most important opinion-shaping committees of the post–World War II era denied any connection to the Council on Foreign Relations, but papers and correspondence related to the organization reveal otherwise (Wala 1994).

To create an atmosphere in which the general public more readily accepts policy changes, these committees attempt to picture the situation as one of great crisis. For example, this is what the Committee on the Present Danger did in the mid-1970s in order to gain public support for increased defense spending, claiming that government estimates of Soviet defense spending and military capability were far too low. Both claims proved to be patently false (Sanders 1983). Similarly, the perception of a health care crisis in the late 1980s was in good part the product of corporate concern about the rising costs of their health benefit plans (Bergthold 1990).

One of the most important goals of the opinion-shaping network is to influence public schools, churches, and voluntary associations by establishing a supportive working relationship with them. To that end, organizations within the network have developed avenues into these institutions by offering them movies, television programs, books, pamphlets, speakers, advice, and financial support. However, it is important to stress that the schools, churches, and voluntary associations are not part of the opinion-shaping network. They are independent settings within which the power elite must constantly contend with spokespersons from the liberal-labor coalition and the Christian Right. To assume otherwise would be to overlook the social and occupational affiliations of the members of these groups, along with the diversity of opinion that often exists within them.

In the attempt to prevent the development of attitudes and opinions that might interfere with the acceptance of policies created in the policy-planning process, leaders within the opinion-shaping process also attempt to build upon and reinforce the underlying principles of the American belief system. Academically speaking, these underlying principles are called *laissez-faire liberalism,* and they have their roots in the work of several European philosophers and the American Founding Fathers. These principles emphasize individualism, free enterprise, competition, the fairness of economic markets, equality of opportunity, and a minimum of reliance upon government in carrying out the affairs of society. This package of beliefs developed gradually during the centuries-long rise of the capitalist system in Europe and then arrived in America in nearly finished form. Laissez-faire liberalism had no serious rivals in a small new nation that did not have a feudal past or an established state church (Hartz 1955; Lipset 1963).

Although this individualistic and antigovernment belief system remains pervasive, it is an independent and uncontested factor in shaping the opinions and behavior of Americans in part because the liberal-labor coalition and leftists have not been able to develop an organizational base in unions, churches, or a political party from which they could advocate a more communal, cooperative, and pro-government alternative in which government is portrayed as a way to solve common societal problems. American cultural beliefs that are thought to be a timeless part of culture by pluralist theorists are in fact sustained by the efforts of organizations created and funded by the power elite, as shown in this chapter. Put another way, general belief systems are communicated by organizations even though they are often articulated and written down by philosophers. Such beliefs, in other words, are *institutionalized,* turned into taken-for-granted habits and customs.

Most citizens know these unchallenged values as "Americanism." They are thought to be part of human nature or the product of good common sense. If Americans can be convinced that some policy or action is justified in terms of this emotion-laden body of beliefs, they are more likely to accept it. Thus, the organizations that make up the opinion-shaping network strive to become the arbitrators of which policies and opinions are in keeping with good Americanism and which are not. They struggle against the liberal-labor coalition and the Christian Right to define what policies are in the national interest and to identify those policies with Americanism.

The efforts of the opinion-shaping network sometimes reach a more subtle level as well. Even though many people do not accept the overt messages presented in ads, speeches, and booklets, they often accept the implicit message that their problems lie in their own personal inadequacies. Because of its strong emphasis on personal effort and responsibility, an individualistic ideology not only rewards the successful, it blames the victims of how the economic system operates. (An *ideology* is the complex set of rationales and rationalizations through which a group, class, or nation interprets the world and justifies its actions; an ideology usually is fervently believed by those who espouse it.)

Educational failure and other social problems, which are best understood in terms of the way in which a class system encourages some people and discourages others, are turned into reproaches of the victims for their alleged failure to correct personal defects and take advantage of the opportunities offered to them (Lane 1962; Ryan 1971). A classic study based on in-depth interviews explains how an individualistic ideology leaves many working people with a paralyzing self-blame for their alleged failures even though they know the social system is not fair to them:

> Workingmen intellectually reject the idea that endless opportunity exists for the competent. And yet, the institutions of class force them to apply the idea to themselves: If I don't escape being part of the woodwork, it's because I didn't develop my powers enough. Thus, talk about how arbitrary a class society's reward system is will be greeted with general agreement—with the proviso that in my own case I should have made more of myself (Sennett and Cobb 1973, pp. 250–251).

This self-blame is important in understanding the reluctant acquiescence of wage earners in a hierarchical system with extreme economic inequalities:

> Once that proviso (that in my own case I should have made more of myself) is added, challenging class institutions becomes saddled

with the agonizing question, Who am I to make the challenge? To speak of American workers as having been "bought off" by the system or adopting the same conservative values as middle-class suburban managers and professionals is to miss all the complexity of their silence and to have no way of accounting for the intensity of pent-up feeling that pours out when working people do challenge higher authority (Sennett and Cobb 1973, p. 251).

There is a further problem for most Americans: It is very hard to imagine that the overall socioeconomic system, with all its many integrated parts, could be the problem because the world is fair and sensible—it's a "just world" (Jost and Major 2001). For example, there was initial sympathy for people who lost their homes in the mortgage meltdown that began in late 2006, but many people who did not lose their homes soon came to think it was the homeowners' fault for not being hardheaded or frugal enough. The pressures, enticements, deceptive advertising, and regulatory failures of banks, mortgage companies, and government regulatory agencies were lost from view (see Baker 2009, for a step-by-step account of how appraisers, mortgage bankers, credit rating agencies, and captive government regulatory agencies created the problems now blamed on the victims). Since the system is mostly fair, the average American ends up in the conflicted position of having many critical observations about how things work mixed with an overall attitude of acceptance. The result is usually a focus on the pleasures of everyday life and a grumbling acceptance of the political status quo. It is only when people are part of collective efforts in opposition to conditions they think are unfair that they overcome their tendency to blame themselves.

Public Relations/Public Affairs

Public relations is a multibillion-dollar industry created by the power elite in the 1920s for the sole purpose of shaping public opinion (Ewen 1996). There are hundreds of important independent firms, but a few large ones do the major work, taking in hundreds of millions of dollars in fees each year. Advertising companies of even greater size in turn own most public relations firms. Public relations firms usually do not run general campaigns aimed at shaping overall public opinion. Instead, they are hired to work on very specific issues and are asked to focus on relatively narrow target audiences. The goal is not to change general public opinion, but to block any activities that might harm the image or threaten the profits of their clients. To accomplish that goal, it is often enough to give the impression that there are many contending voices or that there is uncertainty about how to proceed. Spreading confusion and uncertainty, a practice that provides the necessary cover while an issue is being debated, comprises the underlying mission of public relations.

For example, Burson-Marsteller, one of the largest of these firms, created the National Smokers Alliance in the early 1990s for the tobacco industry, sending its paid canvassers into bars to find members and potential activists. Another firm, National Grassroots and Communications, specializes in creating local organizations to oppose neighborhood activists. Still another, Nichols-Dezenhall Communications Management Group, concentrates on helping corporations by "aggressively exposing and discrediting" their critics (Stauber and Rampton 1995). Its founder is the author of *Rules for Corporate Warriors: How to Fight and Survive Attack Group Shakedowns*, which was published by the Center for the Defense of Free Enterprise in 2001.

Public relations sometimes operates through the mass media, so it is not surprising that one-third of its 175,000 practitioners are former journalists and that about half of current journalism school graduates go into one form of public relations work or another. Some public relations experts with journalism backgrounds put their contacts to work by trying to keep corporate critics from appearing in the media. One company keeps files on practicing journalists for possible use in questioning their credibility. Public relations experts use their skills to monitor the activities of groups critical of specific industries, everyone from animal rights groups opposed to the use of animals in testing cosmetic products to antilogging groups. Some of the actions taken against these groups, which include infiltration of meetings and copying materials in files, add up to spying (Stauber and Rampton 1995). (See www.prwatch.org for recent accounts of campaigns organized by public relations firms.)

Public affairs, on the other hand, is a generally more benign form of public relations practiced by departments within the large corporations themselves. Here the emphasis is on polishing the image of corporations rather than criticizing journalists and opposition groups. These departments are more frequently staffed by women and minorities than other corporate departments, in order to provide the company with a human face more reflective of the larger community. In one large corporation, the employees in public affairs refer to their department as the "velvet ghetto" because the job is a pleasant one with an excellent salary and expense account, but one that rarely leads to positions at the top of the corporation (Ghiloni 1987).

The first task of employees in public affairs departments is to gather newspaper stories and radio and TV transcripts in order to monitor what is being said about their own corporation at the local level. They then try to counter any negative commentary by placing favorable stories in local newspapers and giving speeches to local organizations.

They also join with members of other public affairs departments in an effort to shape public opinion in the interests of local corporations in general. The general goal of public affairs personnel is "looking good and doing good" (Himmelstein 1997).

The efforts of public affairs departments are supplemented by the financial gifts they are able to provide to middle-class charitable and civic organizations through the corporations' foundations. About one-third of this money goes to educational programs, another quarter to health and charitable services, and the rest to community and cultural organizations. The emphasis on improving the image of the corporation and cultivating good will is seen most directly in the fact that it is cigarette companies and corporations with poor environmental reputations that give the most money to sporting events, the arts, and the Public Broadcasting System (Ermann 1978).

Reading through the list of grants to highly visible voluntary and charitable organizations in the *Foundation Directory Online*, it is clear that few if any of these organizations could survive for very long without financial support from corporate and family foundations. For example, between 2003 and early 2008 Big Brothers Big Sisters of America, which works with disadvantaged children, received $17.3 million from the Clark Foundation in New York, based on the Clark family's Avon Products fortune, along with $2.1 million from the MetLife Foundation. (For a detailed account of the full range of donations claimed by 3,000 company-sponsored foundations and 1,300 corporate giving programs, see the *National Directory of Corporate Giving 2008*.) At the least, foundations provide a stable funding base for most charitable and voluntary organizations and the discretionary money that makes it possible for them to test out new programs. They provide the seed money for fundraising with the general public and they ensure that the officers will receive good salaries. Table 5.1 presents a sample of major

Table 5.1 Top Donations to Nonprofit Groups by Selected Foundations between 2003 and Early 2008

Foundation	Recipient	Size of Grant
Wal-Mart	Children's Miracle Network	$14.8 million
Citigroup	Habitat for Humanity	$8.0 million
General Electric	American Red Cross	$6.0 million
JPMorgan Chase	United Negro College Fund	$4.6 million
ExxonMobil	Save the Children Federation	$3.0 million
Kellogg	Ms. Foundation for Women	$2.5 million

Source: Foundation Directory Online (New York: The Foundation Center, 2008).

donations by corporate foundations to nonprofit groups in the years before this book was published.

Perhaps the best evidence for the essential role that corporations play in most nonprofit groups can be seen in the funding of the United Way, which raises a significant share of the money spent by charities and local volunteer groups around the country. In addition to their foundation grants to the United Way, the corporations organize campaigns to collect money from their employees. By way of thanks, the United Way runs full-page ads in major newspapers each year to acknowledge the help provided by corporations and trade associations, which is also a form of good will advertising for the corporate community. In 2008 the ad listed 117 companies in rank order that raised $15 million or more, which added up to "more than $1 billion to improve lives and strengthen communities" (*The New York Times*, December 11, 2007, p. A6). At the top of the list at presumably well more than $15 million were UPS, Microsoft, IBM, Bank of America, Publix Supermarkets, General Electric, Wells Fargo, AT&T, and Pfizer.

In addition, top corporate executives or their public affairs vice presidents sit on the boards of trustees of these organizations. In a study of director interlocks in 1998 between the 100 largest industrial corporations and national nonprofit groups, there were 37 links with the United Way in various regions of the country, 14 with the Boys and Girls Clubs of America, and 14 with the Boy Scouts of America (Moore, Raffalovich, Whitt, Sobieraj, Dolan and Beaulieu 2003). In 2008 a retired executive from one of the country's largest accounting firms chaired the board of the United Way of America, where he was joined by executives from UPS, FedEx, and several other firms. The board of trustees of Big Brothers Big Sisters of America is headed by the chief executive officer of Cargill, a privately owned agricultural commodities firm that is one of the 20 largest corporations in the country; over half the board members are current or retired corporate executives, supplemented by representatives from professional sports associations and former sports stars.

The attempt to establish good relationships with a wide range of voluntary organizations through both public relations departments and board memberships reinforces the ethic within these organizations to steer clear of conversations about politics. They therefore can rarely if ever play any role in creating a political debate concerning new ways to deal with the social problems their organizations are meant to overcome. It seems doubtful that very many voluntary associations any longer carry out the important function of political socialization that has been claimed for them by theorists of democracy since the nineteenth century. Instead, they encourage the avoidance of politics (Eliasoph 1998).

Although public relations specialists backed by corporate largesse cannot overcome general negative opinions toward corporations, they have been able to create a positive attitude toward specific corporations in the communities where they are located, or at least a reluctance to bite the hand that feeds local voluntary associations. They thereby make it difficult to mobilize average citizens against local corporations on a particular grievance. People may be critical of corporations in opinion polls, but they usually do not want to confront the corporations in their own cities. This is one example of why general public opinion often does not lead to any specific actions, which is an acceptable outcome for corporations. Corporations may not be loved, but their top executives did not have to endure any sustained criticism between 1975 and 2008 except by small liberal and leftist advocacy groups that were not able to gain any widespread public backing.

The Advertising Council

Although it is not feasible to discuss very many of the numerous small organizations that attempt to shape public opinion, the Advertising Council, usually called the Ad Council, provides a good example of how they operate. In effect, it sells the free-enterprise system through public-interest advertising on a wide range of issues. In 2000 its outgoing president claimed that "over the decades the Ad Council has fought totalitarianism and racism, saved lives, healed the environment and made life measurably better for all Americans" (Berger 2000). Whether that glowing self-praise is true or not, the Ad Council is a case study in how individualism and Americanism are called into service on behalf of the power elite.

The Ad Council began its institutional life as the War Advertising Council during World War II, founded as a means to support the war effort through advertising in the mass media. Its work was judged to be so successful in promoting a positive image for the corporate community that it was continued in the postwar period. In recent years the Ad Council has been enlisted by the American Red Cross, Big Brothers Big Sisters of America, the Girl Scouts of the USA, the National Urban League, the American Cancer Society, the Department of Homeland Security, and the United States Army to conduct ad campaigns on their behalf. With an annual budget of only a few million dollars, the council also places over $1.5 billion worth of free advertising each year through radio, television, magazines, newspapers, billboards, and public transportation. After the council leaders decide on what campaigns they want to undertake, the specifics of the program are given to one or another Madison Avenue advertising agency, which does the work without charge.

Corporations provide most of the Ad Council's funding. Like the United Way, the Ad Council uses full-page ads to thank its corporate sponsors and remind newspaper readers that corporations are good citizens ("we made a difference, you made it possible"). Topping the list of 260 contributors in 2008, which ranges from American Express to Facebook to NASCAR, were five donors of $150,000 or more: Coca-Cola, Johnson & Johnson, Microsoft, PepsiCo, Time Warner, and Yahoo.

Most council campaigns seem relatively innocuous and in a public interest that nobody would dispute. Its best-known figures, Smokey the Bear and McGruff the Crime Dog, were created for the campaigns against forest fires and urban crime, respectively. However, as one media analyst demonstrated in a detailed study of some of these campaigns, many of them have a strong slant in favor of corporations. The council's environmental ads, for example, suggest that "people start pollution, people can stop it," thereby putting the responsibility on individuals rather than on a system of production that allows corporations to avoid the costs of disposing of their waste products by dumping them into the air or water. A special subcommittee of the council's Industry Advisory Committee gave very explicit instructions about how this particular ad campaign should be formulated: "The committee emphasized that the advertisements should stress that each of us must be made to recognize that each of us contributes to pollution, and therefore everyone bears the responsibility" (Hirsch 1975, p. 69). Thus, the Keep America Beautiful campaign is geared to show corporate concern about the environment while at the same time deflecting criticism of the corporate role in pollution by falling back on the individualism of the American creed.

The Ad Council reacted to the shock of 9/11 in 2001 by reorganizing itself to reflect its original wartime footing, creating a Coalition Against Terrorism headed by a recently retired executive from one of the public relations/advertising conglomerates. It now sees its primary mission as "supporting the country and the war effort" through ad campaigns that stress the importance of freedom and the dangers of losing it. At the same time, the council mounted a campaign extolling the virtues of diversity, showing people of different racial and religious backgrounds who proclaim "I am an American" (Levere 2002).

The effectiveness of such campaigns is open to question. It is not clear that they have a direct influence on very many opinions. Studies by social scientists suggest that advertising campaigns of a propagandistic nature work best "when used to reinforce an already existing notion or to establish a logical or emotional connection between a new idea and a social norm" (Hirsch 1975, p. 78). Even when an ad campaign can be judged a failure in this limited role, it has filled a vacuum that might have been used by a competing group. This is especially the case with television, where the council is able to capture a significant percentage of the public-service advertising time that television networks provide. Thus, the council has the direct effect of reinforcing existing values while simultaneously preventing groups with a different viewpoint from presenting their interpretation of events. (For more on the Ad Council and its current campaigns, see www.adcouncil.org.)

The Ad Council is typical of a wide variety of opinion-shaping organizations that function in specific areas. For example, the National Right to Work Committee and related antiunion organizations constantly run print ads criticizing labor unions for everything that goes wrong with the American economy, including the movement of companies overseas, which they say would not have been necessary if union wages were not so exorbitant. On a more positive note, there is the Business Committee for the Arts, recently folded into Americans for the Arts, which has encouraged the artistic endeavors of low-income children since the 1960s as a way to boost the morale of those who live in inner-city neighborhoods. Whether the strategy is to criticize or encourage, the functions of these organizations are basically three in number:

1. They provide think-tank forums where academics, journalists, and other cultural experts can brainstorm with corporate leaders about the problems of shaping public opinion on a specific issue.
2. They help to create a more sophisticated corporate consciousness on social problems through forums, booklets, speeches, and awards.
3. They disseminate their version of the national interest and good Americanism to the general public on issues of concern to the power elite.

STRIVING TO SHAPE OPINION ON FOREIGN POLICY

The opinion-shaping network achieves its clearest expression in the area of foreign policy, where most people have little information or interest and are predisposed to accept unilateral or bellicose actions by top leaders out of patriotism or fear of the foreign, even though polls show that the general public has more liberal and less militaristic views than those members of the power elite and the policy-planning network who focus on foreign policy (Jacobs and Page 2005; Moore 2007; Page 2008). Moreover, foreign policy experts believe that people in general agree with them and have little knowledge of specific issues, so there is little need to consult them in devising policies. The power elite's major efforts in opinion shaping on foreign policy are therefore aimed toward a small stratum of highly interested and concerned citizens with college educations who might become a thorn in their side.

The most prominent organization involved in trying to shape upper-middle-class public opinion on foreign affairs is the Foreign Policy Association (FPA), based in New York. About one-third of its governing council are also members of the Council on Foreign Relations. Although the FPA does some research and discussion work, its primary focus is on shaping opinion outside the power elite, a division of labor with the Council on Foreign Relations that is well understood within foreign-policy circles. The FPA's major effort is an intensive program to provide literature and create discussion groups in middle-class organizations and on college campuses, working closely with local World Affairs Councils. Both independent and corporate foundations support its general activities. Between 2003 and early 2008, it received $4.7 million through sixty-nine grants from twenty-seven different foundations, the largest of which came from the Starr Foundation, founded by an insurance magnate ($1.7 million), and the Annenberg Foundation, created by the family that owns *TV Guide* and many other publications ($1.5 million).

Although the efforts of the foreign-policy groups are important in shaping opinions among the most attentive publics, the actions of the president and his top foreign-policy officials are the strongest influences on public opinion on specific foreign policy issues. Public opinion polls conducted before and after an escalation in the war in Vietnam still provide one of the most dramatic examples of this point. Before the bombing of Hanoi and Haiphong began in late spring 1966, the public was split fifty-fifty over the question of bombing, but when asked in July, 1966, after the bombing began, if "the administration is more right or more wrong in bombing Hanoi and Haiphong," 85 percent were in favor (Mueller 1973). College-educated adults and people in younger age groups are most likely to show this change in opinion shortly after a presidential initiative.

However, there are limits to the shaping of public opinion on foreign policy when social stability is threatened and there is potential for social protest. Opposition to both the Korean and Vietnam wars grew consistently as the number of American casualties continued to mount. Demonstrations and teach-ins at universities in the mid-1960s helped consolidate a large minority against the Vietnam War by 1967 and probably played a role in halting the escalation of the ground war (Mueller 1973). At the same time, opinion polls showed that the general public disliked the antiwar protesters even more than they disliked the war (Mueller 1984).

Despite a massive public relations effort on the part of the Bush Administration and a generally supportive press, in 2005 public opinion also turned against the war in Iraq as the military's death toll mounted. According to a political scientist who has done sustained work on public opinion concerning American involvement in wars since World War II, there was only one difference from the past: This time the critical attitudes developed much faster (Mueller 2005). Nevertheless, it was not until September 2006, shortly before the midterm congressional elections, that it seemed likely that this growing disapproval of the war might affect the election. Most analysts were caught unawares when people reported in exit polls that their number one concern was the war and that they had voted to put the Democrats back in charge of both houses of Congress for the first time since 1994.

The findings on public opinion and foreign policy present a major problem for pluralist theory. The general public has more liberal views than elected and appointed officials, but their views have had no impact. Instead, polls showing approval of presidential actions shortly after they occur, such as bombing in Vietnam, are used to legitimate the actions that have been taken. Even when both exit polls and the electoral outcome in 2006 showed that the American public wanted to wind down the war in Iraq, the Bush Administration used a plan proposed by ultraconservatives at the American Enterprise Institute to increase troop strength over the next two years. Pluralist theory is not able to explain this outcome.

TRYING TO SHAPE OPINION ON ECONOMIC POLICIES

Corporate leaders find the generally liberal opinions on economic issues held by a majority of people to be very annoying and potentially troublesome. They blame these opinions in good part on a lack of economic understanding. They label this alleged lack of understanding *economic illiteracy,* a victim-blaming term that implies that people have no right to their opinions because of their educational deficiencies. They claim these ill-informed liberal opinions would change if people had the facts about the functioning of corporations and the economy, so they have spent tens of millions of dollars trying to present the facts as they see them. However, attempts to shape public opinion on domestic economic issues, where people feel directly involved and have their own experiences to rely upon, are even less successful than in the area of foreign policy.

Table 5.2 Largest Donations to the National Council for Economic Education by Foundations between 2003 and Early 2008

Foundation	Amount
Kaufman Foundation	$3,498,000
Bank of America Foundation	$3,000,000
Goldman Sachs Foundation	$1,535,000
Citigroup Foundation	$1,250,000
Allstate Foundation	$770,000
Templeton Foundation	$628,200
3M Foundation	$371,000
Nasdaq Stock Foundation	$363,000
Moody's Foundation	$309,000
Murphy Oil Foundation	$289,800
Total	**$12,013,800**

Source: The Foundation Directory Online (New York: The Foundation Center, 2008).

These points can be demonstrated by a look at the central organization in the field of economic education, the National Council on Economic Education (NCEE). It is only one of many organizations that attempt to shape public opinion on domestic economic issues, but its efforts are typical in many ways. Founded in 1949 by leaders within the Committee for Economic Development who wanted to counter the strident ultraconservative economic educational efforts of the National Association of Manufacturers, the NCEE received much of its early funding from the Ford Foundation. Most of its financial support now comes from corporations and corporate foundations. Table 5.2 lists its major foundation supporters for the previous five years.

The NCEE's twenty-nine-person board reflects the fact that it is part of the opinion-shaping network. It includes Harold Burson, the founder of the public relations firm, Burson-Marsteller; the president of the American Council of Life Insurers; vice presidents from General Mills, State Farm Insurance, and Wells Fargo; and professors of economics from Harvard, Princeton, and Vanderbilt. The NCEE attempts to influence economic understanding by means of books, pamphlets, videos, and press releases. Its most important effort is aimed toward elementary and high schools through its "Economics America" program. This program provides schools with the curriculum plans and materials that are needed to introduce basic economic ideas at each grade level. To prepare teachers to carry out the curriculum, the NCEE has created a network of state councils and several hundred university centers to coordinate the training of teachers in the nation's colleges and universities. The NCEE claims that:

> Each year the network trains about 120,000 teachers serving 8 million students. More than 2,600 school districts, teaching about 40 percent of the nation's students, conduct comprehensive programs in economic education with assistance from the network (NCEE 1997).

As this brief overview shows, the NCEE's program begins in corporate boardrooms and foundation offices, flows through affiliated councils and university centers, and ends up in teacher-training programs and public school curricula. In that regard, it is an ideal example of the several steps and organizations that are usually involved in attempts to shape public opinion on any domestic issue. And yet, after all this effort, the level of "economic illiteracy," according to polls taken for the corporations, remained as high in the 2000s as it was in the 1940s. As a large-scale survey in 2007 showed once again, Americans agree that private enterprise is a good way to run an economic system and they are wary that government can grow too large. But according to the political scientists who analyzed the survey, Americans are conservative egalitarians who want far more job-creation programs, financial support for college educations, and social insurance programs than most members of the power elite think is sensible (Page and Jacobs 2009).

This inability to engineer wholehearted consent to the views of the power elite on economic issues reveals the limits of the opinion-shaping process in general. These limits are in good part created by the work experiences and general observations of average citizens, which lead them to be skeptical about many corporate claims. Then, too, the alternative analyses advocated by trade unionists, liberals, and the Christian Right also have a counteracting influence.

Although the power elite is not able to alter the liberal views held by a majority of Americans on a wide range of economic issues, this does not necessarily mean that the liberal opinions have had any influence. To the contrary, a large body of evidence suggests that the majority's opinion is often ignored. This point is made most clearly by the conservative directions taken by the Carter and Reagan administrations from 1978 to 1983 despite strong evidence that the public remained liberal on the issues under consideration: "Throughout that period the public consistently favored more spending on the environment, education, medical care, the cities, and other matters, and it never accepted the full Reagan agenda of 'deregulation'" (Page and Shapiro 1992, p. 117). An even more detailed analysis of survey data relating to the alleged rightward shift found little support for the claim except on issues of crime. It concludes Democratic and Republican leaders embraced conservatism in the 1970s, but that the American electorate did not follow their lead (Gold 1992).

It is usually possible to ignore public opinion on domestic economic issues for several intertwined reasons. First, as stated earlier in the chapter, the general public lacks an organizational base for making direct contact with legislators, which makes it very hard for people to turn their general opinions into specific positions on complex and detailed legislation. Second, as will be explained in Chapter 6, the nature of American political parties has made it difficult to influence policy through the electoral process. Third, as also explained in Chapter 6, most liberal initiatives that did make it to the floor of Congress were blocked between 1938 and 2008 by a conservative voting bloc that was by and large invulnerable to majority public opinion.

CREATING DOUBT ABOUT SCIENTIFIC FINDINGS

For corporations that use dangerous chemicals in their production process or sell products that are detrimental to people's health, the opinion-shaping process plays a major role in their resistance to any changes by casting doubt on the credibility of scientific findings. Since science involves the gradual development of a consensus through a wide range of studies by different investigators, the goal of the corporations that want to maintain the status quo is to generate uncertainty about the consensus that has in fact developed about the dangers of tobacco, asbestos, lead, vinyl chloride, and many other substances. Building on the principles of spreading confusion and creating cover, they admit that "doubt is our product," as one tobacco company executive wrote in a memo to public relations specialists in 1969, "since it is the best means of competing with the 'body of fact' that exists in the public mind" (Mooney 2008, p. 80). The tobacco companies' campaign was so successful that every corporation that faced similar challenges adopted its methods.

The way in which these campaigns are carried out by non-profit think tanks and advocacy groups can be seen in the case of ExxonMobil's reaction to calls for legislation to slow global warming. Between 1998 and 2005 ExxonMobil donated $16 million to a mixture of ultraconservative think tanks and opinion-influencing organizations with the expressed goal—stated in memos that were leaked to media outlets—of creating doubt about the emerging consensus on the role of fossil fuels in bringing about the climate crisis (see Table 5.3 on page 136 for a partial list of these organizations and

Table 5.3 Alphabetical List of Some of the Organizations Funded by ExxonMobil from 1998 to 2005 That Opposed Legislation Dealing with the Climate Crisis

Organization	Amount Received
American Council for Capital Formation	$1,604,523
American Council on Science and Health	$125,000
Annapolis Center for Science-Based Public Policy	$763,500
Atlas Economic Research Foundation	$680,000
Cato Institute	$105,000
Center for the Defense of Free Enterprise	$230,000
Center for the Study of Carbon Dioxide and Global Change	$90,000
Citizens for a Sound Economy Educational Foundation	$380,250
Committee for a Constructive Tomorrow	$472,000
Competitive Enterprise Institute	$2,005,000
Foundation for Research on Economics and the Environment	$210,000
Fraser Institute	$120,000
Free Enterprise Action Institute	$130,000
Frontiers of Freedom Institute	$1,002,000
George C. Marshall Institute	$630,000
Heartland Institute	$561,500
Heritage Foundation	$460,000
Institute for Energy Research	$177,000
International Policy Network	$295,000
National Center for Policy Analysis	$420,900
National Center for Public Policy Research	$280,000
National Environmental Policy Institute	$75,000
Pacific Research Institute for Public Policy	$355,000
Total	**$11,180,773**

Source: Union of Concerned Scientists, *Smoke, Mirrors & Hot Air*, 2007, pp. 31–32.

the amount of funding they received). Many of the smaller organizations funded by ExxonMobil have overlapping boards of directors and staff members; they all hire the same few contrarian scientists and free-market economists—who usually have little or no training or expertise on climate change—to write their reports and appear in forums arranged by the nonprofit groups. Staffers and consultants from these groups also testified before Congress and worked as lower-level appointees in government agencies during the Bush Administration (UCS 2007). (For greater detail on the Exxon network, see "Map Exxon's Network" at www.exxonsecrets.org.) By the end of 2008, however, the top executives at ExxonMobil were acknowledging the existence of human-generated global warning.

SOCIAL ISSUES

Highly charged social issues received great attention in the mass media and figured prominently in political campaigns over the past forty years. Some of these issues are now history, some of them were still burning hot in 2008: abortion, affirmative action, busing, the death penalty, gun control, pornography, protection against discrimination for gays and lesbians, same-sex marriage, school prayer, and sex education in the schools. Despite the time and energy that goes into these issues, they are not ones that are of direct concern to the power elite. There is no power elite position on any of them. Some individuals within the power elite may care passionately about one or more of them, but these issues are not the subject of discussion at the major policy groups or of position papers from the mainstream think tanks because they have no direct bearing on the corporate community.

Nonetheless, these issues are often front and center in battles between the Democrats and Republicans because liberals seek changes on all of them and social conservatives resist such changes. Although the Christian Right is deeply and genuinely concerned with moral issues as a matter of principle, such issues are seen by most conservative political consultants as "cross-cutting" issues that can be used as "wedges" in trying to defeat liberal-labor candidates in the electoral arena. A disenchanted Christian conservative who was surprised by the cynicism of the Bush Administration's political advisers reveals this point once again in a tell-all memoir of his years in the Office of Faith-Based Initiatives at the White House. (Kuo 2006). These issues are thought to be useful to conservative political candidates because voters who agree with the liberal-labor coalition on economic issues often disagree with it on one or more social issues, which provides an opportunity for conservatives to win their allegiance. Although a majority of Americans were liberal or tolerant on most of these issues by the 1980s, conservative political consultants nonetheless stress them because they hope to gain support from a few percent of the most emotional opponents to each of the liberal social initiatives who might otherwise vote Democratic. If each of these issues can win over just 1–2 percent of voters, the cumulative effect can make a large difference in close elections. Social issues therefore have been an integral part of the Republican's electoral strategy since the mid-1960s, as discussed in more detail in the final chapter. Most recently, Senator John McCain decided to embrace the Christian Right during his 2008 Republican presidential campaign, as seen most clearly in his choice of running mate, even though he had earlier denounced some of its leaders as agents of intolerance.

Ultraconservative think tanks and public relations groups contribute to the effective use of social issues in the electoral arena by running a variety of seemingly nonpartisan media campaigns. In the process they link their dislike for gender equality, abortion, greater sexual freedom, and gay rights with economic issues such as poverty and welfare spending. They do so by claiming that childhood poverty and youth violence are caused by an alleged decline in family values and responsible fatherhood, not by low incomes and unemployment (Coltrane 2001). A "marriage movement" and a National Fatherhood Initiative were one result of this effort in the 1990s through a coordinated campaign by the Institute for American Values, the Family Research Council, Focus on the Family, the Heritage Foundation, and the Hudson Institute.

Both initiatives were financed in part by the same handful of foundations that support ultraconservative think tanks that concentrate on economic issues. For example, the Bradley Foundation gave $870,000 to the National Fatherhood Initiative and $664,000 to the Institute for American Values in the 1990s and the Sarah Scaife Foundation gave $990,000 to the National Fatherhood Initiative, $580,000 to the Institute for American Values, and $100,000 to Marriage Savers during the same decade (Coltrane 2001, p. 413). However, an even larger portion of the marriage movement and responsible fatherhood money came from several smaller foundations created by the highly religious multimillionaire owners of privately held corporations, such as the DeVos family, owners of Amway, and the Prince family, then owners of the Prince Corporation, a manufacturer of interior parts for automobiles. These foundations focus almost exclusively on conservative Christian causes. (See Russell 2005 for a detailed financial study of 327 foundations that gave $168 million to approximately 150 evangelical nonprofit organizations between 1999 and 2002. For the wider involvement of evangelicals in power issues, some of whom are wealthy ultraconservatives who converted, others of whom are evangelicals who became wealthy, see the interview and survey studies carried out by sociologist D. Michael Lindsay [2007; 2008].)

THE ROLE OF THE MASS MEDIA

Ownership and control of the mass media—newspapers, magazines, books, radio, movies, and television—are highly concentrated and growing more so all the time. Members of the upper class own all of the large media companies and these companies have extensive inter-locks with other large corporations. In addition, the media rely on cor-porate advertising for the lion's share of their profits, making them dependent on other corporations (e.g., Bagdikian 2004; Chomsky and Herman 1988, for detailed information on these points).

The large media play their most important role in the power equation by reinforcing the legitimacy of the social system through the routine ways in which they accept and package events. Their style and tone usually takes the statements of business and government lead-ers seriously, treating any claims they make with great respect. This respectful approach is especially noticeable and important in the area of foreign policy, where the media cover events in such a way that America's diplomatic aims always seem honorable, corporate involve-ment overseas is necessary and legitimate, and any large-scale change in most countries is undesirable and must be discouraged.

However, beyond these very general influences, which can fall by the wayside in times of social or economic disruption, the media are not an essential part of the opinion-shaping process or a key building block in a class-domination theory. The corporate community was powerful in the United States long before there were any mass media except newspapers, which were more widely and locally owned in the late nineteenth century in any case. In addition, the relationship between the media and the rest of the corporate community is com-plicated by several factors. From the corporate community's point of view, the problems begin with the fact that there are differences of opinion between corporate leaders and media professionals on some issues, as revealed in opinion surveys of top leaders from busi-ness, labor, media, and minority group organizations. These studies show that representatives of the mass media tend to be more liberal on foreign policy and domestic issues than corporate and conserva-tive leaders, although not as liberal as the representatives of minor-ity groups and liberal organizations. On questions of environment, which are very sensitive to corporate leaders, the media professionals hold much the same liberal views as people from labor, minority, and liberal organizations (Gans 1985).

The net result is an often-tense relationship between media execu-tives and the rest of the corporate community, with corporate leaders placing the blame on the mass media for any negative opinions about corporations held by the general public. This rift seemed especially large in the 1970s, leading the corporations and foundations to fund conferences and new journalism programs that would lead to new understandings. The corporations also began to run their own analyses and opinion pieces as advertisements on the editorial pages in major newspapers and liberal magazines, thereby presenting their viewpoints in their own words on a wide variety of issues. Since that time they have spent several hundred millions of dollars a year on such "advocacy advertising" (Dreier 1982).

Nor does the concentration of ownership necessarily mean that the range of opinions available through the media is narrowed. For example, large newspaper chains may have less negative effects than some critics fear. Using survey responses from 409 journalists at 223 newspapers, a journalism professor found that their reporters and editors report high levels of autonomy and job satisfaction. Further, he discovered that a diversity of opinions appears in them, including critical ones. In comparison to small local newspapers, he also found that large newspapers and newspaper chains are more likely to publish editorials and letters that are critical of mainstream groups and institutions, or that deal with local issues the growth coalitions would rather ignore (Demers 1996).

Despite the generally conservative biases of newspaper owners, systematic studies by sociologists of how the news is gathered and produced show that journalists are by and large independent professionals who make use of the freedom of the press that was won for them by journalists of the past, often in battles with the federal government. Studies of the socialization of newspaper journalists show that they make every effort to present both sides of a story and keep their own opinions separate (Gans 1985; Schudson 1995). Although there are blatant examples of attempts at censorship by their publishers or editors, perhaps especially in the case of special investigative programs on television, the relative independence of journalists is first of all seen in the many newspaper and magazine stories on corporate and government wrongdoing within the long tradition of investigative journalism, which always has been strongly resisted by corporate and political leaders alike. Thanks to their great resources, the major newspapers do as many critical studies of corporate malfeasance and governmental favoritism to big business as do scholars and activists. The detailed journalistic coverage of the federal government by *CQ Weekly* and *National Journal* is also invaluable to scholars. These varied print sources provide much of the evidence for social scientists who analyze corporate power, as can be seen in many of the references in this book.

Then, too, the evidence shows that what appears in the media is most importantly shaped by forces outside of them, which means that the corporate leaders, politicians, experts, and celebrities with the ability to make news have more impact on what appears in the media than editors and reporters. A political scientist who specializes in media studies concluded that the media are "to a considerable degree dependent on subject matter specialists, including government officials among others, in framing and reporting the news" (Zaller 1992, p. 319). His findings suggest that it is necessary to understand the politics of specialized expert communities in order to explain any influence on public opinion by the mass media, which is where the policy-planning and opinion-shaping networks come into the picture again. They supply the experts, including those corporate leaders who have been legitimated as statesmen on the basis of their long-time involvement in policy-discussion groups. The media's dependence on government leaders and outside experts as sources constrains any inclination independent-minded journalists might have to inject their personal views, but it is also true that they have some leeway to pick the outside experts they want to feature.

The importance of outside experts and government officials in shaping what appears in the media is best seen in the case of defense spending, where public opinion has been shown to move "in tandem" with "shifts in media coverage" (Zaller 1992, p. 15). Since it is unlikely that journalists advocated the vast increases in defense spending from 1978 to 1985 and since 2001, this finding supports the conclusion that government officials and experts are the main influences on media content on most issues of political importance. Indeed, the rise in defense spending in the late 1970s fits nicely with the intense media scare campaign by the Committee on the Present Danger and related organizations, which were creations of leaders in the policy-planning network (Sanders 1983).

When it comes to the idea that the corporate media only report what they want people to hear, there are many qualifications that have to be considered. First, political leaders, corporate executives, and policy experts are unable to shape stories when there are unexpected accidents, scandals, or leaks, which lead to stories that tell readers and listeners about corporate wrongdoing, oil spills, illegal payments to government officials, torture of prisoners by the American military, and much else. By early 2004, for example, shocking new revelations about the war in Iraq were being reported every day. In these situations readers learn how the power structure actually operates. Most of all, they are reminded to take the claims by politicians and the public relations industry with a huge grain of salt (Molotch 1970; Molotch 2004; Molotch and Lester 2004).

Generally speaking, then, the media probably do not have the independent impact on public opinion that is often attributed to them by leftists and ultraconservative critics, a conclusion that may come as a surprise to many readers. While it is true that social psychologists have carried out experimental studies with doctored television news programs showing that where stories are placed on the evening news may influ-ence the importance that people give to an issue, there is also real-world evidence that the news is often not watched even though the television is on and that people don't remember much of what they do see. The declining audience for serious television news programs has led to even more emphasis on human interest stories on television as people turn to alternative sources on the Internet, talk radio, and late-night comedy news shows for their information. Thus, news is increasingly seen as a form of entertainment by television executives in the face of their compe-tition with the new media, which tend to speak to the already converted on both the liberal and conservative sides. Moreover, several studies sug-gest that most people actually retain more politically relevant informa-tion from what they read in newspapers and magazines. In addition, the potential effects of television seem to be counteracted by people's beliefs and membership identifications, their ability to screen out information that does not fit with their preconceptions, and their reliance on other people in developing their opinions (Erikson and Tedin 2005; Iyengar and Reeves 1997; Iyengar and Simon 2000).

There is also evidence that people sometimes ignore overt attempts by the media to influence them. This is best seen in several well-known instances. For example, most newspapers were against the reelection of President Franklin D. Roosevelt in 1936, but he won by a landslide. The media were against the reelection of President Harry Truman in 1948, but he squeezed by in an upset victory. The limits on the own-ers and managers of the mass media in shaping public opinion were demonstrated once again in 1998 by the unwillingness of the public to endorse the impeachment of President Bill Clinton, even though it was enthusiastically advocated by most of the Washington pundits who appear on television. In addition, over 140 newspapers called for his resignation. However, to the surprise of media leaders, a strong majority of Americans opposed impeachment despite their highly negative opinion of the president's personal behavior. They made their own distinction between job performance and personal morality. One polling expert concluded that the campaign against President Clinton might have increased public resentment toward the media. The same expert also thought that this event "proves just the opposite of what most people believe: how little power the media elite have over public opinion." (Schneider 1998, p. 2350).

Moreover, thanks to the willingness of journalists to report on the events of the day, the media sometimes played a role in the successes small bands of reformers enjoyed in past decades on a few specific issues. These lawyers, experts, and activists developed information on the issue of concern to them, found a way to present that information at just the right moment in one or another governmental setting, such as congressional hearings, and then depended on press releases, press conferences, and staged events to encourage the media to spread their story. In short, their formula for success was information plus good timing plus use of the media. There is ample evidence that this formula can still be an effective one, once again demonstrating that a few focused activists can have an impact out of all proportion to their numbers or resources if they know how to use the media.

When all is said and done, as a textbook written by leaders in the field of public opinion research states, the direct evidence from surveys for a strong media influence on public opinion in general is surprisingly weak (Glynn, Herbst, O'Keefe and Shapiro 1999). Another authoritative text on public opinion, now in its seventh edition, concludes its chapter on mass media effects on public opinion by saying there is no clear evidence that this relationship is more than minimal (Erikson and Tedin 2005). Finally, a detailed analysis by a social psychologist of how people in focus groups react to various media stories suggests that "a) people are not so passive, b) people are not so dumb, and c) people negotiate with media messages in complicated ways that vary from issue to issue" (Gamson 1992, p. 4). Perhaps ironically, it is likely that the media have their greatest importance as a way for rivals within the power elite to try to influence each other. The opinion pages of *The New York Times*, *The Washington Post*, and *The Wall Street Journal* provide readers with a front-row seat when these differences are aired.

Whatever emphasis readers of this book may decide to put on the influence of the mass media on the general public, the important point for now is that none of the claims for a class-dominance theory relies on the mass media or on any theory which suggests that people do not understand the power system within which they live. Contrary to Marxists and many other leftist theorists, who explain the failure of their predictions about social change to come true by saying that most people do not realize they are being exploited, the people are not bamboozled. People's opinions are in good part grounded in their lives and the opinions of those closest to them; their opinions make sense to social scientists who conduct participant-observation studies or construct careful surveys (Flacks 1988; Page and Jacobs 2009).

Although the mass media reach more people than any other outlet that is available for the dissemination of the pamphlets, speeches, and infomercials created by the opinion-shaping network, the people they reach are those who matter the least from the point of view of the power elite. The media can amplify the messages of the people who have the power to gain access to them and can marginalize, trivialize, or ignore the concerns of the less powerful, but the messages the media provide also can be ambiguous or confusing, and they are often ignored.

THE ROLE OF PUBLIC OPINION SURVEYS

Public opinion surveys are a good way for social scientists to obtain useful information, as many examples in this chapter demonstrate, but they also can be used by political leaders and advocacy groups to influence public opinion. For example, interviews with former congressional and White House aides suggest that polling data about public opinion is used to decide how to present and package the votes the elected officials intend to make because of their strong policy preferences (Jacobs and Shapiro 2000). Then too, polls are sometimes constructed so that their results can be used to shape public opinion when they are reported to the public via the media. This is accomplished by using loaded terms or political labels. For example, in a study asking the public about a law that did not really exist, public opinion differed by 20 to 30 percentage points depending on whether it was alleged to be of interest to Democratic or Republican leaders (Morin 1995).

Opinion surveys also can be used to suggest that a public opinion exists on issues where there is none. This does not mean people do not have general opinions, but that they often "make it up as they go along" when responding to specific questions about policy preferences. If questions about affirmative action or oil drilling are framed in one way, they yield one answer, but framed in another way they yield a different answer, especially for those without knowledge or firm opinions (Zaller 1992). It therefore becomes relatively easy for advocacy groups to obtain whatever results they wish when they conduct a survey.

Findings such as these suggest that the alleged public opinion on a specific issue is sometimes a myth based on the results of questionable polls reported in newspapers. In those cases, the alleged public opinion reported by the media is only another tool in the ongoing conflict between the corporate community and the liberal-labor coalition. Although there is a sensible public opinion on many general issues of great importance to average Americans, it is not easily discerned in the heat of a battle where both sides are out to win, not to respond to majority opinions.

THE ENFORCEMENT OF PUBLIC OPINION

There are limits to the tolerance that exists within the power elite for the general public's disagreements about public issues, although these limits vary from era to era and are never fully clear until they are tested.

Although pluralists who regard public opinion as the product of discussion and deliberation often ignore the fact, members of the power elite make many attempts to enforce public opinion, which means there are serious personal costs for people who move outside the general consensus. These attempts to enforce the limits on disagreement begin with strong criticism in the media and the angry use of labels such as "extremist" or "un-American." The next steps are exclusion from events and dismissal from jobs. Such punishments are relatively minor for activists who are extremely committed to their points of view, but most people are very uncomfortable when they are in any way excluded or criticized by their peers.

The use of scorn, isolation, and other sanctions is seen most directly in the treatment of "whistleblowers," employees of corporations or government agencies who expose wrongdoing by their superiors. Contrary to the impression that they are rewarded as good citizens for stepping forward, they are treated as pariahs, relieved of their responsibilities by higher authority figures in the organization, and shunned by peers out of fear of guilt by association. Their lives are often turned upside down. Many regret they took the action they did, even though they thought it was the honest or moral course to take. Their fate serves as a warning for others that speaking out is personally risky (Miethe 1999; Rothschild and Miethe 1994). Those who become prominent public critics of some aspect of conventional wisdom receive similar harsh treatment. Their motives are questioned and negative stories appear in the media, which attempt to demonstrate they are acting from irrational psychological motives.

Government officials sometimes resort to severe sanctions in an attempt to discredit liberal and leftist leaders who attempt to influence public opinion and inspire public demonstrations. In the case of Martin Luther King, Jr., and many other civil rights activists, the government not only spied on them, it planted false information and issued false threats in order to disrupt their efforts. Such actions may not seem at first glance to be part of an opinion-shaping process, but they are because they serve as another reminder that attempts to change opinions and laws can have serious negative consequences. Government violence and other extralegal methods are seldom used on dissenters in times of domestic tranquility, but they are often employed in times of social upheaval when members of the power elite appointed to the government feel it is necessary to do so. One of the most prominent historical examples concerns the liberal attorney general of the early 1960s, Robert F. Kennedy, the son of a multimillionaire and the brother of President John F. Kennedy. He authorized wiretaps on Martin Luther King, Jr., at the height of the Civil Rights Movement in 1963 in an effort to discredit King and keep him from making demands that would disrupt the voting coalition that supported the Democratic Party.

WHEN PUBLIC OPINION CAN AND CANNOT BE IGNORED

Public opinion does not have the routine importance often attributed to it by pluralist theory. Even though most people have sensible opinions, it is unlikely that any focused public opinion exists on most of the complicated legislative issues of concern to the corporate community or on the volatile foreign policy issues that often arise suddenly. Under the umbrella of crisis talk, confusion, and doubt that is in part the result of organizations in the opinion-shaping network, the power elite and politicians therefore enjoy a great deal of leeway on most policy questions. Furthermore, public opinion usually can be ignored because people's beliefs do not lead them into opposition or disruption if they have stable roles to fulfill in the society or see no clear organizational path to social change on issues that would spring them into action. Routine involvement in a compelling and enjoyable daily round of activities, the most crucial of which are their families, their jobs, their friends, and their forms of entertainment, are more important in understanding people's acquiescence to power elite policies than attempts by the power elite to shape public opinion.

What happens in the economy and in government has far more impact on how people act than what is disseminated through the opinion-shaping network and the mass media. This point is perfectly demonstrated by the fact that the Bush Administration lost favor with the great majority of the American people between 2005 and 2008 because of the rising American casualties in Iraq and the decline of the economy in spite of massive attempts by power elite organizations with complete access to the mass media to claim that the war was going well and that the economy was on the right track. Nonetheless, public opinion can have an impact when people are forced out of their routines by economic upheaval, wars, and other forms of social disruption. In those cases, public opinion can have an impact because it leads to election defeats for political incumbents and to social movements that threaten one or another aspect of the established order, which in turn leads members of the power elite to seek solutions—sometimes reformist, sometimes repressive—that will restore social stability.

Although this chapter suggests there is usually a large amount of latitude for the power elite to operate as they wish to, this conclusion is incomplete in one important respect. It has not considered the routine effects of public opinion through the electoral process. It is now time to see if newly elected officials fulfill their campaign promises or instead adopt policies advocated by the corporate community within the special-interest and policy-planning processes.

6

Parties and Elections

Elections hold the potential that citizens can shape public policy through support for candidates who share their policy preferences. But have elections delivered on their promise in the United States? To provide perspective on this question, it is useful to begin with the gradual development of elections in Western history and then explain why they have not mattered as much as they might have in the United States.

WHEN AND HOW DO ELECTIONS MATTER?

Historically, the first function of elections was to provide a mechanism for rival power groups, not everyday people, to resolve disputes in a peaceful way. This does not mean that elite rivals willingly accepted elections. To the contrary, elections were not adopted in any European country until these rivals had compromised their major differences in a pact or settlement, usually after years of violence or in the face of extreme economic crisis (Burton and Higley 1987a; Higley and Burton 2006; Higley and Burton 1989).

In the United States, the Constitution was the equivalent of these elite peace agreements. It dealt with several issues that rival colonial leaders said were not negotiable. Most important, Northern wealth holders had to make several concessions to the Southern slave owners to win their agreement to the Constitution. Even in this example, the limited nature of elections in restraining rival segments of the American ownership class is revealed by the Civil War. The slaveholders decided to secede from the union and risk the costly and devastating war that soon followed rather than see their way of life gradually eroded by an inability to expand slavery westward, which shows how quickly a society can descend into violence when elected officials cannot compromise the disagreements that divide rival power groups.

It was not until rival elite groups in Europe and the United States accepted elections in the eighteenth and nineteenth centuries that they became a way to engage more of the population in governance, which does not imply that the inclusion of an expanded electorate was willingly accepted by elites. Instead, it usually took a long battle to extend the franchise beyond the top layers of society. This desire by elites to exclude common people from voting—especially those who own no property or are members of minority groups—is still seen today in the United States through the many documented methods the Republican Party uses to suppress voter participation by people of color (Davidson, Dunlap, Kenny and Wise 2004). Within the context of stable power-sharing pacts, elections gradually came to have another function. They allowed average citizens to help determine which of the rival power groups would play the lead role in government. In the case of the United States, this meant that different occupational, religious, and ethnic groups became part of different corporate-led coalitions that contended for office on a wide range of appeals. At the least, though, voters were often able to eliminate candidates they perceived as extremists.

More recently, elections came to provide the opportunity to register disapproval of government policies. This role for elections was demonstrated dramatically in the United States in 2006 when independent voters—those who say they are not affiliated with either major political party—registered their disapproval of the war in Iraq by supporting Democratic candidates by a 59 percent to 40 percent margin for Congress. It was demonstrated again in 2008 when a majority of citizens took a decisive turn to Senator Obama in late September after the financial turmoil made the perilous state of the economy by far the overriding issue in most people's minds. According to weekly polls, the change was especially pronounced among whites who worried about the economy, 54 percent of whom came to favor Obama compared to a mere 10 percent of whites not worried about the economy (Balz and Cohen 2008). Independents also shifted 53–39 percent for Senator Obama at this point after showing a small preference for Senator John McCain shortly after the Republican convention. (Senator Obama's 52–43 percent lead in late September was not much different from exit poll results on Election Day, 53–46.)

Elections also make it possible for citizens in many countries to have an influence on economic and social issues by forming their own political parties. This is best seen in those European countries where social democrats have won a majority and created social insurance systems for unemployment, disability, health, and old age that are far larger and more inclusive than American programs. Finally, elections came to matter as a way to introduce new policies in times of social disruption caused by extreme domestic problems. In the nineteenth and early twentieth centuries, this role was often fulfilled in the United States by third parties that appeared suddenly on the scene, such as the new parties of the 1840s and 1850s that first advocated the abolition of slavery. By the second decade of the twentieth century, the main electoral arena for new ideas became the primary elections of the two major parties.

The development of primaries gave American voters the opportunity to decide which individuals from rival groups and classes would have the opportunity to compete in the general elections. Primaries force candidates to mingle with everyday people and pay attention to them. In the process, even incumbents are graphically reminded that they can be deposed if they are not attentive. The need for political candidates to interact with individuals from the general public puts limits on the degree to which money, advertising, and name recognition can shape the outcome of elections.

Hillary Clinton had the most money and the best organization going into the Democratic Party primaries in early 2008. She and her husband had strong-armed many of the people who owed them political favors to make an early endorsement of Hillary. Media pundits assured one and all that she was the frontrunner and then became even more convinced of this claim when early polls gave her the lead. But her refusal to grant that she might have made a mistake in voting to give President Bush the discretion to invade Iraq made her unpopular with antiwar liberals, who are often overrepresented in Democratic primaries. After her equivocation on the war was combined with the appeal that Barack Obama had in small-group meetings with Democrats in Iowa, at a time when he was also best known for his antiwar views, Obama went on to win the primary and the whole race changed.

So elections can and do matter. They allow for at least some input by citizens who are not wealthy, and they provide an opening for critics of the social system to present their ideas. In the United States, however, elections have yielded far fewer successes for the liberal-labor coalition than might be expected on the basis of social-democratic victories in most Western democracies. The reasons for this difference are explained in the remainder of this chapter.

WHY ONLY TWO MAJOR PARTIES?

In some democratic countries, there are three or more substantial political parties with clearly defined programs understood by voters, who therefore are able to vote on the basis of their policy preferences if they so desire. In sharp contrast, there have been only two major parties for most of American history. The only exceptions were a brief one-party era from about 1812 to 1824 after the Federalist Party collapsed and a few years in the 1850s when the conflict over extending slavery into Kansas and Missouri led to the breakup of the Whig Party (the party that, roughly speaking, replaced the Federalist Party). Even the Republican Party that developed in the 1850s does not really qualify as a third party because it replaced the Whigs in the space of just one or two elections.

Why are there only two major parties despite the country's tumultuous history of regional, religious, and class rivalries? Two fundamental features of American government lead to a two-party system. The first is the selection of senators and representatives from states and districts in elections that require only a plurality of votes, not a majority. Such an arrangement is called a "single-member district plurality system," and it has led to two-party systems in most countries that used this system (Lipset and Marks 2000; Rae 1971; Rosenstone, Behr and Lazarus 1996). The exceptions tend to be in countries where a third party has some strength in a single region for ethnic or religious reasons. The second reason for the American two-party system is relatively unique in the world: the election of a president. The election of a president is in effect a strong version of the single-member district plurality system, with the nation serving as the only district. Due to the enormous power of the presidency, the pull toward two parties that exists in any single-member district system is even greater in the United States. The result is that third parties are even more uncommon and smaller than in other countries with district/plurality elections.[*]

The fact that only one person can win the presidency, or be elected to Congress from a given state or district, which seems trivial and is taken for granted by most Americans, leads to a two-party system by creating a series of "winner-take-all" elections. A vote for a third-party

---

[*]As shown dramatically in the 2000 election, the president is selected by the electoral college, where each state has a number of electors equal to the size of its congressional delegation. The minimum number of electors a small state can have is three—two senators plus one representative. Electors cast their ballots for the candidate who wins in their state. The focus on electoral votes forces candidates to concentrate on winning a plurality in as many states as possible, not simply on winning the most votes in the nation overall. This system creates a further disadvantage for third parties.

candidate of the right or left is in effect a vote for the voter's least-favored candidate on the other side of the political spectrum. Because a vote for a third-party candidate of the left or right is a vote for "your worst enemy," the usual strategy for those who want to avoid this fate is to form the largest possible pre-election coalition even if numerous policy preferences must be abandoned or compromised. The result is two coalitional parties.*

Third parties of the left or right rarely last for more than one or two elections and rarely receive more than 1–2 percent of the vote when they do persist, but they can have dramatic impacts on the overall results. In 2000, Ralph Nader and the Green Party contributed to President Bush's triumph by taking just enough votes from Democrat Al Gore in New Hampshire and Florida to give their electoral votes—and the presidency—to Bush. It was the first time in history that a leftist party had a major impact on a presidential election, which led to deep and lasting anger on the part of liberals, feminists, environmentalists, and civil rights activists and the near-total exclusion of Nader and his supporters from any forums that might have had more inclusionary policies in the past. What is less known is that the tiny Libertarian Party to the right of the Republicans cost the Republicans a Senate seat in Nevada in 1998, a Senate seat in Washington state in 2000, a Senate seat in South Dakota in 2002, and the governorships of Oregon and Wisconsin in 2002 by winning far more votes than the margin by which the Republican challengers lost to their Democratic opponents (Domhoff, 2003, chapter 2; Miller, 2002).

By way of contrast, a parliamentary system provides some room for third parties even in single-member district plurality electoral systems. This is because a prime minister is selected by the parliament after the elections. There is therefore less pressure toward two pre-electoral coalitions, thus making the existence of three issue-oriented parties possible or for a new third party to grow over the period of several elections. Even more parties are likely to exist if the parliament is elected through a system of proportional representation, which allots seats in proportion to a party's nationwide vote once a certain minimum is reached (usually about 5 percent). Thus, comparative studies of the relationship between electoral rules and the number of political parties suggest how candidate selection in the United States came to

---

*The fact that H. Ross Perot received 19 percent of the vote in 1992 and nearly 9 percent in 1996, running as the candidate of his Reform Party, does not contradict this analysis because his party was positioned between the two major parties. As a centrist party, it drew votes from partisans of both parties, and hence was not more threatening to one than the other. Perot's success was also possible because he spent $72 million of his own money to promote his candidacy in 1992.

be conducted through a two-party system despite the existence of similar class, regional, and ethnic conflicts that have led to three or more parties in other countries.

Although the American system of single-member congressional districts and presidential elections generates a strong pull toward a two-party system, it was not designed with this fact in mind. The Founding Fathers purposely created a system of checks and balances that would keep power within bounds, especially the potential power of an aroused and organized majority of farmers and artisans. However, a party system was not among their plans. Indeed, the Founding Fathers disliked the idea of parties, which they condemned as "factions" that are highly divisive. Parties are a major unintended consequence of their deliberations, and it was not until the 1830s and 1840s that a new generation of political leaders finally accommodated themselves to the idea that the two-party system was not disruptive of rule by the wealthy few (Hofstadter 1969).

A two-party system does not foster parties that articulate clear images and policies in good part because rival candidates attempt to blur their differences in order to win the voters in the middle. It causes candidates to emphasize personal qualities rather than policy preferences. It may even lead to collusion between the two parties to avoid some issues or to avoid competition in some districts. Moreover, there is reason to believe that a two-party system actually discourages voting because those in a minority of even 49 percent receive no representation for their efforts. Voting increases considerably in countries where districts have been replaced by proportional representation (Hamilton 1972; Lipset 1963).

For all these reasons, then, a two-party system leads to the possibility that there may be very little relationship between politics and policy. Candidates can say one thing to be elected and then do another once in office, which of course gives people with money, access, and information the opportunity to shape legislation. In short, a two-party system creates a set of circumstances in which the parties may or may not reflect citizen preferences. However, none of this explains why the liberal-labor coalition does not have a party of its own. The historic difference between the Northern and Southern economies, one based in free labor, the other in slavery, provides the explanation for this unusual situation.

REPUBLICANS AND DEMOCRATS

Two contrasting claims predominated in discussions of the Republican and Democratic parties in the past. One suggested that "there's not a dime's worth of difference between them," which reflects the need to appeal to the centrist voters in a two-party system. The other said that the Republicans represented big business and the Democrats represented the liberal-labor coalition, a belief that comes equally from the scare tactics of ultraconservatives and the mythmaking by liberals about their party's allegedly progressive past. In fact, different factions within the power elite controlled both parties for most of their history. It is important to tell this story at a time when the two parties have never been more different because it helps to explain why 2008 marked a unique turn in American electoral history (McCarty, Poole and Rosenthal 2006; Poole and Rosenthal 1997).

Although the Constitutional Convention of 1787 settled the major issues between the Northern and Southern segments of the ownership class, at least until the 1850s, it did not take long for political parties to develop. From the day in 1791 when wealthy Virginia plantation owners made contact with landowners in upstate New York to create what was to become the first incarnation of the Democratic Party, the two parties represented different economic interests within the upper class. For the most part, the Democrats were originally the party of agrarian wealth, especially in the South, the Republicans the party of bankers, merchants, and industrialists (Domhoff 1990, chapter 9).*

As with all generalizations, this one needs some qualification. The Democratic-Republican Party, as it was first known, also found many of its adherents in the North among merchants and bankers of Irish origins, who disliked the English-origin leaders in the Federalist Party for historical reasons. Then, too, religious dissenters and Protestants of low-status denominations often favored the Democratic-Republicans over the "high church" Federalist Party. These kinds of differences (based on the power principle that the enemy of my enemy is my friend) persist down to the present. In terms of social status, the Federalist-Whig-Republican party has been the party of the secure and established, the Democrats the party of those who were in the out-group on some dimension. Today it is most strongly supported by African-Americans, Hispanics, Jews, Muslims, and single women who work outside the home (Manza and Brooks 1999; Mayer 1996).

---

*The South is defined for purposes of this book as the seventeen states that had state laws requiring school segregation until the *Brown vs. Board of Education* decision by the Supreme Court in 1954: Alabama, Arkansas, Delaware, Florida, Georgia, Kentucky, Louisiana, Maryland, Mississippi, Missouri, North Carolina, Oklahoma, South Carolina, Tennessee, Texas, Virginia, and West Virginia. In addition, all of them were slave states in 1860 with the exception of West Virginia, which was part of the slave state of Virginia until it broke away to become a separate state in 1863, and Oklahoma, an Indian territory that allowed slavery. This definition emphasizes that "the South" was once much larger, and hence much more powerful, than it is in people's minds today, when the focus is on a few states in what was once called the "Deep South."

The characterization of the Democratic Party as a coalition of out-groups even fits the slaveholders who controlled the party in its first sixty-nine years because they were agrarians in an industrializing society, slaveholders in a land of free labor. Although they controlled the presidency in thirty-two of the first thirty-six years of the country's existence by electing slave owners like Thomas Jefferson, James Madison, and Andrew Jackson, the plantation capitalists were on the defensive, and they knew it. Following the Civil War, the Democratic Party became even more completely the instrument of the Southern segment of the upper class when all wealthy white Southerners moved into that party. They correctly saw this move as the best strategy to maximize their impact in Washington and at the same time force the Southern populists to accept marginalization within the Democratic Party or else start a third party that could go nowhere (Woodward 1966).

After the Civil War, the white Southerners gained new allies in the North with the arrival of millions of ethnic Catholic and Jewish immigrants, who were often treated badly and scorned by the Protestant Republican majority. When some of these new immigrants grew wealthy in the first half of the twentieth century, they became major financial backers of urban Democratic organizations (called "machines" in their day). Contrary to ultraconservatives and liberals, the liberal-labor coalition that developed within the Democratic Party in the 1930s was no match for the well-established Southern rich and their wealthy urban ethnic allies (Alston and Ferrie 1999; Webber 2000).

Still, the liberal-labor coalition did begin to elect about 100 Democrats to the House starting in the 1930s, where they joined with roughly 100 Southern Democrats and fifty machine Democrats from Northern urban areas to form a strong Democratic majority in all but a few sessions of Congress before 1994. By 1938, however, the Southern Democrats and Northern Republicans had formed a conservative voting bloc that stopped the liberal Democrats from passing legislation concerning union rights, civil rights, and the regulation of business. These are precisely the issues that defined class conflict at the time. This generalization includes civil rights because that was a code phrase for issues concerning the coercive control of the low-wage African-American workforce in the South (Patterson 1981; Potter 1972).

For the most part, the liberal-labor coalition had to settle for small victories on economic issues, such as housing subsidies, where it could attract the support of some Southern Democrats. More generally, the Democratic Party became a pro-spending alliance in which Northern Democrats supported agricultural subsidies and price supports that greatly benefited Southern plantation owners. The Southerners in turn were willing to support government spending programs for roads, public housing, hospital construction, school lunches, and even public assistance, but with three provisos. The spending programs would contain no attack on segregation, they would be locally controlled, and they would differentially benefit Southern states. This arrangement hinged on a tacit agreement that the liberal-labor coalition in the North would not vigorously oppose the continuing segregation in the South (Clausen 1973; Brown 1999).

The fact that Democrats formally controlled Congress for most of the years between 1932 and 1994 is therefore largely irrelevant in terms of understanding the domination of government policy by the power elite. The important point is that a strong conservative majority was elected to Congress throughout the twentieth century and always voted together on the issues that relate to class conflict. There are two crucial exceptions to this generalization, the mid-1930s and the mid-1960s, times of great social turmoil. The activism of workers in the 1930s led to the passage of pro-union legislation in 1935 and the efforts of the Civil Rights Movement of the 1960s led to the Civil Rights Act of 1964 and the Voting Rights Act of 1965. The pro-union legislation is discussed at the end of Chapter 7 and the civil rights legislation at the beginning of Chapter 9.

There is, of course, far more to the story of the Democratic Party, including the details of how a voting majority is assembled for each particular piece of legislation through complex deals and trade-offs. But enough has been said to explain why the liberal-labor coalition does not have a party of its own, as it does in most democratic countries. The electoral rules leading to a two-party system, in conjunction with control of the Democrats by wealthy Southern whites until the last few decades, left the liberal-labor coalition with no good options. It cannot form a third party without assuring the election of even more Republicans, who are its sworn enemies, but it was unable to win control of the Democratic Party. The result was a sordid bargain with Southern racists from the point of view of leftists and young left-liberal activists.

The control of both political parties by members of the power elite as the twenty-first century began reinforced the worst tendencies of a two-party system: avoidance of issues, collusion, and an emphasis on the character and personality of the candidates. There is an important political science literature on how elected officials from both parties employ a variety of strategies within this context to vote their policy preferences, even when they are opposed by a majority of voters, and at the same time win reelection (Jacobs and Shapiro 2000). This literature shows the complexity of politics and electioneering at the intersection between the power elite and ordinary citizens. It is at this intersection that crafting the right strategies and using the most emotionally salient media images can matter. This is the province of political consultants who advise candidates and of political scientists who analyze the factors leading to electoral success in specific elections.

For the purposes of this book, the important point of this literature is that in at least some situations and with the right use of divisive issues, ultraconservatives have been able to persuade many people in the United States to vote on the basis of their race, religion, or ethnicity rather than their social class. Once again, this is in good part because liberals and organized labor were not able to create a political party that could develop and popularize a program appealing to the economic interests of everyday salary and wage workers. This is the main reason why the electoral system is best understood from a power perspective as a "candidate-selection process." Its primary function is one of filling offices with the least possible attention to the policy aspects of politics, which of course provides openings for the policies developed within the special-interest and policy-planning networks.

PARTY PRIMARIES AS GOVERNMENT STRUCTURES

The inexorable two-party logic of the American electoral system led to another unique feature of American politics, the use of primary elections regulated by state governments to determine the parties' candidates. The system was first legislated in 1903 by reformers in Wisconsin, who became convinced there was no hope for a third party (Lovejoy 1941). About the same time, a system of white primaries was adopted in the segregationist Southern states as a way for rival white candidates to challenge each other without allowing African-Americans to vote (Key 1949).

As primaries grew in frequency, they gradually became an accepted part of the overall electoral system due to pressures from liberal reformers. It has now reached the point where the use of state-regulated primaries, when combined with long-standing governmental control of party registration, has transformed the two major parties into the official office-filling agencies of the government. From a legislative and legal point of view, the party primaries labeled *Republican* and *Democratic* can be seen as two different pathways legitimated by the government for obtaining its elected officials. Thus, government-sponsored primaries reinforce the point that American politics is a candidate-selection process.

Put another way, parties are no longer fully independent organizations that control membership and choose their own leaders. Since anyone can register with the government to be a member of a party, party leaders cannot exclude people from membership based on political beliefs. Furthermore, people registered in the party can run in its primaries for any office, so party leaders and party conventions have very little influence on the policies advocated by its candidates. In effect, a party stands for what the successful candidates in primaries say it stands for. Party leaders can protest and donors can withhold crucial campaign funds, but the winners in the primaries, along with their many political consultants and fundraisers, are the party for all intents and purposes. This is a major difference from political parties in other countries. It is also very different from the situation a few decades ago in the United States when urban bosses selected Northern Democratic candidates.

The use of primaries by insurgents led to some surprising victories early in the twentieth century. In North Dakota, for example, a one-time Socialist Party organizer developed the Non-Partisan League to run candidates in party primaries on a radical platform. The platform called for state-owned grain elevators, a state-owned bank, public housing for farm workers, and other policies that would make farmers less dependent on railroads and grain companies, which were viewed as highly exploitative. Despite vehement opposition from business leaders and mainstream politicians, the Non-Partisan League swept to power in North Dakota in 1916 and instituted much of its program. The Bank of North Dakota, which focuses on credit for farmers and low-income rural people, is still the only publicly owned bank in the United States. Even though the Non-Partisan League has been gone for many decades and is almost completely forgotten, it had a large impact. As the historian who studied it most closely concludes: "Not only was it to control for some years the government in one state, elect state officials and legislators in a number of midwestern and western states, and send several of its representatives to the Congress—its impact was to help shape the destinies of a dozen states and the political philosophies of an important segment of the nation's voters" (Morlan 1985, p. 1).

In 1934, in the midst of the Great Depression, the most famous leftist of his day, the prolific author Upton Sinclair, switched his party registration from Socialist to Democrat and announced that he would run for governor of California on a detailed program to End Poverty In California (EPIC), which featured a mixture of socialist and self-help ideas. He organized his supporters into EPIC clubs, thereby giving them an identity that distinguished them from other Democrats with whom leftists did not want to be associated. He proceeded to win the primary with 51 percent of the vote in a field of seven candidates. After an extraordinary campaign in which the incumbent Republican governor promised to embrace many New Deal programs, Sinclair lost the general election with 37 percent of the vote, but the Democratic Party was thereafter liberalized in California because many young liberal and socialist activists ran for other offices as part of his campaign (Mitchell 1992). Despite this apparent success, most leaders in the Socialist and Communist parties bitterly denounced Sinclair's approach because of their strong belief that a separate leftist party was needed. As a result of these criticisms, his model of creating a separate identity within the Democratic Party through a club structure—in effect, a party within the party—was never adopted by other leftists.

The first major insurgency in Democratic presidential primaries came from a Tennessee senator who shocked party leaders in 1952 by advocating integration in the South and opposing the influence of organized crime in Democratic machines in many large cities in the North. Although he won several primaries and fared well in polls, too many convention votes were still controlled by party leaders for him to receive the nomination (Fontenay 1980). In 1968, antiwar liberals entered Democratic presidential primaries to register their strong opposition to the Vietnam War and did so well that the incumbent president, Lyndon B. Johnson, chose not to run (Rising 1997). This effort, in conjunction with insurgent campaigns at other levels of the party in 1970 and 1972, led to major changes in the party rules for selecting delegates to the presidential nominating convention, along with a greater use of primaries to select candidates at all levels. The result was the nomination of a very liberal candidate for president in 1972, George McGovern (Miroff 2007). More recently, a major civil rights leader, Jesse Jackson, ran solid presidential campaigns in the 1984 and 1988 primaries. In fact, he received more votes in the 1988 primaries than either future president Bill Clinton or future vice president Al Gore and thereby established his credibility with white Democratic politicians who previously ignored him. However, the suspicions and tensions between him and his leftist allies were too great for them to build a lasting organization (Barker and Walters 1989; Celsi 1992).

The most successful use of party primaries was carried out by ultraconservative Republicans, who first took their platform and strong separate social identities as "Young Americans for Freedom" and "Goldwater Republicans" into Republican primaries in 1964, where they secured the presidential nomination for Senator Barry Goldwater of Arizona. Although Goldwater lost badly, his "states' rights" platform (a code word signifying that the Republicans would not try to end segregation in Southern states) started the movement of the solid Democratic South into the Republican Party in response to the Civil Rights Act of 1964. His campaign also recruited new cadre and steeled the determination of his followers to take over the party at the grassroots level (Himmelstein 1990; Perlstein 2001). They continued to challenge moderate Republicans in primaries throughout the next three decades, deriding them as "RINOs," Republicans In Name Only.

In 2004 an ultraconservative Republican running on a strong antitax and antiabortion platform nearly defeated the incumbent Republican senator in Pennsylvania, Arlen Specter. In early 2009 the same ultraconservative Republican, who served in the House of Representatives from 1999 to 2005, began making plans to challenge Specter once again in the 2010 primaries.

The institutionalization of primaries in conjunction with the transformation of the South as a result of the Civil Rights Movement led to the break-up of the New Deal coalition and the gradual Republican ascendancy in American politics. At the same time, these changes created new possibilities for the liberal-labor coalition within the Democratic Party. These points are elaborated upon in the final chapter.

THE CRITICAL IMPORTANCE OF CAMPAIGN FINANCE

In an electoral system in which party differences become blurred for structural and historical reasons, the emphasis on the character and image of each candidate becomes very great, along with a concern about her or his stance on symbolic social issues. In fact, personalities and social issues often become more important than policies related to jobs, health, and other substantive issues, even though systematic voting studies suggest that most voters are more concerned about policies that affect their everyday well-being than they are about personalities (Miller and Shanks 1996). This tendency to focus on personality and social issues has been increased somewhat with the rise of the mass media, in particular television, but it is a reality of American politics that has existed far longer than is understood by the many newspaper columnists and television pundits who until 2008 lamented what they always called "the recent decline of political parties."

Because the candidate-selection process is relatively individualistic and therefore dependent upon name recognition and personal image, it has been in good part controlled by members of the power elite through large campaign contributions. Serving as big donors and fundraisers, the same people who finance and direct corporations play a central role in the careers of most politicians who advance beyond the local level in states of any size and consequence. The role of wealthy donors and fundraisers is especially crucial in determining which candidates enter primaries and do well in them.

This does not mean that the candidate with the most money usually wins. Far from it, as seen in case studies of big-spending losers who are usually new to politics and think that money is everything. Instead, the important point is that it takes a very large minimum, now as much as $1,000,000 in a campaign for the House of Representatives, to be a viable candidate even with the requisite political experience and skills. It is like a high-stakes poker game: Anyone is welcome as long as they can place millions of dollars on the table.

Several reforms in campaign finance laws were instituted by a coalition of liberals and moderate conservatives during the 1970s to limit the impact of big donors by restricting the size of donations and creating a system of optional public financing for both primaries and regular elections at the presidential level. However, the reforms did not diminish the influence of the corporate community. If anything, they increased it quite inadvertently. Before the reforms, a handful of owners and executives would give hundreds of thousands of dollars (the equivalent of millions of dollars today) to candidates of interest to them. Since the reforms, the same few people organize receptions, luncheons, and dinners at which all of their colleagues and friends gave a few thousand dollars for specific candidates and party finance committees. (They are now called "bundlers" because they collect many hundreds of checks, which they bundle together and turn over to the campaign finance chair.) Corporate leaders also borrowed a page out of organized labor's playbook and formed Political Action Committees (PACs) so their stockholders and executives could give another several thousand dollars each year. In addition, trade associations and professional societies organized PACs to which their members can contribute. PACs, in turn, contribute to individual candidates and other PACs. More recently elected officials have formed their own PACs so they can give donations to fellow politicians. It is now a full-time job to figure out the networks through which political money flows, as shown by the existence of nonpartisan organizations such as the Campaign Finance Institute (http://www.cfinst.org/), the Center for Responsive Politics (http://www.opensecrets.org), and Newsmeat (http://www.newsmeat.com/).

Moreover, the restrictions on the size of individual donations were in effect lifted as long ago as 1979 when the Federal Election Commission ruled that unrestricted donations to state parties for "party building" were permissible, although the money could not be used to support a particular candidate. In practice, this distinction boiled down to the fact that the party's candidate could not be named even though his or her opponent could be named (and pilloried). This "soft money," as it came to be called, climbed to $46 million for both parties combined in 1992, then jumped to $150 million in 1996, and to over $250 million in 2000. Still, the "hard" money of regular donations remained much larger. Some of the soft money loopholes were closed in 2002, but in the process the cap on donations to individual candidates was doubled from $1,000 to $2,000 and indexed to inflation.

Although big donations from wealthy people will continue to be important in the future, the 2004 and 2008 elections also showed the possibilities of raising significant amounts of money over the Internet in amounts of $10 to $1,000 from large numbers of people. In 2004, when Democratic presidential hopeful Howard Dean raised $41 million from 340,000 donors for his insurgent campaign in the primaries, mostly by means of the Internet, other candidates soon followed his lead. Similarly, it was the possibility of small donations solicited by means of the Internet that convinced many wealthy liberals to provide groups such as MoveOn.org with start-up money. Moreover, the Internet fund-raising campaigns also led to the possibility of new meet-up groups of like-minded voters where more money can be raised and campaign volunteers recruited.

However, even with the new fund-raising efforts through the Internet, the less than 1 percent of American adults who give $1,000 or more remain important in political campaigns, and they are most often members of the corporate community and the growth coalitions. Business groups contribute twelve to fourteen times as much as organized labor, and they are the major donors to Democrats as well as Republicans. In 2008, for example, business PACs (which includes some small businesses as well as large corporations and financial institutions) gave $301.1 million to all federal candidates, almost half of which went to Democrats, whereas the 213 labor union PACs gave less than one-fourth as much, $67.0 million, 91 percent of which went to Democrats. Even within the Democratic Party, corporations outspent organized labor by 2.4:1 (see "2008 Overview: Business-Labor-Ideology Split in PAC & Individual Donations to Candidates and Parties" at http://www.opensecrets.org for details).

Although the corporate community and the growth coalitions are the largest donors to Democratic as well as Republican candidates, detailed analyses of PAC donation patterns at the congressional level provide strong evidence that the differences between the corporate community and the liberal-labor coalition manifest themselves in the electoral process. They show that corporate PACs usually support one set of candidates, liberal and labor PACs a different set, and that corporate PACs almost never oppose each other. Corporate PACs do not necessarily give to the same candidate, but they seldom give to two different candidates in the same race (Neustadtl, Scott and Clawson 1991). These conclusions, based on sophisticated statistical analyses, have been bolstered by interviews with PAC executives, which reveal there is indeed a large amount of coordination among corporate PACs. Furthermore, these studies report that corporate PACs support Democrats for one or more of three reasons: (1) because the Democrat is a moderate or conservative, usually from a rural area; (2) to maintain access to a Democrat who sits on a congressional committee important to the corporation; or (3) as a favor to another corporation that wants to maintain access to the Democrat (Clawson, Neustadtl and Weller 1998).

Studies that compare the degree to which legislators vote the same way with the degree to which they receive money from businesses or trade unions suggest that business PAC donations always have an influence, but the same cannot be said for labor PACs. These analyses of thousands of roll call votes in the House of Representatives between 1991 and 2006 show that business PACs had a significant impact in every two-year session, but that labor PACs had an influence in only a few sessions; in addition, the business influence was always greater than the labor influence (Peoples 2007). Another study in this series showed that neither business nor labor donations had any impact in the Canadian House of Commons in the late 1990s, which suggests that the American government is less independent of outside influences than the Canadian government (Peoples and Gortari 2008).

The large amount of money spent on campaigns is a source of great concern to liberal reformers. As part of their reform package, which includes tighter limits on individual donations and the expansion of public funding, some of them also call for the abolition of PACs, but that makes their allies in organized labor very uneasy. Although labor is greatly outspent by business in most elections, the union leaders believe that they would lose the little influence they have if they were not allowed to accumulate a war chest and then make donations to a few favored candidates. Similarly, several campaigns by women have been successful at least in part due to the collection of funds by feminist PACs, so women activists are also wary of restrictions on how money is raised.

Because it is so difficult to fashion effective campaign finance reforms that are constitutional, acceptable to all elements of the liberal-labor coalition, and acceptable to a congressional majority, it seems likely that large donations from members of the corporate community and the growth coalitions will continue to be a central element in determining who enters politics with any hope of winning a nomination at the federal level. In particular, it is the need for a large amount of start-up money—to travel around a district or the country, to send out large mailings, to schedule television ads in advance—that gives representatives of the power elite a very direct role in the process right from the start and thereby provides them with personal access to politicians of both parties. Even though they rarely try to tie specific strings to their donations, they are able to ensure a hearing for their views and to work against candidates they do not consider sensible and approachable. At a more psychological level, they create a sense of obligation in the recipients of their contributions because they are a form of gift. There is evidence that human beings everywhere feel a sense of debt upon receiving a gift, which leads them to want to reciprocate to rid themselves of the feeling of obligation (Gordon 2005; Mauss 1924/1969).

THE OBAMA FINANCIAL NETWORK

President Obama's network of donors is similar to those of most other successful political candidates in the United States in that it builds on wealthy contributors. His original financial network developed after he received his law degree from Harvard in 1992 and returned to the South Side of Chicago, where from 1985 to 1988 he had been a community organizer, to take charge of a voter registration project in African-American neighborhoods. This effort brought him into contact with middle-class African-Americans and well-to-do white liberals who would later become his political supporters. For example, Bettylu Saltzman, an heir to a large real estate fortune, was impressed with his political skills, introduced him to as many wealthy donors as she could, and talked him up to David Axelrod, a campaign manager who ten years later ended up managing his campaigns for the U.S. Senate and then for the presidency (Becker and Drew 2008).

The future president strengthened his ties to black executives and financiers through his wife, who grew up on the South Side. As also mentioned in Chapter 2, she left corporate law and took a job in city government, where she worked for another African-American lawyer who had left corporate law, Valerie Jarrett, who had degrees from Stanford and the University of Michigan. Jarrett also had many well-to-do friends throughout the Hyde Park neighborhood around the University of Chicago because her father was among the first black professors in the medical school. Obama's financial network soon included the founder of the largest black-owned money management firm in the country, the chief executive officer of a commercial real estate development firm, black executives in major Chicago corporations, and not least, James Nesbitt, an African-American vice president in the Pritzker Realty Company and the Parking Spot, two of many companies owned by the Pritzker family briefly discussed in Chapter 3.

However, support from the Pritzkers and other large corporate owners was still in the future when Obama ran for the state senate from the Hyde Park area in 1996 with the help of donations from his African-American business friends, a few wealthy white liberals such as Saltzman, and most importantly at the time, the developers who were in the process of gentrifying part of the area encompassed by his state senate district. As Obama explained to a reporter in the late 1990s after he won the seat in the state senate, the developers, brokerage houses, and law firms supported political candidates who in turn helped them gain government contracts for urban renewal: "They do well, and you get a $5 million to $10 million war chest" (Lizza 2008, p. 58; Murray 2008). His own war chest was never that big, but developers were a key element in his success.

Obama's financial network expanded after Democratic victories in 2000 made it possible for him to ask the Democratic leader in the state senate to redraw his district so that it included the wealthy Gold Coast district along Chicago's lakefront as well as Hyde Park and part of the black ghettoes to its south. At this point Saltzman took him to meet the Ladies Who Lunch, a group of nineteen women executives and heiresses "who see themselves as talent scouts and angel investors for up-and-coming liberal candidates and activists" (Lizza 2008, p. 61). One of them, Christie Hefner, who ran Playboy Enterprises, a company she inherited from her father, until early in 2009, said that "I was very proud to be able to introduce him during the Senate race to a lot of people who have turned out to be important and valuable to him, not just here but in New York and L.A." (Lizza 2008, p. 61). He also came to know members of the billionaire Crown family discussed briefly in Chapter 3. In particular, he gained the confidence of the president of the family holding and investment company, James S. Crown, the member of the family who sits on the boards of General Dynamics and JPMorgan Chase.

When Obama brought his group of African-American friends together to surprise them with the news that he intended to run for the U.S. Senate in 2004, he assured them he could win if he could raise several million dollars. They agreed to back him, but they also knew that he would have to tap much deeper pockets as well. It was at this point that Nesbitt arranged for Obama and his wife to spend two days with Penny Pritzker and her husband, an eye surgeon, at the Pritzkers' weekend home 45 minutes east of Chicago. Although Pritzker told Obama's biographer that she and her husband had met the Obamas before, the visit was in many ways an audition because she asked the candidate many questions about his general philosophy and campaign plans. By the end of the weekend she had agreed to help raise money for him (Mendell 2007, p. 155). Pritzker, who ranked 135th on the 2007 Forbes list of the richest 400 in America, with an estimated net worth of $2.8 billion, gave the campaign immediate credibility in the Chicago business community, in part because she is described as a centrist who provides financial support to candidates in both parties.

Other Obama fundraisers reached out to the national level, starting with his friend Valerie Jarrett. Jarrett's cousin is married to one of the most prominent African-Americans in the corporate community, Vernon Jordan, a corporate lawyer and former chief counsel to

President Bill Clinton. Jordan sat on the boards of five corporations in 2007 (American Express, Asbury Automotive Group, JCPenney, Sara Lee, and Xerox) and his wife, Ann Dibble Jordan, sat on three corporate boards: Automatic Data Processing, Citigroup, and Johnson & Johnson. The result was a fundraiser in Washington where Obama gained new bundlers and first met people who subsequently became members of his administration (Silverstein 2006). With the help of Pritzker, Saltzman, Crown, Jordan, and many other wealthy donors, the campaign raised over $5 million, half of which came from just 300 people (Street 2008, p. 15).

The same network was in place as Senator Obama prepared to enter the presidential primaries in 2007. This time Pritzker was the national campaign finance chair. The senator also raised money on Wall Street through a friend from Harvard Law School who worked as an executive for Citigroup. In addition, he raised money in Los Angeles and Hollywood through several other friends, including Christie Hefner of Playboy Enterprises. By March 2008 his 79 top money raisers, five of them billionaires, had collected at least $200,000 each (Mosk and MacGillis 2008).

As the campaign picked up steam late in the summer, the Obama forces set up a special party committee, the Committee for Change, so that donors who had given the maximum to the candidate ($2,300) and to the Democratic National Committee ($28,500) could provide money that would go directly to state-level parties in eighteen battleground states. The new funds made it possible to pay for transportation, lodging, and meals for the large army of young get-out-the-vote activists who had been recruited through e-mail, Facebook, YouTube, and text messaging (Melber 2008). Individual checks for $5,000 to $66,000 poured in from the financial sector, lawyers, corporate leaders, and celebrities. Members of the Crown family, who already had raised $500,000 and donated $57,000 to the Obama Victory Fund, gave another $74,000 to the Committee for Change (Mosk and Cohen 2008).

When President Obama disappointed many liberals by deciding not to accept public funding of his campaign, as he had promised to do in 2007 if his opponent also agreed to do so, he justified his decision in part with the claim that his campaign had created a parallel public financing system of small donors via the Internet and door-to-door campaigning. Although President Obama did raise approximately $200 million in donations of under $200 over the Internet and had more donors (3.1 million) than any previous candidate, his dependence on small donors turned out to be exaggerated. Closer scrutiny of his campaign finance reports showed that many of the seemingly small donors gave $200 or more several times in the course of the campaign. Only 26 percent of his donations actually came from people who gave

$200 or less, which was about the same as the percentage of small donors for George W. Bush in 2004; almost half of the money donated to Obama came from people who gave $1,000 or more (Luo 2008b; Malbin 2008).

Although President Obama's campaign once again showed that large sums of money can be raised in small amounts via the Internet, the fact remains that a relative handful of large donors in the corporate community were the key to his success in both his senatorial and presidential campaigns. Moreover, his decision to forego public money for his presidential campaign so that he could raise unlimited amounts probably put an end to that particular reform and to the general reform thrust that began in the 1970s. Big money is back in American politics as never before.

If the past tells us anything, it tells us that the positions favored by President Obama's supporters in the corporate community will be taken into account when it comes time to make decisions on policies put forward by liberals and labor. It is not a foregone conclusion, however, that he will always, or even usually, decide in favor of the corporate position. The economic structure is up for grabs until such time as the economy is stabilized. The liberal-labor coalition may be able to build upon this fact if the Obama Administration's economic stimulus, bank bailouts, and health care plans fall short of their goals.

OTHER CORPORATE SUPPORT FOR CANDIDATES

As important as large campaign donations are in the electoral process, there are also numerous other methods by which members of the corporate community provide support to the politicians they favor. One of the most direct is to give them corporate stock or to purchase property from them at a price well above the market value. In 1966, for example, just this kind of favor was done for a future president, Ronald Reagan, shortly after he became governor of California. Twentieth Century Fox purchased several hundred acres of his land adjacent to its large outdoor set in Malibu for nearly $2 million, triple its assessed market value and 30 times what he had paid for it in 1952. The land was never utilized and was later sold to the state. It was this transaction that gave Reagan the financial security that made it possible for him to devote himself full-time to his political career (Horrock 1976).

A very direct method of benefiting the many politicians who are lawyers is to hire them or their law firms as legal consultants or to provide them with routine legal business. Corporations can be especially helpful to lawyer/politicians when they are between offices. For example, the chairman of PepsiCo retained former vice president and future president Richard M. Nixon as the company's lawyer in 1963, while Nixon was out of office. He thereafter paid for every trip Nixon made overseas in the next two years. This made it possible for Nixon to remain in the political limelight as a foreign-policy expert while he quietly began his campaign to become president in 1968 (Hoffman 1973, p. 106).

In an era when campaign donations to each candidate are limited in size and widely publicized via Internet sites, corporations and their lobbyists help boost the public profiles of candidates and elected officials by giving large donations to foundations, scholarship funds, and charities that politicians set up in their home congressional district or state. In Johnstown, Pennsylvania, for example, the defense companies General Dynamics and Northrup Grumman each gave $50,000 to an endowment for the Johnstown Symphony Orchestra set up by John P. Murtha, the Democratic congressman from that district, who is chair of a House committee that has a major impact on the awarding of defense contracts (Hernandez and Chen 2008).

The corporate community provides the services of lobbyists from the special-interest process (briefly explained at the end of Chapter 2 and discussed again in Chapter 7) to candidates in both political parties, where they serve as political strategists, campaign managers, and fundraisers. Although 2008 Republican presidential candidate John McCain emphasized that he was an opponent of lobbyists and of the favors won by them through the special-interest process, his campaign was managed and financed by several of the most important lobbyists in Washington. For example, his chief political strategist, who had worked in Republican presidential campaigns since the 1980s, has a client list that includes AT&T, Alcoa, JPMorgan Chase, United Technologies, and US Airways. Similarly, Senator McCain's campaign manager was the cofounder of a lobbying firm that worked for Verizon and other telephone companies. His top fundraiser worked as a lobbyist for Saudi Arabia, Toyota, Southwest Airlines, and the pharmaceutical manufacturers' trade association. Seventeen of the 106 people who collected $100,000 or more for the campaign as of early spring 2008 were lobbyists (Luo and Wheaton 2008; Shear and Birnbaum 2008).

Politicians also know from past experience that they can be richly rewarded after their careers in office if they are seen as reasonable and supportive. Between 1998 and 2004, for example, 45 percent of the members of Congress who departed from Congress became lobbyists, mostly for corporations and trade associations, usually at salaries many times what they made while they were in government. Those who do not become lobbyists may become corporate executives or join corporate advisory boards. Former House speaker Newt Gingrich, a Republican, joined the advisory board of Forstmann Little and Company, an investment banking firm run by one of the party's largest contributors, after he resigned from Congress under a cloud in November 1999. When a Republican representative from Louisiana retired after twenty years in the House, where he wrote Medicare legislation in 2004 that forbids the federal government from bargaining about the prices for the prescription drugs it purchases, he was appointed president of the Pharmaceutical Research and Manufacturing Association, the industry's trade group, at a reported $2 million a year. Former president Bill Clinton has earned tens of millions of dollars for speeches to business associations and foreign governments since he left office.

THE RESULTS OF THE CANDIDATE-SELECTION PROCESS

What kinds of elected officials emerge from a candidate-selection process that puts great emphasis on campaign finance and media recognition? The answer is available from numerous studies. First, politicians are from the top 10 to 15 percent of the occupational and income ladders, especially those who hold the highest elective offices. Only in a minority of cases are they from the upper class or corporate community, but they often share a business or legal background with members of the upper class (Matthews 1967; Zweigenhaft 1975). Nonetheless, politicians feel a need to stress the humble nature of their social backgrounds whenever it is possible.

As shown by a study comparing the rhetoric and reality of the early lives of American presidents, most of the presidents were wealthy or connected to wealth by the time they reached the White House. George Washington was one of the richest men of his day, partly through inheritance, partly through marriage. Andrew Jackson, allegedly of humble circumstances because his father died before he was born, was raised in a well-to-do slaveholding family and he became even wealthier as an adult. He "dealt in slaves, made hundreds of thousands of dollars, accumulated hundreds of thousands of valuable acres in land speculation, owned racehorses and racetracks, bought cotton gins, distilleries, and plantations, was a successful merchant, and married extremely well" (Pessen 1984, p. 81). Abraham Lincoln became a corporate lawyer for railroads and married into a wealthy Kentucky family.

Few presidents since 1900 have come from outside the very wealthiest circles. Theodore Roosevelt, William H. Taft, Franklin D. Roosevelt, John F. Kennedy, George H. W. Bush, and George W. Bush are from upper-class backgrounds. Herbert Hoover, Jimmy Carter, and Ronald Reagan were millionaires before they became deeply involved in national politics. Lyndon B. Johnson was a millionaire several times over through his wife's land dealings and his use of political leverage to gain control of a lucrative television license in Austin. Even Richard M. Nixon, whose father ran a small store, was a rich man when he finally attained the presidency in 1968 after earning high salaries as a corporate lawyer between 1963 and 1968.

Bill Clinton, elected president in 1992 and 1996, tries to give the impression he is from an impoverished background, claiming he is just a poor boy from little Hope, Arkansas, born of a widowed mother. But Clinton was gone from Hope, where he lived in comfortable circumstances with his grandparents, who owned a small store, by the age of six. At that time his mother married Roger Clinton, whose family owned a car dealership in the nearby tourist town of Hot Springs. He grew up playing golf at the local country club and driving a Buick convertible. His mother sent him money throughout his years in college. Clinton is not wealthy or from the upper class, but he has a very solid middle-class upbringing and education that he artfully obscures.

The second general finding about elected officials is that a great many of them are lawyers. Between 50 and 60 percent of congressional members have been lawyers, although the number has slipped below 50 percent in recent years, and twenty-eight of the forty-four American presidents earned law degrees, including Bill Clinton, who attended Yale Law School, and President Obama, who graduated from Harvard Law (Eulau and Sprague 1984; Miller 1995). The large percentage of lawyers in the American political system is highly atypical when compared with other countries, where only 10 to 30 percent of legislators have a legal background. Comparing the United States with a deviant case at the other extreme, Denmark, where only 2 percent of legislators are lawyers, provides insight into this overrepresentation. The class-based nature of Danish politics since the late nineteenth century and the fact that political careers are not pathways to judicial appointments are thought to discourage lawyer participation in that country. The Danish situation thus suggests that the marginalization of class issues by the two main American political parties, combined with the intimate involvement of the parties in the judicial system, creates a climate for strong lawyer involvement in the political system (Pederson 1972).

Whatever the reasons for their involvement, lawyers are the occupational grouping that by training and career needs are ideal go-betweens and compromisers. They have the skills to balance the relationship between the corporate community that finances them on the one hand and the citizens who vote for them on the other. They are the supreme "pragmatists" in a nation that prides itself on a pragmatic and can-do ideology. They have an ability to be dispassionate about "the issues" and they are generally respectful of the process by which things are done.

Whether elected officials are from business or law, the third general result of the candidate-selection process is a large number of very ambitious people who are eager to "go along to get along." To understand the behavior of a politician, one political scientist concluded after studying many political careers that "it is more important to know what he wants to be than how he got to where he is now" (Schlesinger 1966, p. 5). This great ambition, whether it is for wealth or higher office, makes politicians especially available to those people who can help them realize their goals. Such people are often members of the corporate community or upper class, who have money to contribute and connections to other districts, states, or regions where striving candidates need new friends. Thus, even the most liberal or ultraconservative of politicians may develop a new circle of moderate supporters as they move from the local to the congressional to the presidential level, gradually becoming more and more involved with leading figures within the power elite.

The *Chicago Tribune* reporter assigned to cover Barack Obama from the day he announced in 2002 that he would enter the U.S. Senate primaries in 2004 was struck by his overwhelming ambition: "He is an extraordinarily ambitious, competitive man with persuasive charm and a career reach that seems to know no bounds; he is, in fact a man of raw ambition so powerful that even he is still coming to terms with its full force" (Mendell 2007, p. 7). Indeed, keeping his ambition under wraps and suppressing his "privately haughty manner" is his most difficult problem (Mendell 2007, pp. 353–354). "I'm LeBron, baby, I can play on this level. I got some game," President Obama suddenly remarked to the *Tribune* reporter as he was about to take the stage to give the keynote speech at the 2004 presidential convention that brought him nationwide attention and a large number of young and enthusiastic supporters who wanted him to be president some day (Mendell 2007, p. 2). He was referring to LeBron James, the National Basketball Association superstar who plays for the Cleveland Cavaliers. Ambition aside, President Obama also fits the general pattern because he moderated his liberal positions on many issues when he ran for the U.S. Senate in 2004 and then for the presidency in 2008; some of the liberal activists in Hyde Park who helped him win his first campaign have resigned themselves to the fact that he took more moderate positions when he started to raise money in wealthy financial circles, but others have become disappointed and no longer support him (Becker and Drew 2008; Lizza 2008).

The fourth generalization about most successful political candidates is that they try to straddle the fence or remain silent on the highly emotional social issues. Basically, very few candidates can win if their views fall outside the limits that have been set by the actions and television advertising of the ultraconservatives. As long as 75 percent of the people say they believe in the death penalty, for example, it is unlikely that anyone who openly challenges that position can be elected to any office except in a few liberal districts and cities. Here, then, is an instance where public opinion has a direct effect on the behavior of candidates and elected officials, even though it is also true that most voters make their voting decisions based on their party identification and degree of satisfaction with the state of the economy (Miller and Shanks 1996).

The fifth general finding, alluded to earlier in the chapter, is that the majority of elected officials at the national level have been pro-business conservatives. For most of the twentieth century, this conservative majority consisted of Northern Republicans and Southern Democrats. In the 1980s and early 1990s, Republicans replaced Southern Democrats in both the House and the Senate, which contributed heavily to the Republican takeover of Congress in 1994. As late as 1996, however, with conservative white Southern Democrats accounting for less than thirty votes in the House, the conservative voting coalition still formed on 11.7 percent of the congressional votes and was successful 98.9 percent of the time. The Southern Democratic votes were essential to thirty-three of fifty-one conservative victories in the House and nineteen of thirty-seven such victories in the Senate, offsetting defections by the handful of moderate Republicans from the Northeast who were still in office at the time (CQ 1996).

But that was then and this is now. Most strong conservatives are now part of the Republican Party and the two parties are very different on many issues. The only wealthy people who will remain in the Democratic Party will be those who are moderate conservatives or liberals because of their religious affiliations or social values, or who feel threatened by ultraconservative Republican positions on abortion, feminist issues, gay rights, or immigration.

THE LIBERAL-LABOR COALITION IN ELECTORAL POLITICS

The liberal-labor coalition has very little independent influence at the presidential level. Fearing the antiunion and antiliberal stance of the Republican Party, it ends up trying desperately to turn out voters for the centrist or moderate conservative who wins the Democratic presidential nomination. However, the liberal-labor coalition has been able to elect more sympathizers and supporters to both the House and Senate in recent years. According to studies of congressional voting records by the liberal Americans for Democratic Action, the percentage of Democratic representatives with liberal voting records has been growing steadily since the late 1990s. Using the organization's standard that voting liberal 80 percent of the time on key issues defines a liberal, nearly half the members of the Democratic caucus in the House were liberals in 2007 and perhaps as many as 40 percent in the Senate (Riddiough and Card 2008).

Moreover, politicians who are supported by and feel sympathetic toward the power elite may be inclined to vote with the liberals and labor under some conditions, which means that a majority of elected officials can and sometimes do disagree with the power elite on specific issues. These defeats for the corporate community once again show, as emphasized at the end of Chapters 2 and 4, that there is too much uncertainty and volatility in the workings of government for the power elite to leave anything to chance. The power elite therefore have to be able to influence government directly in order to augment their structural economic power, their status power, their large reservoir of respectable policy options, and their access to the pro-corporate majorities that existed in Congress at least until the 2008 elections. They cannot risk the possibility that the liberal-labor minority in Congress will be able to create coalitions that defeat them on key issues. The explanation for the handful of past liberal-labor successes on some issues of concern to the corporate community, including the passage of pro-union legislation in 1935, is presented as part of the next chapter.

7

How the Power Elite
Dominate Government

At least up until the 2008 elections, the power elite has built on their structural economic power, their status power, their storehouse of policy recommendations, and their success in the electoral arena to dominate the federal government on the issues they care about. Lobbyists from corporations, law firms, and trade associations played a key role in shaping government on narrow issues of concern to specific corporations or business sectors and the policy-planning network supplied new policy directions on major issues, along with top-level governmental appointees to implement those policies.

However, these victories within government have been far from automatic. The power elite face opposition from a significant number of liberal elected officials and their supporters in labor unions and liberal advocacy groups. These liberal opponents are sometimes successful in blocking the social initiatives advocated by the Christian Right, such as making abortion illegal, but the corporate community and the conservative voting bloc in Congress seldom lost in the years between 1877 and 2008 when they were united. In fact, as noted at the end of the previous chapter, many of the relatively few victories for the liberal-labor coalition came because of support from moderate conservatives, usually in situations of extreme social disruption, such as economic depression, wars, or the civil rights era.

There is only one major issue that does not fit these generalizations, labor legislation, which is one of the areas that the corporate community cares about the most. In particular, the National Labor Relations Act of 1935 passed over its extreme objections. This legislation gave employees the right to join unions and enter into collective bargaining with their employers. However, as a section toward the end of this chapter explains, there was one other crucial ingredient in this victory besides labor militancy and a large number of liberals in Congress. The liberal-labor coalition accepted the exclusion of agricultural and domestic workers from the purview of the legislation in order to win the support of the Southern plantation capitalists who had great power in Congress at the time. In effect, the power elite lost because its Northern and Southern segments were divided on this issue. This explanation is supported by the fact that they were able to limit the power of the National Labor Relations Act when they united against it just three years after it passed.

THE ROLE OF GOVERNMENTS

Governments are potentially autonomous in just the way historical institutionalists suggest because they have a unique function: territorial regulation. They set up and guard boundaries and then regulate the flow of people, money, and goods in and out of the area for which they have responsibility. They also have regulatory functions within a territory, such as settling disputes through the judicial system and setting the rules that shape the economic marketplace. In a world in which one country is prone to invade and conquer another, governments also have the crucial function of protecting the home territory and fending off rival states.

Neither business, the military, nor churches are organized in such a way that they could provide these necessary functions. The military sometimes steps in—or forces its way in—when a government is weak or collapsing, but it has a difficult time carrying out routine regulatory functions for very long. Nor can competing businesses regulate themselves. As the years between 2000 and 2008 showed all too well, there is always some business that will try to improve its market share or profits by adulterating products, reducing wages, colluding with other companies, or telling half-truths. As most economists and all other social scientists agree, a business system could not survive without some degree of market regulation by government. Contrary to assertions about markets being "free," which is the key claim of conservative economists and their ultraconservative supporters in the power elite, markets are historically constructed institutions dependent upon governmentally sanctioned enforcement of property and contract rights (e.g., Massey 2005, for a recent summary and synthesis). When these regulatory agencies are captured by the corporate community, the result is often the kind of speculative frenzy in financial markets that led to the bankruptcy of Enron in 2001 and Lehman Brothers in 2008, as well as accounting scandals, insider dealing among stock brokers, excessive fees by mutual funds, kickbacks by insurance companies, false applications by mortgage companies, and fraudulent ratings of stocks and bonds by stock analysts and credit rating companies.

Governments are also essential in creating money, setting interest rates, and shaping the credit system. Although Wall Street bankers tried to manage the money system without a government central bank for much of the nineteenth century, the problems caused by a privately controlled money system were so great that the most powerful bankers of the early twentieth century worked together to create the Federal Reserve System in 1912 (Greider 1989; Livingston 1986). The system was improved during the 1930s and has been an essential institution in keeping a highly volatile business system from careening off in one direction or another. When the stock market crashed in 1987, for example, the Federal Reserve made sure that stockholders would not lose their wealth, and that there would be no repeat of the mistakes leading to the Great Depression, by instructing large New York banks to keep making loans to temporarily insolvent debtors. Similar bailouts were performed in the 1990s due to problems in Mexico, Korea, and a Wall Street investment firm, Long Term Capital Management, which could have caused large-scale bankruptcies (Woodward 2000). Only massive efforts by the Federal Reserve System, this time in conjunction with the Department of Treasury, staved off a potentially disastrous meltdown of the entire financial system in late 2008.

The federal government also is essential in providing subsidy payments to groups in trouble, such as farmers and low-income workers, in ways that bolster the market system and benefit large corporations. For example, farmers receive tens of billions in direct payments, which is half of all farm income in some years, and low-income employees who work full time and have children also receive tens of billions through a program called the "Earned Income Tax Credit." Both corporate leaders and Republicans prefer these year-end government bonus payments to the old system of welfare payments because they increase the labor pool and reinforce the work ethic.

Nor is government any less important in the context of a globalizing economy. If anything, it is even more important because it has to enforce rules concerning patents, intellectual property, quality of merchandise, and much else in an unregulated international arena. The film industry, publishers, and drug companies, among several, are absolutely dependent on the government to protect them against cheaply produced copies and knock-offs. Furthermore, the international economy simply could not function without the agreements on monetary policy and trade that the governments of the United States,

Japan, Canada, and Western Europe uphold through the International Monetary Fund, World Trade Organization, and other international agencies. For these reasons, all of which belie the idea of "free markets," domination of the federal government on domestic and international economic issues is essential for the corporate community.

THE SPECIAL-INTEREST PROCESS

The special-interest process, as noted at earlier points in the book, consists of the many and varied means by which specific corporations and business sectors gain the favors, tax breaks, regulatory rulings, and other governmental assistance they need to realize their narrow and short-run interests. The process is based on a great amount of personal contact, but its most important ingredients are the information and financial support that the lobbyists have to offer. It is carried out by people with a wide range of experiences: former elected officials, experts who once served on congressional staffs or in regulatory agencies, employees of trade associations, corporate executives whose explicit function is government liaison, and an assortment of lawyers and public relations specialists (Goldstein 1999; Luger 2000). In reaction to the growing number of women in elected and appointed government positions, there are also a number of women lobbyists, many of them experts on taxes and finance (Benoit 2007).

Corporations spend far more money on lobbying than their officers give to political candidates or their company's Political Action Committee, by a margin of 10 to 1. In 2000, for example, the tobacco industry, facing lawsuits and regulatory threats, spent $44 million on lobbyists and $17 million on the Tobacco Institute, an industry public relations arm, but gave only $8.4 million to political campaigns through Political Action Committees. More generally, a study of the top twenty defense contractors showed that they spent $400 million on lobbying between 1997 and 2003, but only $46 million on campaign contributions (de Figueiredo and Snyder 2003; POGO 2004).

The most powerful lobbyists are gathered into a few large firms that are large businesses in and of themselves, bringing in tens of millions of dollars each year. Several of these firms, in turn, are owned by the public relations firms that have a major role in the opinion-shaping network discussed in Chapter 5. Two former Senate majority leaders, one Democratic, one Republican, are the leading figures in the second-largest lobbying firm, where their many clients include Citigroup, Merrill Lynch, and Brown & Williamson Tobacco. The narrow but financially significant issues these firms handle are typical of the special-interest process. For example, Pfizer paid one firm $400,000 to try to work against a National Transportation Safety Board proposal to ban the use of antihistamines by truck drivers. The Magazine Publishers of America paid another firm $520,000 to oppose a possible 15 percent increase in magazine postal rates (Zeller 2000).

Intricate and arcane tax breaks are one of the most important aspects of the special-interest process. Thanks to successful efforts in 1993 to relax rules concerning minimum corporate taxes and changes in 1997 making it possible for corporations to spread tax breaks over several years, 12 of 250 profitable large firms studied for the years 1996–1998 paid no federal income taxes. Seventy-one of the 250 paid taxes at less than half the official rate during those three years (Johnston 2000). The trend to increasingly large tax breaks continued during the Bush Administration, with the effective tax rate on corporations declining from 21.7 percent during the last years of the Clinton Administration to 17.2 percent in 2003. Forty-six of 275 major companies studied for 2003 paid no federal income taxes, a considerable increase from a similar study in the late 1990s (Barshay and Wolfe 2004; Browning 2004; McIntyre 2004).

Special interests also work through Congress to try to hamstring regulatory agencies or reverse military purchasing decisions they do not like. When the Federal Communications Commission tried to issue licenses in 2000 for over 1,000 low-power FM stations for schools and community groups, Congress blocked the initiative at the behest of big broadcasting companies, setting standards that restricted new licenses to a small number of stations in the least populated parts of the country (Labaton 2000).

Some special-interest conflicts pit one sector of business against another, such as when broadcasters jockey for advantage against movie or cable companies. Sometimes the arguments are within a specific industry, as occurred when smaller insurance companies moved their headquarters to Bermuda in 1999 and 2000 to take advantage of a tax loophole worth as much as $4 billion annually. Since the bigger insurance companies could not take advantage of this opportunity, they supported bipartisan legislation to end the tax benefits of setting up in Bermuda. They hired a lobbying firm, several law firms, and a public relations firm to press their cause. The small companies countered by hiring a different set of law firms and public relations companies (Stone 2000). The loophole stayed open and the bigger companies were still fighting against it seven years later (Johnston and Treaster 2007).

The special-interest process often is used to create loopholes in legislation that is accepted by the corporate community in principle. "I spent the last seven years fighting the Clean Air Act," said a corporate lobbyist in charge of Political Action Committee donations for his company, and then went on to explain why he gave money to elected officials who voted for the strengthening of the Clean Air Act in 1990:

> How a person votes on the final piece of legislation is not repre-sentative of what they have done. Somebody will do a lot of things during the process. How many guys voted against the Clean Air Act? But during the process some of them were very sympathetic to some of our concerns (Clawson, Neustadtl and Weller 1998, p. 6).

Translated, this means there were forty pages of exceptions, exten-sions, and other loopholes in the 1990 version of the act after a thirteen-year standoff between the Business Roundtable's Clean Air Working Group and the liberal-labor coalition's National Clean Air Coalition. For example, the steel industry was given thirty years to bring twenty-six large coke ovens into compliance with the new standards. Once the bill passed, lobbyists went to work on the Environmental Protection Agency to win the most lax regulations possible for implementing the legislation.

Although most studies of the special-interest process recount the success of one or another corporation or trade association in gaining the tax or regulatory breaks it seeks, or discuss battles between rival sec-tors of the corporate community, there are occasional defeats for cor-porate interests at the hands of liberals and labor within this process, but most of them were long ago. In 1971, for example, environmen-talists convinced Congress to end taxpayer subsidies for construction of a supersonic transport. In 1977, a relatively strong anti–strip mine bill was adopted over the objections of the coal industry. Laws that improved auto safety standards were passed over automobile industry objections in the 1970s, as were standards of water cleanliness opposed by the paper and chemical industries (Luger 2000; Vogel 1989).

The liberal-labor coalition also can claim some victories for its own initiatives in Congress. For example, the Family and Medical Leave Act of 1993 allows both male and female employees of companies with fifty or more employees to take up to twelve weeks of unpaid leave a year for child care or family illness. Corporate groups opposed the bill when it was first introduced in 1986 and President George H.W. Bush vetoed it twice before President Clinton came into office. The fact that the leaves are unpaid limits the number of workers who can take advantage of them and conservatives were able to exempt small companies and reduce the amount of leave from eighteen weeks to twelve, but health benefits are still in place during the leave. Although the act is popular with workers, especially in companies that do not grant sick leave or disability coverage, the U.S. Chamber of Commerce and specific trade associations complain that its is abused and want to add more restrictions on its use. As the Bush Administration neared its final months, the Department of Labor was hoping to issue new guidelines, but Democratic control of Congress by that point made it possible to block that effort (Trejos 2008).

The special-interest process is the most visible and frequently studied aspect of governmental activity in Washington. It also consumes the lion's share of the attention devoted to legislation by elected officials. Although the special-interest process is very important to the corporate community, it is not the heart of the matter when it comes to a full understanding of corporate power in the United States. There is general agreement among a wide range of theorists about the operation of this dimension of American politics: Everyone concludes that organized business groups have great power in this arena. But as far as pluralists and historical institutionalists are concerned, this is not enough to show dominance of the federal government in general. It fits well with the emphasis on interest groups in pluralist theory. From the point of view of historical institutionalism, it can be interpreted as the way in which government keeps business as an ally. This means that the policy-making process is very important in dealing with these theoretical disputes.

THE POLICY-MAKING PROCESS

General policy-making on issues of concern to the corporate community as a whole represents the culmination of work done in the policy-planning network described in Chapter 4. However, the differences between moderate conservatives and ultraconservatives sometimes lead to major conflicts over new policies within the executive branch and the legislative process. In addition, the power elite have to fend off alternative legislative proposals put forward by the liberal-labor coalition at this point in the policy process.

The recommendations developed in the policy-planning network reach government in a variety of ways. On the most general level, their reports, news releases, and interviews are read by elected officials and their staffs, if not in their original form, then as they are summarized by commentators and columnists in *The Washington Post*, *The New York Times*, and *The Wall Street Journal*. Members of the policy organizations also appear before congressional committees and subcommittees that are writing legislation or preparing budget proposals. However, the most important contacts with government are more direct and formal in nature. First, people from the policy-planning network are often members of the many unpaid committees that advise specific departments of the executive branch on general policies. In the most

recent and detailed study of this linkage, 83 percent of twelve prominent thinks tanks and policy planning groups and 72 percent of the 100
largest corporations had members on federal advisory committees, far
more than the foundations, universities, and charities in the database.
For example, the Defense Policy Advisory Committee on Trade within
the Department of Defense comes primarily from the defense industry,
while the National Security Telecommunications Advisory Committee
in the Department of State comes from telecommunication, information, and electronic companies. CEOs make up the entire membership
of some of these advisory committees. Every government department
that is of potential interest to the corporate community has such committees (Moore et al. 2002). (For further information on these advisory
committees, see the document on "Federal Advisory Committees" at
www.whorulesamerica.net.)

Second, corporate executives and experts from the policy-planning
network have been prominent on the presidential and congressional
commissions that have been appointed from time to time since World
War II to make recommendations on a wide range of issues from highway construction to changes in social security to a new missile defense
system. Third, corporate leaders have personal contact with both
appointed and elected officials as members of the two policy organizations with the most access to government, the Business Council and
the Business Roundtable. Fourth, they serve as informal advisers to
the president in times of foreign policy crisis. Finally, as shown in the
next section of this chapter, they are appointed to government positions that put them in a position to endorse the policy suggestions put
forth by their colleagues and former employees in the policy-planning
network.

Proposals developed in the policy-planning network led to several new government agencies in the twentieth century. Contrary to the
historical institutionalists' assertion that elected officials and government administrators expanded and strengthened the American government, it is more accurate to say that new agencies were created by
the corporate community in response to specific crises and pressures,
beginning with the Federal Trade Commission and the Bureau of the
Budget (now called the Office of Management and Budget to reflect
its expanded duties) during the Progressive Era (Kahn 1997; Weinstein
1968). Then the Agricultural Adjustment Administration and the Social
Security Administration emerged from the policy-planning network
during the New Deal (Domhoff 1996, chapters 3 and 5). As mentioned
in the discussions of the Council on Foreign Relations and the Committee for Economic Development in Chapter 4, members of the policy-
planning network created the framework for American foreign policy
and trade policy for the post–World War II era. Here it can be added

that members of the policy-planning network had a major role in reorganizing the Department of Defense after the war and then establishing the National Security Council and the CIA (Huntington 1961). (For a detailed account of the origins of the Social Security program that is now under constant attack by ultraconservatives in the corporate community, see the document on "How and Why Corporate Moderates Created the Social Security Act" at www.whorulesamerica.net.)

During the twentieth century, the positions taken by moderate conservatives determined the outcome of policy battles. If they did not wish to see any change, they sided with their ultraconservative counterparts in the power elite to defeat any programs suggested by liberals or labor, with considerable help from the conservative voting bloc in Congress. There were only a few instances in the twentieth century when the conservative voting bloc did not unite to stop class-oriented liberal-labor legislation through an outright majority, maneuvering within key congressional committees, or a filibuster in the Senate. On the other hand, if the moderate conservatives favored policy changes that were opposed by the ultraconservatives, they sought the backing of liberal-labor elected officials for a program developed in moderate think tanks or policy-discussion groups, or else they modified a plan advocated by liberals. They were especially likely to take this course in times of extreme social disruption such as the 1960s when they were dealing simultaneously with an antiwar movement, major upheaval in inner cities, and an overheated economy.

Sometimes general policy battles pit one or two industries against the rest of the corporate community, with the aggrieved industries eventually losing out. This is what happened to a large extent in the 1950s and 1960s when the textile and chemical sectors blocked attempts to reduce tariff barriers and increase world trade. When leaders from the Committee for Economic Development were able to forge a compromise with textile and chemical spokespersons, the opposition in Congress disappeared immediately (Domhoff 1990, chapter 8). The same thing happened in 1987 when the U.S. Chamber of Commerce and the National Federation of Independent Business objected on general principle to a call by the American Electronics Association, the Chemical Manufacturers Association, and organized labor for a federal program to monitor and notify workers exposed to toxic substances in the workplace. The legislation was defeated by a Republican filibuster in the Senate because the corporate community as a whole feared that such a program might provide a thin entering wedge for further demands for regulation (Jacobs 1999).

None of this means that congressional voting coalitions develop any more quickly and easily on large-scale issues than they do on special-interest ones. Instead, each coalition has to be carefully constructed by

elected officials with the help of corporate lobbyists and grassroots publicity. It is here that the political leaders do their most important work.
They are specialists in arranging trades with other politicians for votes
and in being sensitive to the electoral risks for each colleague in voting
for or against any highly visible piece of legislation. They are also experts
at sensing when the moment is right to hold a vote, often keeping the
final outcome hanging in the balance for weeks or months at a time.
Sometimes they wait until a lame-duck session shortly after elections
have been held, or slip controversial legislation into omnibus bills that
are hard for voters to fathom. Finally, their constant interaction with
constituents and the media gives them the experience and sensitivity to
use the rhetoric and metaphors needed to make the new legislation palat-
able to as many people as possible.

However, important parts of this picture changed significantly
when President George W. Bush was elected in 2000 in the context
of Republican control of the Congress and a conservative majority on
the Supreme Court. From the outset his administration ignored the
suggestions of the moderate conservatives, casting aside international
treaties that they had patiently negotiated concerning weapons control and global warming. The Bush Administration's initial determination to govern in a strong and forceful manner despite its questionable
mandate was strengthened by the terrorist attacks of September 11,
2001, which were interpreted as a major threat and reacted to as such.
As an elite theorist who studies ruling elites in a historical and comparative perspective observed, "When war or the threat of war impinge,"
it is usually the case that the "ruling elite becomes more bellicose and
prone to use force," making appeals to "patriotic, religious, and xeno-
phobic sentiments to mobilize mass support for the reliance on force"
(Higley 2003, p. 25).

Virtually all foreign policy experts, whether liberal hawks, moderate conservatives, or ultraconservatives, supported the retaliatory
attack on Afghanistan and Al Qaeda after 9/11 and the general public accepted the Bush Administration's arguments. But the invasion of
Iraq in March 2003 was undertaken amidst the opposition of moderate
conservatives and without the support of either the United Nations or
the nation's usual Western European allies. More optimistic and inex-
perienced ultraconservative planners at the Pentagon ignored plans
for the occupation worked out by moderate conservatives in the State
Department. Most of these decisions were openly disputed by leading moderate conservatives in debates at the Council on Foreign Relations, which spilled onto the opinion pages of *The New York Times* and
The Washington Post. Nor did the Bush Administration feel any need
to offer the liberal-labor coalition the kinds of concessions on employment and welfare issues that were often made in past wars in the name

of national unity. Except for the need for sixty votes in the Senate to end a filibuster, the ultraconservatives in the corporate community and their Christian Right allies were in complete control of the policy agenda in Washington until independent voters unexpectedly turned against them in 2006 due to the continuing war in Iraq.

With the arrival of the Obama Administration and large Democratic majorities in Congress in 2009, it may be that the moderate conservatives in the corporate community will once again have a pivotal position in the shaping of general policies. With the American military stretched to the limit and the country facing an economic crisis that they fear will last for at least a year or two, it is unlikely that they will side with the ultraconservatives except on issues having to do with the power of organized labor. The more interesting question is whether the Democrats will pass any legislation that is vigorously opposed by the moderate conservatives.

As of early 2009, however, as shown by the historical information in this section, the pluralists and historical institutionalists have been wrong to ignore the importance of the corporate-dominated policy-planning network. This network provides the answer to their major theoretical hesitations concerning a class-domination theory. It also shows that the experts who are important in policy-making are not independent of the corporate community.

APPOINTEES TO GOVERNMENT

The final way to see if and how the power elite has shaped the federal government is to look at the social, educational, and occupational backgrounds of the people who are appointed to important positions in the government. If the power elite are as important as this book claims, such appointees should come disproportionately from the upper class, the corporate community, and the policy-planning network.

There have been numerous studies of top-level governmental appointees under both Republican and Democratic administrations. These studies usually focus on the appointees in the departments that are represented in the president's cabinet, with a special emphasis on the State, Treasury, and Defense departments because they have great power in the areas of most concern to the power elite. These studies are unanimous in their conclusion that most high-level appointees in both Republican and Democratic administrations have been corporate directors or corporate lawyers, and hence members of the power elite. This point holds true through the recent Bush Administration. Moreover, they are often part of the policy-planning network as well, supporting the claim in Chapter 4 that the network plays a central role in preparing members of the power elite for government service (Salzman and Domhoff 1980).

An exhaustive three-volume historical study provides relevant background information on cabinet appointees, diplomats, and Supreme Court Justices from the founding of the country through the Carter Administration (Burch 1980; Burch 1981a; Burch 1981b). It defines the "economic elite" as those who were among the top wealth holders or who sat on the boards of the largest companies of their era, then shows that (1) 96 percent of the cabinet and diplomatic appointees from 1780 to 1861 were members of this economic elite, with a predominance of landowners, merchants, and lawyers; (2) from 1862 to 1933, the figure was 84 percent, with an increasing number of financiers and corporate lawyers; and (3) from 1934 to 1980, the overall percentage was 64, but with only 47 percent during the New Deal. A second large-scale study, which focused on the 205 individuals who served in presidential cabinets between 1897 and 1972, reported that 60 percent were members of the upper class and 78 percent members of the corporate community. There are no differences in the overall percentages for Democrats and Republicans or for the years before and after 1933 (Mintz 1975).

The most systematic study of the factors leading to appointments in the 1960s and 1970s showed that corporate executives who had two or more outside directorships were four times more likely to serve in a federal government advisory position than executives from smaller companies. In addition, the participation of corporate directors in at least one policy group increased their chances of an appointment by a factor of 1.7. An accompanying interview study supported the quantitative findings by showing that chief executive officers often mention participation in a policy group as a qualification for an appointment to government (Useem 1980b; Useem 1984).

Findings on the Reagan, Clinton, and George W. Bush administrations compiled for previous editions of this book are consistent with the earlier studies (Domhoff 1983, pp. 139–141; Domhoff 1998, pp. 251–255; Domhoff 2006, pp. 167–170). They show the same patterns as the earlier studies. For example, the four people who served as secretaries of state for the Clinton and Bush administrations are almost indistinguishable in their credential even though they differ by race and gender, as revealed by the following brief summaries of their corporate and policy-planning network connections.

President Clinton's first secretary of state, Warren Christopher, was a director of Lockheed Martin, Southern California Edison, and First Interstate Bancorp, a trustee of the Carnegie Corporation, a recent vice chair of the Council on Foreign Relations, and officially a corporate lawyer. His second secretary of state, Madeleine Albright, is the daughter of a Czechoslovakian diplomat who immigrated to the United States and became a dean at the University of Denver. Albright married into great wealth, earned a Ph.D. in international relations, raised money for the Democratic Party, and became active in several foreign policy groups in the policy-planning network, including the Council on Foreign Relations.

President Bush's first secretary of state, retired army general Colin Powell, an African-American, made millions after his retirement as a speaker to corporate audiences at $60,000 to $75,000 per appearance. He served as a director of Gulfstream Aerospace until its merger with General Dynamics in 1999, where he earned $1.49 million from stock options in exchange for helping the company sell its corporate jets in Kuwait and Saudi Arabia. He was a director of America Online at the time of his appointment to the State Department, walking away with $8.27 million in stock options. He was also a member of the Council on Foreign Relations at the time (and became one of its trustees after he left the Bush Administration).

The second person to serve as secretary of state in the Bush Administration, Condoleezza Rice, an African-American woman brought up in a middle-class home in Birmingham, Alabama, earned a B.A. and a Ph.D. in international relations from the University of Denver, where she studied with Madeleine Albright's father, joined the faculty at Stanford University in 1981, and received a fellowship from the Council on Foreign Relations in 1986 to work for the Joints Chiefs of Staff at the Pentagon. She served in a secondary position on the National Security Council during the presidency of George H. W. Bush, and then returned to Stanford, where she soon became the second-ranking officer in the university and joined the boards of directors of ChevronTexaco and Transamerica. She is a fellow of the Hoover Institution and a member of the Council on Foreign Relations. She left her administrative role at Stanford in 1999 to become George W. Bush's personal tutor on foreign relations and then served as his National Security Advisor until she was put in charge of the State Department.

Appointees to the Department of the Treasury also have a considerable overlap. President Clinton's first secretary of the treasury, Lloyd Bentsen, inherited millions from his rancher father and founded his own insurance company in Texas. He was succeeded by a Wall Street Democrat, Robert E. Rubin, who at the time was a codirector of Goldman Sachs and a trustee of the Carnegie Corporation; he had a net worth between $50 and $100 million when he was appointed. The Bush Administration's first secretary of the treasury, Paul H. O'Neill, was the recently retired chair of Alcoa and a director of Lucent Technologies. He owned over $50 million in Alcoa stock. He was a member of the Business Council and the Business Roundtable, the chair of the board of trustees at the Rand Corporation, and a trustee of the American Enterprise Institute. The second secretary of treasury, John W. Snow, was the CEO of CSX, a freight transportation company, and a director of Circuit City, Johnson & Johnson, and Verizon. He was a member of the Business Roundtable. The third secretary of the treasury, Henry Paulson, was the chairman of Goldman Sachs and a director of the Business Roundtable.

Both the Clinton and George W. Bush administrations did show greater gender and ethnic diversity than past administrations. Five women and three Latinos served at one point or another in both administrations. There were five African-Americans in the Clinton Cabinet and four in the Bush Cabinet. Clinton appointed the first Asian-American to a cabinet position in the final months of his second term and the Bush Administration retained him in a different cabinet post. President Bush also appointed the first Asian-American woman to the cabinet (see Zweigenhaft and Domhoff 2006, pp. 63–66, 115–117, 157–159, for information on these appointees).

Several of the people of color came from backgrounds similar to those of the white cabinet members. On the Clinton side, the secretary of agriculture, Michael Espy, was an African-American from the Mississippi Delta whose grandfather and father were major landowners and business owners. Clinton's secretary of commerce, Ronald Brown, also an African-American, came from a family that owned a hotel in Harlem; at the time of his appointment he was a lawyer with one of the leading corporate firms in Washington, which paid him $580,000 in 1992 even though he spent most of his time as chairman of the Democratic Party. The former secretary of energy, Hazel O'Leary, is both an African-American and female; she was also the former executive vice president of Northern States Power, a utility company in Minnesota, and the daughter of two physicians. The secretary of housing and urban development, a Mexican-American who had been mayor of San Antonio, was the chair of an investment firm, the head of an air charter company, and a trustee of the Rockefeller Foundation at the time of his appointment.

From the Bush Administration side, Elaine Cho, the secretary of labor for eight years, is the daughter of wealthy Chinese immigrants from Taiwan. She graduated from Mount Holyoke and the Harvard Business School, worked in management for Bank of America and Citigroup, and served as deputy secretary of transportation and then head of the Peace Corps in the George H. W. Bush Administration. She has been on the boards of Clorox, Dole Foods, and Northwest Airlines, and is a fellow of the Heritage Foundation and a member of the Council on Foreign Relations. Carlos M. Gutierrez, President Bush's second secretary of commerce, was born into a wealthy Cuban family that came to the United States when Fidel Castro came to power. He worked his way up from an entry-level position in marketing to the top echelons of the Kellogg Corporation, where he became president in 1998 and CEO in 1999. He was also a director at Colgate-Palmolive.

Norman Mineta served in both the Clinton and the George W. Bush administrations. He is a Japanese-American and former Democratic Congressman who inherited his father's insurance agency in San Jose, where he was elected to the city council and the office of mayor before going to Congress in 1975. He resigned from Congress in 1995 and then worked as a vice president at Lockheed Martin until he joined first the Clinton Administration as secretary of commerce and then the Bush Administration as secretary of transportation.

There were also some differences between the two administrations. President Bush's secretaries of defense had more corporate and policy-planning connections and his attorneys general were far more conservative. Overall, the Bush Administration had more corporate connections. Counting former vice president Dick Cheney in the mix, there were eight former CEOs and 28 former board directors among them. On the other hand, a very large number of Clinton appointees were members of the Council on Foreign Relations, even in positions that had nothing to do with foreign affairs (Domhoff 1998, Table 7.4).

Reflecting the different coalitions that make up the two parties, there were often striking differences between the second-level and third-level appointees in Republican and Democratic administrations in the years between 1932 and 2008. Republicans appointed ultra-conservatives to agencies that they thoroughly disliked, such as the Environmental Protection Agency, the Occupational Safety and Health Administration, the National Highway Traffic Safety Commission, or the Office of Civil Rights. These appointees proceeded to do everything they could to limit the effectiveness of the agencies. Democrats, on the other hand, often placed liberals in the same agencies. The Clinton Administration's lower-level appointments to the Office of the Attorney General, for example, were far more vigorous in using the antitrust laws to challenge monopolistic corporate practices than those of the Reagan and George H. W. Bush Administrations. As an even more dramatic example, the Food and Drug Administration took on the tobacco companies during the Clinton years and won, to the amazement of everyone (Kessler 2000).

IS THE OBAMA ADMINISTRATION DIFFERENT?

Does the Obama Administration fit the historic pattern? Liberals and leftists were disappointed by many of his appointments because they were for the most part centrists with Ivy League educations who had worked in the Clinton Administration, some of them in very high positions. The relief with which many conservatives greeted President Obama's appointments, including two Republicans, one a holdover at the Department of Defense, the other at the Department of Transportation, fits with the idea that President Obama's top appointees are centrist. The modest diversity of the people in the fifteen traditional cabinet positions—ten Euro-Americans (three of whom are women), one Latina,, three Asian-Americans, and one African-American—also suggests a centrist continuity. According to administration publicists, however, the cabinet is more diverse than in the past, but that is because it was expanded to include the UN ambassador, the trade representative, and the chair of the Environmental Protection Agency, which added three more African-Americans (two of them women) to the overall picture.

The administration's foreign policy team believes in American global leadership as much as previous administrations, which it hopes to accomplish through a more cooperative approach, respect for the United Nations, and multilateralism, but it still adds up to a dominant role rather than a mutual one with China, Japan, India, Russia, Brazil, and the nations of Western Europe. The team also believes in overwhelming American military superiority, which may mean increased defense spending even if some highly expensive weapons systems are cancelled (Dreyfuss 2008; Leeman 2008). As for the economic team, several of its members were strong proponents of the financial deregulation and reliance on the market that contributed to the excesses on Wall Street between 1998 and 2008. They played a critical role through their high positions in the Department of Treasury in blocking regulations suggested by concerned officials at a lower rung on the power ladder (Failoa, Nakshima and Drew 2008). Instead, they jettisoned President Clinton's liberally oriented campaign platform and followed a set of financial strategies that brought about prosperity through a stock market bubble, which brought them great acclaim at the time (Baker 2009, chapter 2).

Nevertheless, as the following brief biographies show, the Obama Administration appointees are different from past appointees in two major respects as far as a class-dominance theory is concerned. First, they are far more likely to have spent most of their careers in government service than business; eight have held elective office as governors, senators, or members of the House of Representatives. Second, they are less likely to have served on corporate boards than appointees in previous administrations.

Secretary of State Hillary Rodham Clinton, a graduate of Wellesley and Yale Law School, worked as a lawyer for the largest corporate law firm in Little Rock and served on the board of directors of Wal-Mart for six years while her husband was the governor of Arkansas. After eight years as first lady, she was elected to a senatorial seat from New York. Secretary of Defense Robert M. Gates, a holdover from the Bush Administration, sat on several corporate boards before his appointment, as noted in the previous section. Both of these appointments fit the usual mold, but from this point on the corporate connections become fewer and fewer.

Secretary of the Treasury Timothy Geithner, the son of a Ford Foundation official who worked for several decades as a program officer in Asia, followed his father's path by going to Dartmouth and Johns Hopkins, then went to work as an assistant to President Richard Nixon's former secretary of state, Henry Kissinger, at Kissinger & Associates, a consulting firm that advises corporations and foreign governments. He was a director of policy development at the International Monetary Fund and then worked as an assistant in the U.S. Department of the Treasury during the Clinton Administration after changing his political affiliation from Republican to Independent. In 2002 he joined the Council on Foreign Relations as a senior fellow in international economics and in 2003 he was appointed head of the New York Federal Reserve Bank, where he worked closely with President Bush's secretary of the treasury, Henry Paulson, and the chair of the Federal Reserve Board, Ben Bernanke, on the bailouts in the fall of 2008.

The attorney general, Eric Holder, an African-American, is the son of a real estate broker from Barbados and an Episcopal Church secretary from New York. He received his undergraduate and law degrees at Columbia University in his native New York City, did an internship at the NAACP Legal Defense and Education Fund, and then joined the Justice Department in the late 1970s, rising to the position of deputy attorney general in the Clinton Administration. During the early 2000s he became a partner at a Washington law firm, where he earned $4.6 million in his last two years there, including deferred compensation and a separation payment. He listed his assets at the time of his confirmation hearings at $5.7 million, most of them accumulated during the eight years he practiced corporate law in Washington.

The secretary of commerce, Gary Locke, grew up in Seattle as the son of Chinese-Americans of modest income. He has an undergraduate degree from Yale University and a law degree from Boston University. He was elected to the legislature in the state of Washington in 1982 at age 32 and served as the elected chief executive of King County, which encompasses Seattle, from 1993 to 1997. He then served as governor of the state from 1997 to 2005. After retiring from government office, he joined the Seattle office of an international corporate law firm, where he worked to develop trade relations with Chinese companies. He also joined the board of directors of Safeco, the twenty-third largest insurance company in the United States in 2008.

The secretary of health and human services, Kathleen Sebelius, is the daughter of a former Democratic governor of Ohio and the daughter-in-law of a former Republican member of the House of Representatives from Kansas. With an undergraduate degree from Trinity College in Washington, D.C., and a master's in public administration from the University of Kansas, she served on several commissions in Kansas between 1974 until 1986, at which point she was elected to the Kansas legislature. She was elected state insurance commissioner in 1996 and served until 2002, when she won the governorship of the state and then won reelection in 2006.

The secretary of the interior, Kenneth Salazar, comes from a prominent family of ranchers in Colorado that traces its history back to the Spanish settlers in Santa Fe in the late 1500s. Technically, perhaps, he can be called a Latino, as the Obama Administration identifies him, but his Spanish heritage makes him as much a European descendant as people whose ancestors came from Italy, France, and other European countries many generations ago. After receiving his undergraduate degree from Colorado College, he earned his law degree at the University of Michigan and practiced law for 11 years, specializing in water and environmental issues before going into government service as chief legal council for the governor of Colorado. He returned to private practice in the early 1990s and then was elected attorney general of Colorado in 1998 and 2002. He was elected to the U.S. Senate in 2004.

The secretary of transportation, Ray LaHood, is a centrist Republican from Illinois who had decided to retire in 2008 from the House seat he held for 14 years. After he graduated from Bradley University in 1971, he taught social studies in junior high school for six years before being elected to the Illinois legislature and subsequently serving as chief of staff for a top Republican leader in the House of Representatives.

The secretary of agriculture, Tom Vilsack, is a native of Pennsylvania who moved to Des Moines, his wife's hometown, after earning an undergraduate degree at Hamilton College in upstate New York and a law degree at Albany Law School. He worked as a trial lawyer in Des Moines while starting in politics on a suburban city council, and ended up as the governor of Iowa from 1998 to 2006. At that point he became a partner in a corporate law firm in Des Moines, advising clients in the energy and agribusiness industries, and he became cochair of the Council on Foreign Relations' task force on climate change.

The secretary of housing, Shaun Donovan, graduated from Harvard with a B.A. and an M.A. in public administration and architecture. He worked for a nonprofit developer of affordable housing before taking a position as deputy assistant secretary for multifamily housing in the Clinton Administration. He then did research on housing at New York University and Harvard before working for a brief time as a managing director at Prudential Mortgage Capital Company, where he focused on affordable housing loans. His most recent position was as the head of the Department of Housing Preservation and Development in New York City, where he tried to encourage the creation of affordable housing.

The secretary of veterans affairs, General Erik K. Shinseki, is a retired army general of Japanese-American heritage born in Hawaii. He was almost instantly pushed out of his post as army chief of staff in 2003 by Secretary of Defense Donald Rumsfeld when he dared to tell Congress that it would take far more troops to put down insurgencies after the fighting was over in Iraq than Rumsfeld and his think tank advisors—mostly from the American Enterprise Institute and the Center for Strategic and International Studies—thought necessary. Deeply respected by the soldiers who served under him, his appointment to this position was a powerful repudiation of Rumsfeld's leadership on the war, but it also showed respect for the many contributions Asian-Americans have made in the military services.

The secretary of energy, Steven Chu, is a physicist who shared a Nobel Prize in his field in 1977 for research on supercooled atoms. A graduate of the University of Rochester and the University of California, Berkeley, he served as head of the electronic research laboratory at AT&T's Bell Labs and as chair of the physics department at Stanford before becoming director of the government's Lawrence Labs, which are managed by the University of California, where he brought about greater emphasis on research on energy issues because of his concerns about the climate crisis.

The secretary of homeland security, Janet Napolitano, is a graduate of Santa Clara University in California and the University of Virginia Law School. She was appointed as a U.S. attorney during the Clinton Administration, won office as state attorney general of Arizona in 1998, and became governor of the state in 2003. The secretary of education, Arne Duncan, received his undergraduate degree at Harvard and sits on its board of overseers. He played professional basketball in Australia from 1987 to 1991, and then became director of the Ariel Education Initiative in Chicago, which tries to create better schooling opportunities for low-income children on Chicago's South Side. Financier John P. Rogers, one of President Obama's wealthy African-American financial supporters, created this program. After several years at Ariel Education Initiative, Duncan became director of magnet schools and deputy chief of staff to the chief executive officer of the Chicago school system until 2001, when he took over as the chief executive officer.

The secretary of labor, Hilda Solis, the daughter of Latino immigrants who both belonged to unions, received a B.A. in political science from California State Polytechnic University, Pomona, and a Master of Public Administration degree at the University of Southern California, and worked briefly in Washington for the Office of Hispanic Affairs and the civil rights division of the Office of Management and Budget. She then returned to California to work in a local school district, win election to a community college board of trustees, and receive an appointment to the Los Angeles County Commission on Insurance. She was elected to the California state legislature in 1992 and to the House of Representatives in 2000. She has been strongly supported by organized labor throughout her political career. Susan Rice, an African-American, is the ambassador to the United Nations. She is a graduate of the elite National Cathedral School in Washington, as well as Stanford University and Oxford, where she was a Rhodes Scholar and earned a Ph.D. in international relations. After working as a management consultant for McKinsey & Associates, she became senior director for African affairs at the National Security Council during the Clinton Administration. In the years before her appointment, she was a fellow at the Brookings Institution.

Lisa Jackson, the director of the Environmental Protection Agency, grew up in a low-income African-American neighborhood in New Orleans, graduated from Princeton with a degree in engineering, and worked for many years for the Environmental Protection Agency before becoming head of the state environmental agency in New Jersey. The trade representative, Ron Kirk, graduated from Austin College and the University of Texas Law School, worked for the former Democratic senator from Texas, Lloyd Bentsen, and was elected as the first black mayor of Dallas. More recently he worked for the corporate law firm of Vinson & Elkins, where his clients included Southwest Airlines and the Texas Association of Realtors.

As these brief biographical sketches show, this cabinet group is very different from those of the past in that there are no long-term corporate executives and very few corporate directors. Most of the appointees have careers in government or go back and forth between government and the corporate world. They often have elite educations and an advanced degree, and they have worked with members of the power elite in the policy-planning network. But there is hardly a true interlocking overlapper of the old school among them with the exception of Gates, who may have been replaced at the Department of Defense by the time this book is being read.

Perhaps President Obama's top staff appointments at the White House, who may play as large a role as his cabinet, have more connections to the corporate community. His chief of staff, Rahm Emanuel, who worked after college with a public interest group and then as an aide to elected officials, including six years in the Clinton White House, joined the private sector for a few years in 1998. As a dealmaker in the Chicago office of a Wall Street banking firm, Wasserstein Perella & Co., he brokered several lucrative mergers that earned him $16.2 million, including the merger of two smaller utility firms into Exelon, now the largest utility company in the country (Luo 2008a). In 2002 he left Wasserstein Perella & Co. to run for the House of Representatives from a Chicago district, receiving major campaign backing from the securities and investment industry. Once elected, he quickly became a Democratic leader in the House. He raised campaign contributions from investment and mortgage bankers to help fund moderate Democrats who won House seats in Republican-leaning states in 2006 and 2008.

Valerie Jarrett, the president's friend and fundraiser since the early 1990s, is a key White House adviser with general liaison duties. By the time of her appointment she had become the CEO of a real estate management firm, a director for USG (a Chicago-based building materials company), the vice chair of the board of trustees at the University of Chicago, and a trustee of the Joyce Foundation (the sixty-third largest foundation in 2008, where President Obama served as a trustee a few years earlier). Obama's national security advisor, James L. Jones, a career Marine who served as chief commander of that service, has very hawkish credentials and also has good corporate connections in that after his retirement from the military he became the director of the U.S. Chamber of Commerce's Institute for 21st Century Energy and joined the boards of ChevronTexaco and Boeing (Dreyfuss 2009). The White House legal counsel, Gregory B. Craig, a graduate of Harvard, Cambridge, and Yale Law School, was responsible for President Clinton's defense during his impeachment trial in 1998. Known as a "power lawyer," which is one step beyond a political or corporate lawyer, he became a partner in a corporate law firm in Washington in recent years after many years as a government aide (Stolberg 2009). He has been a supporter of the president since he met him at Vernon Jordan's Obama fundraiser in Washington in 2003 (Silverstein 2006).

The director of the president's Office of Management and Budget, Peter Orszag, received his B.A. in economics from Princeton and his Ph.D. in that subject from the London School of Economics. After serving as an economic adviser in the Clinton Administration, he was a fellow at the Brookings Institution and worked on the Hamilton Project before he became director of the Congressional Budget Office in 2007. Larry Summers, one of the president's main White House economic advisers, has degrees in economics from Harvard and MIT, taught at both those schools, and then received an appointment in the Department of Treasury during the Clinton Administration, where he became secretary of the treasury in 1999. He then served as president of Harvard until he resigned under pressure in 2006. He then took part in the Hamilton Project at the Brookings Institution and worked as a partner in D. E. Shaw, a hedge fund, where he earned $5.2 million in 2008. He also earned $2.7 million in 2008 giving speeches to Wall Street firms.

Carol M. Browner, the White House adviser on environmental policy, who received her undergraduate and law degrees at the University of Florida and headed the Environmental Protection Agency in the Clinton Administration, has consulted with Coca-Cola and Merck about their foreign operations as a member of the Albright Group, a consulting firm founded by former secretary of state Madeleine Albright. She also had a stake in Albright Capital Management, an investment advisory group (Hendrix and Shear 2008; Luo 2008a).

Dennis C. Blair, President Obama's director of national intelligence, served as president of the Institute of Defense Analysis, a nonprofit organization financed in good part by the federal government, after retiring from a 34-year Navy career as a four-star admiral. He sat on several corporate boards while working at the Institute of Defense Analysis.

Taken as a group, a few more of the White House appointees have worked in business or served on corporate boards than those appointed to the cabinet, and three of them have been part of the policy-planning network, but the general pattern is much the same as the cabinet appointees. They have spent more time in government than in the corporate community.

Looking at President Obama's cabinet and staff appointees as a total package, their greater involvement in government is notable. So is the absence of any corporate chieftains. They are thus more of a political elite than a corporate-based elite such as was found in most previous administrations, including the Clinton Administration. When the failures of the Bush Administration, the seriousness of the economic downturn, and the moderate-to-liberal composition of the Democratic delegation in both houses of Congress are added to the picture, it might be that the Obama Administration has more potential for autonomy from the corporate community than any administration since the New Deal, which was in any case hampered by the Southern Democrats' domination of Congress through the control of key committees and the threat of the filibuster.

Putting aside for a moment the 41-member Republican minority in the Senate that might be able to block legislation through the repeated use of filibusters, as it did to a record degree in the 2007–2008 session of Congress, and the moderate-to-conservative Democrats who might join them on some issues, the biggest problem the Obama Administration may face is an internal one. It has to deal with the demands from labor leaders and organizers who want more government support for union organizing as well as more employment opportunities and a strengthening of the social safety net. They backed the Obama-Biden ticket strongly and they may have made the difference in Indiana, Ohio, and Pennsylvania, where meetings at union halls and door-to-door visits with white union members helped to overcome any white reluctance to vote for an African-American candidate.

But a political elite rooted in the Ivy League and other elite educational institutions may balk at providing a bigger and better power base for the 73 percent of adults over the age of 25 who do not have a four-year college degree and work at blue-collar and white-collar jobs for wages that are not keeping up with inflation. This conflict between the Obama political elite and workers without college degrees may be especially the case on issues where members of the corporate community, Democratic and Republican alike, will oppose any government support for organized labor as strongly as they can. To gain perspective on just how intensive the class conflict over this issue will be, this chapter takes a look at labor history in the twentieth century after an analysis of Supreme Court appointments and the role the justices play in relation to the corporate community.

SUPREME COURT APPOINTMENTS

The Supreme Court has a unique role in the American system of governance. As the final arbiter in major disputes, it has been imbued with a mystique of reverence that makes it the backstop for the American power elite. While its members are to some extent constrained by legal precedent, there is in fact a fair degree of discretion in what they decide, as seen in the numerous "great reversals" of opinion down through the years (Ernst 1973). Such reversals have occurred most dramatically on the issue of rights for African-Americans. Then, too, a switch in votes in 1937 by two members of the court legitimated crucial legislation having to do with union recognition, discussed in the next section (Cortner 1964). More recently, the independent power of the Supreme Court was on display for all Americans in the 2000 elections: A highly conservative court that preached against "judicial activism" and emphasized states' rights nonetheless overrode the Florida Supreme Court and found a way to stop the counting of uncounted votes that might have tipped the presidential election to the Democrats. As constitutional scholars argued vociferously about the legal reasoning behind the court's majority, the Democratic Party and most ordinary Americans quietly accepted the decision.

As the court's prevention of the Florida recount shows, Supreme Court appointees and deference to their decisions do matter, which is yet another reason why the power elite work so hard to win elections.

As standard sources conclude from an examination of Supreme Court appointments, virtually all appointees have shared the ideological and political views of the presidents who appointed them, although some appointees have surprised those who appointed them by being more liberal than the Republican president expected or more conservative than the Democratic president expected. Still, the Supreme Court has reflected the range of acceptable opinion within the corporate community on the issues of concern to it (Baum 1998; Carp and Stidham 1998). The appointees are also primarily from the upper and upper-middle classes and an "inordinate number had served as corporate attorneys before their appointments" (Carp and Stidham 1998, p. 217). In addition, they also tend to have attended elite law schools, to have abandoned the practice of corporate law for lower-level judicial appointments or professorships at prestigious law schools, and to have been active in a political party. Once they are nominated for the court, they are subject to strong scrutiny by leaders of the American Bar Association and confirmation by the Senate.

The current court reflects most of these generalities. Five are graduates of Harvard Law School, including four Republican appointments, two are from Yale Law School, and one is from Columbia Law School. The justice most clearly from the upper class, John Paul Stevens, a corporate lawyer appointed by President Gerald Ford, received his law degree at Northwestern after doing his undergraduate work at the University of Chicago. Most of the current court members had corporate law experience, with two exceptions. The one female justice on the court, Ruth Bader Ginsburg, found it difficult to find a position in a law firm despite her high class ranking upon graduation from Columbia. President Bush's 2007 appointment, Samuel Alito, Jr., spent his entire career working as a United States attorney (including positions in President Reagan's Department of Justice from 1981 to 1987) before he became a judge on the Court of Appeals in 1990. Five of the nine are millionaires, including the two Clinton appointees, Ginsburg and Stephen Breyer. Some inherited their wealth, some married into wealth, and others acquired wealth from their corporate law practices.

Three of the nonmillionaires, Antonin Scalia, Clarence Thomas, and Alito, are also the most conservative justices. Scalia worked for a corporate law firm for six years after graduation from Harvard, then became a law professor. Thomas's work experience after graduation from Yale included two years as a corporate attorney for Monsanto Chemical Company followed by two years as a legislative assistant to the millionaire Republican Senator from Missouri, John C. Danforth, who later urged Thomas's appointment to the Supreme Court as the African-American replacement for the first African-American ever appointed to the Supreme Court, civil rights lawyer Thurgood Marshall.

The fourth nonmillionaire, Anthony M. Kennedy, is the son of a corporate lawyer, a graduate of Harvard Law School, and a corporate lawyer before he became a judge. He became the swing vote on the court after Sandra Day O'Connor retired in 2005, voting with the ultra-conservatives on most issues, but with the moderates and liberals on others: In the 2007–2008 term he sided with the ultraconservatives on abortion, civil rights, and employment and with the moderates and liberals on the death penalty and treatment of detainees at Guantanamo (Toobin 2008, p. 401).

As the swing votes by Justice Kennedy imply, the biggest differences between the two wings of the court concern volatile social issues. Women's reproductive rights, affirmative action, civil liberties, and the separation between church and state are the main targets of the ultraconservatives on the court. There is much less disagreement among liberals, moderate conservatives, and ultraconservatives on issues of concern to the corporate community. On these issues, court opinions can be seen as the best rationales that can be constructed for the defense of the corporate economic system. Moreover, the court has become even more pro-corporate over the past 20 years on issues concerning shareholder suits against corporate management, antitrust challenges to mergers, lawsuits alleging securities fraud, product-liability lawsuits, and large punitive-damage awards by juries (Rosen 2008).

During this period a new National Chamber Litigation Center at the U.S. Chamber of Commerce has entered the fray by preparing briefs on business-related cases and trying to pressure both parties to appoint pro-business judges. The Chamber's center gave its hearty support to both of President Clinton's appointees because of their sympathy for the business viewpoint on most issues. The new chief justice appointed by President Bush in 2005, John G. Roberts, was "the go-to lawyer for the business community" in the years before his appointment, partly because of briefs he wrote for the Chamber's legal center in 2001 and 2002 (see Rosen 2008, for an excellent analysis and recent court history that also explains how work by conservative economists came to influence legal decisions).

Although the Supreme Court defends corporate interests, it also has protected and expanded individual freedoms by taking an expansive view of the Bill of Rights, thereby solidifying the right to privacy and the protection of freedom of speech. It also has made decisions that ensure the freedom of the press and insisted that states must obey all provisions of the Bill of Rights, which many states had ignored in the past. In short, the Supreme Court has stood for both corporate power and individual rights. At the same time, it has been narrowly divided over the same few social issues that have divided liberals and conservatives in the society in general.

THE GREAT EXCEPTION: LABOR POLICY

An overview of American labor relations in the twentieth century provides an indication of what wage and salary workers will face even with the Obama Administration in office. It also provides a context to explain the biggest setback the corporate community ever suffered in the legislative area, the National Labor Relations Act of 1935. This defeat is often cited by pluralists and historical institutionalists as strong evidence against a class-dominance theory. In addition, the story of how the corporate community gradually overcame this defeat is very instructive for understanding the full scope of corporate domination in the United States.

Labor Relations and Union Organizing

The National Labor Relations Act affirmed the right of workers to organize unions and placed government sanctions behind any illegal attempts to interfere with this right ("unfair labor practices"). At the time, it seemed like the most liberal legislation ever passed, destined to create a powerful union movement in the United States. Since that didn't happen, it may appear irrelevant to discuss an act that seems like ancient history, but the limitations of the act as it was originally passed, along with its subsequent dismantling, help to explain why the liberal-labor coalition is so weak and why the income distribution is more unequal in the United States than in other advanced capitalist democracies.

In a saga with many twists and turns, the first surprise is that all of the precedents for this legislation were created or accepted by moderate conservatives in the early years of the twentieth century. In 1900 they founded the first policy-discussion group, the National Civic Federation, to meet with the leaders of the few unions that existed to see if the violence and volatility of American labor relations in the previous 23 years could be reduced (Domhoff 1990, chapter 4; Weinstein 1968). The new federation, with the help of hired experts, evolved the idea of *collective bargaining*, meaning voluntary meetings between representatives of business and labor to try to come to agreement on matters concerning wages, hours, and working conditions. Although the idea sounds simple, it is actually a complex power relationship that embodies the strengths and weaknesses of both sides. Its narrowness shows the power of corporate leaders to push aside the larger changes that many workers had demanded earlier, including a voice in the production process. Its existence reveals the power of workers through strikes and work stoppages to force corporate leaders to talk with them as a group, which corporate leaders previously had refused to do (Ramirez 1978).

Still, the unionism the corporate leaders were willing to support was a limited one, focused almost exclusively on skilled or craft workers, with no provision for unskilled workers in mass-production industries. Furthermore, they wanted to deal with each craft union separately, and they insisted that collective bargaining be voluntary. Government appointees or special committees sometimes could be called in to mediate, but they could not mandate. This kind of arrangement was given its first serious trial during World War I, when the necessity of regimenting the economy also allowed for a temporary governmental labor mediation board, and it worked well enough. Labor sympathizers were hopeful about the post–World War I era.

But the 1920s were a time of corporate ascendancy and union failure in the midst of a growing economy as the corporate community resorted to a wide range of union-busting strategies based on intimidation and violence. Even the small union movement that had survived in the building trades, coal mining, and garment making seemed on its way to extinction. But the stock market crash in October 1929, which gradually developed into the Great Depression, changed everything. When the Senate unexpectedly passed a bill early in 1933 establishing a 30-hour week at the same weekly pay rate, desperate corporate leaders decided that they had to create a new government regulatory agency, the National Recovery Administration, as an alternative. They believed this agency could help restart the economy by bringing business leaders together to set minimum wages, minimum prices, and maximum levels of productive output. The hope was that the elimination of wage cutting and overproduction, which produced cutthroat competition and a vicious downward spiral in wages and profits, would allow for the reemployment of workers and an increase in purchasing power (Domhoff 1996, chapter 4; Levine 1988).

As one seemingly small part of this plan, there was a clause stating that workers had the right to organize into unions for the purposes of collective bargaining. It was insisted upon by labor leaders as their price for supporting the unprecedented powers the plan would hand to corporate leaders to change the nature of market relations. Although many corporate executives balked, especially those in the National Association of Manufacturers, the weakened labor movement still had the potential to disrupt an already struggling economic system through strikes. It also had the sympathy of many of the Northern Democrats who were first elected in 1930 and 1932, sweeping 21 Republicans out of the Senate and 143 out of the House, which provided the Democrats with a 60–35 majority in the Senate and a 310–117 majority in the House, where they also could count on votes from five Farmer-Labor Party members.

Under these circumstances, the moderate conservatives in the corporate community decided to accept the amendment, which they knew they could not defeat in any case. They saw it as a goodwill gesture toward weak union leaders. They thought *Section 7a*, as the commitment to collective bargaining came to be known, would solidify union support for the act and cause no real problems because there was no enforcement power behind it. They also figured they could fall back on their *employee representation plans*, that is, in-plant consultation groups elected by employees to meet with management on a regular basis to discuss working conditions and other concerns. The several Rockefeller-owned oil corporations and their allies, which were among the biggest and most powerful corporations of that era, had championed this alternative to unions since 1916–1917, installing them shortly after they experienced violent labor battles that led to deaths and property destruction in their antiunion facilities (Gitelman 1988). With the passage of the National Industrial Recovery Act, hundreds of companies that previously had not needed such a plan quickly installed one. But in another unanticipated twist of fate, Section 7a turned out to provide an opening for union mobilization that could not be contained.

The National Recovery Administration was a complete failure because it did not contribute to the recovery and even hampered it in some ways, but Section 7a had an electrifying effect on workers and union organizers. They interpreted it to mean that "the president of the United States wants you to join a union." Within weeks there were strikes and protests in hundreds of locations across the country, with workers demanding the right to join unions of their own choosing. In the midst of this upheaval, surprised corporate leaders from General Electric and Standard Oil of New Jersey (now the core of ExxonMobil) suggested a reincarnation of the wartime mediating board. Then their real troubles began. They had hoped the new National Labor Board would be able to put an end to the disruption, but the simple fact of its existence, as a seeming fulfillment of Section 7a, generated even more labor militancy and a political crisis that the corporate community could not control (McQuaid 1979; McQuaid 1982).

The new labor board consisted of three corporate leaders, three union leaders, and a Democratic senator from New York, Robert F. Wagner, who within a year would surprise the corporate leaders by sponsoring a strong version of the National Labor Relations Act that they vigorously opposed. Ironically, corporate leaders had suggested Senator Wagner as the ideal leader for the board because he was supportive of policy suggestions from moderate-conservative think tanks and at the same time enjoyed the trust of labor leaders (Huthmacher 1968). The board developed a set of rules for bringing business and labor into collective bargaining, including the idea that a union should be recognized if a majority of workers in a factory voted in favor of having it represent them. Members of the board then met with both sides of the dispute to see if they could mediate, but they had no enforcement power.

The labor board had some success in is first few months, in part because it was dealing primarily with small companies that did not have the collective strength to resist. Coal miners and garment workers especially benefited. However, large companies, notably in mass-production industries, began to defy the board's authority as the economy improved. Moreover, union leaders on the board insisted that there should not be more than one union representing workers in each company, which they had not demanded in the past. The corporate moderates resisted this step. They did not want to risk the possibility that most American workers would be organized into inclusive unions that might eventually provide a challenge to corporate power inside and outside the workplace.

Put another way, the idea of collective bargaining was acceptable to the moderate conservatives in the corporate community if it was voluntary, encompassed a few separate craft unions, and allowed plenty of leeway for their employee representation plans to hold on to some workers, which meant in practice that the corporations could divide and conquer. But they continued to bitterly oppose collective bargaining if it was mandated by law and had the potential to unite craft and industrial workers. When Senator Wagner and several liberal Democrats suggested that majority rule should be made into law, and that fines should be levied against those who refused to follow governmentally sanctioned rules that spelled out "good-faith" collective bargaining, the corporate leaders serving on the board turned against it. In addition, many corporations fired union organizers, hired "detectives" to break up strikes, stockpiled weapons and dynamite, and in a few cases made contact with right-wing vigilante groups (Auerbach 1966).

Meanwhile, Senator Wagner's staff and the lawyers working for the National Labor Relations Board, a few of them experienced corporate lawyers who had become liberals, introduced new legislation that would embody and strengthen the practices that they had worked out through experience over the past two years (Gross 1974). The new board would consist of three impartial experts appointed by the president. Instead of trying to mediate, the new board would serve as a mini–Supreme Court for labor disputes. It would have the power to determine whether or not corporations had used illegal means to impede unionization, such as firing or attacking striking workers, and would also have the power to administer fines and to enforce its rulings through the courts.

Deeply disturbed by this unanticipated turn of events, the corporate community mounted a very large lobbying campaign against the proposed National Labor Relations Board. In return, the Senate's Committee on Civil Liberties subpoenaed the papers of the corporate groups coordinating this effort as part of an investigation into anti-union activities. To the great embarrassment of the corporate community, the details of their lobbying plans, including the plans some of them had for violence against union organizers, became known shortly after the legislation passed (Auerbach 1966).

Although there was a large Democratic majority in Congress at this juncture due to Roosevelt's great popularity, and labor unions were gearing up for another big organizing drive after the 1936 elections, these facts do not fully explain why the act passed by a large majority in both the House and Senate in the summer of 1935. They are not sufficient because Southern Democrats controlled the congressional levers of power. Moreover, President Roosevelt was reluctant to oppose the Southerners because they were long-time allies and personal friends who had been among his major supporters when he won the presidential nomination in 1932. In addition, their cooperation was necessary to pass any future legislation he might find essential to nurture the economic recovery. Southern Democrats and their moderate Democratic allies therefore could have sided with the handful of Republicans remaining in the Congress to weaken or block the legislation.

Instead, the Southern Democrats sided with the liberal Democrats. This unusual agreement on a labor issue was possible due to a simple expedient: the exclusion of agricultural and domestic workers from the protection of the act. The exclusion of agricultural workers also made it easier for the Progressive Republicans from the predominantly agrarian states of the Midwest and Great Plains to support the legislation, leaving the employers of northern industrial labor almost completely isolated. In short, the corporate community was isolated from both the plantation capitalists in the South, represented by Southern Democrats, and the farmers of the Midwest and Great Plains, represented by Progressive Republicans.

This compromise was fully understood at the time for the power deal that it was. When the leader of the Socialist Party wrote Senator Wagner to ask why agricultural workers had been excluded from the bill, he replied that he was "very regretful of this," but that they had not been included "because I thought it better to pass the bill for the benefit of industrial workers than not to pass it at all, and the inclusion of agricultural workers would lessen the likelihood of passage so much as not to be desirable" (Domhoff 1990, p. 98).

Further evidence for the pivotal role of the Southern Democrats in this defeat for the corporate community is revealed by the events that unfolded after the legislation passed. Due to disruptive sit-down strikes throughout the North in 1937, along with attempts to create racially integrated industrial unions in some parts of the South, the Southern Democrats turned against the act, doing everything they could to undermine it throughout the years leading up to World War II. When Republicans gained control of Congress for a two-year period in 1946, the Southerners joined with them in passing a package of conservative amendments (called the Taft-Hartley Act) that put severe limitations on the ability of union leaders to organize more workers (Gross 1981). When the liberal-labor coalition helped elect a Democratic Congress and president in 1948, it argued that the Democrats should remove the conservative amendments because of their contribution to the victory. But the Southern Democrats joined with the Republican minority to block any changes.

Unions lost more ground to the conservative voting bloc through further legislative changes and National Labor Relations Board rulings in 1959, 1961, and 1967. Then their attempt to make improvements in the laws relating to union organizing were defeated in 1978 by a filibuster in the Senate, a final blow from which the unions never recovered because the corporate community already had taken the turn to the right described briefly in Chapter 4 (Gross 1995). In effect, the history of union-related legislation since 1935 is as follows: During the New Deal the union leaders conceded the right to regulate methods of union organizing to the federal government in exchange for governmentally protected rights, but then those rights were taken away by a series of legislative amendments, negative rulings by the National Labor Relations Board, and court decisions (McCammon 1990; McCammon 1993; McCammon 1994; McCammon and Kane 1997).

Although the fact remains that the corporate community lost on the National Labor Relations Act, the loss was due to intra-class differences as well as class conflict, which is what critics of class-dominance theory often overlook. Moreover, the aftermath of this defeat provides strong evidence for corporate dominance of the federal government when all parts of the corporate community are united. In 2009, it is clear that the corporate community North and South is united on labor issues.

As Congress convened in January 2009, union-sponsored legislation was on the agenda once again. Unions played a very large role in President Obama's victory in industrial states, just as they did for President Harry Truman in 1948. They also provided financial support and campaign workers to Democrats running for Congress. Now organized labor wants a law, the Employee Free Choice Act, which would give workers the right to express their desire for a union through signing a card to that effect (Greenhouse 2008). If a majority of workers in the company signed such a card, employers would be required to recognize the union and bargain with it in good faith. As a senator,

President Obama voted to bring the bill to the floor of the Senate in 2007, but a Republican filibuster blocked that effort. He also expressed his support for the Employee Free Choice Act during his presidential campaign. In January 2009, he told *The Washington Post* editors in a wide-ranging interview that he still supported the act, but he also said, in what may have been a straw in the wind, "there may be other ways to achieve the same goal without angering businesses" (Shear 2009, p. 1). Specifically, he told the *Post* editors: "If we're losing half a million jobs a month, then there are no jobs to unionize, so my focus first is on those key economic priority items I just mentioned," he said. "Let's see what the legislative docket looks like" (Shear 2009, p. 1).

In anticipation of a congressional vote on the bill in 2009, the corporate community launched a multimillion-dollar media campaign through new organizations with names such as Workplace Fairness Institute and Coalition for a Democratic Workplace, wrongly claiming that the legislation would take away workers' right to vote for or against unionization through use of a secret ballot. (In fact, it is management that has the right to call for an election, and it often delays elections for as long as it can while it cajoles and threatens workers who might be thinking about voting in favor of the union.) The president of the National Association of Manufacturers, a former Republican governor of Michigan, warned that the unionization of Wal-Mart's 1.4 million workers alone would add over $50 million in union dues, part of which would be used to support pro-labor Democratic candidates (Greenhouse 2009). "We like driving the car," the CEO of Wal-Mart told stock market analysts in October, 2008, "and we're not going to give the steering wheel to anybody but us" (Kaplan 2009, p. 10).

Will the Obama Administration encourage congressional leaders to pass the Employee Free Choice Act or will it find a way to delay any decision, as some political analysts speculate it might (Greenhouse 2008)? If the bill comes before the Senate, will Democrats work to overcome a likely filibuster by the ultraconservative Republican senators? The outcome of this conflict will provide a clear test of the intentions and resolve of the Democratic Party when it comes to its labor allies. Readers may already know the answers to these questions by the time they read this book.

WHY DO BUSINESS LEADERS FEEL POWERLESS?

Despite the strong *Who governs?* and *Who wins?* evidence that the power elite have great power over the federal government on the issues of concern to them, many corporate leaders feel they are relatively powerless in the face of government. To hear them tell it, the Congress is more responsive to organized labor, environmentalists, and consumers than it is to them. They also claim to be harassed by willful and arrogant bureaucrats who encroach upon the rightful preserves of the private sector, sapping them of their confidence and making them hesitant to invest their capital.

A journalist and political scientist documented these sentiments when they had the opportunity to observe a series of meetings at the Conference Board in the early 1970s in which the social responsibilities of business were being discussed. The men at these meetings were convinced that government listened to everybody but them. Government was seen as responsive to the immediate preferences of the majority of citizens. "The have-nots are gaining steadily more political power to distribute the wealth downward," complained one executive. "The masses have turned to a larger government." Some even wondered whether democracy and capitalism are compatible. "Can we still afford one man, one vote? We are tumbling on the brink," said one. "One man, one vote has undermined the power of business in all capitalist countries since World War II," announced another. "The loss of the rural vote weakens conservatives" (Silk and Vogel 1976, pp. 50, 75).

The fear corporate leaders express of the democratic majority leads them to view mild recessions as a saving grace, because they help to keep the expectations of workers in check. Workers who fear for their jobs are less likely to demand higher wages or government social programs. For example, different corporate executives made the following comments:

> "This recession will bring about the healthy respect for economic values that the Great Depression did."
>
> "People need to recognize that a job is the most important thing they can have. We should use this recession to get the public to better understand how our economic system works. Social goals are OK, provided the public is aware of their costs."
>
> "It would be better if the recession were allowed to weaken more than it will, so that we would have a sense of sobriety" (Silk and Vogel 1976, p. 64).

The negative feelings these corporate leaders have toward government are not a new development in the corporate community. A study of business leaders' views in the nineteenth century found that they believed political leaders to be "stupid" and "empty" people who go into politics only to earn a living. As for the ordinary voters, they are "brutal, selfish and ignorant." A comment written by a businessman in 1886 could have been made at the meetings just discussed: "In this good, democratic country where every man is allowed to vote, the intelligence and the property of the country is at the mercy of the ignorant, idle and vicious" (Silk and Vogel 1976, p. 193). Even in the 1920s, when everyone agrees that business was at the zenith of its powers, corporate leaders sang the same tune (Prothro 1954). These complaints undercut the claims by pluralists and historical institutionalists that business hostility toward government stems largely from the growth of effective government programs during the New Deal.

Although pluralists and historical institutionalists sometimes take these expressions of impotence as evidence for their claim that business leaders do not have sufficient power to be called a dominant class, the emotional expressions of businesspeople about their lack of power cannot be taken seriously as power indicators. The investigation of power concerns actions and their consequences, which are in the realm of sociology, economics, and politics, not in the realm of subjective feelings. Still, it is worthwhile to try to understand why corporate leaders complain about a government they have dominated up to this point. There are three intertwined aspects to the answer.

First of all, complaining about government is a useful power strategy, a form of action in itself. It puts government officials on the defensive and forces them to keep proving that they are friendly to business so that corporate leaders will not lose "confidence" in economic conditions and stop investing. A political scientist makes this point:

> Whether the issue is understood explicitly, intuitively, or not at all, denunciations serve to establish and maintain the subservience of government units to the business constituencies to which they are actually held responsible. Attacks upon government in general place continuing pressure on governmental officers to accommodate their activities to the groups from which support is most reliable (McConnell 1966, p. 294).

There also seems to be an ideological level to the corporate stance toward government, which is based in a fear of the populist, democratic ideology that underlies American government due to the Revolutionary War period, as discussed in Chapter 1. Since power is in theory in the hands of all the people, there is always the possibility that some day "the people," in the sense of the majority, will make the government into the pluralist democracy it is supposed to be. In the American historical context, the great power of the dominant class is illegitimate, and the existence of such power is vigorously denied (Vogel 1978).

The most powerful reason for this fear of popular control is revealed by the corporate community's unending battle with unions, as described throughout this book. It is an issue-area like no other in evoking angry rhetoric and near-perfect unity among corporate leaders. It has generated more violence than any other issue except civil rights for African-Americans. The uniqueness of the corporate community's reaction to any government help for unions supports the claim made in the introductory chapter that the corporate community, small businesses, and the growth coalitions are antigovernment in good part because they fear government as the only institution that could challenge corporate control of labor markets, thereby changing the functioning of the system to some extent and reducing the power of employers. The federal government can influence labor markets in five basic ways:

1. The government can hire unemployed workers to do necessary work relating to parks, schools, roadways, and the environment. Such government programs were a great success during the New Deal when unemployment reached 25 percent and social disruption seemed imminent, but they were quickly shut down at the insistence of business leaders when order was restored and the economy began to improve (Piven and Cloward 1971/1993; Rose 1994). It will be interesting to see if such programs suffer a similar quick demise if they are instituted to deal with the current economic crisis.

2. It can support the right to organize unions and bargain collectively, as it did when it passed the National Labor Relations Act in 1935. This kind of government initiative is opposed even more strongly than government jobs for the unemployed because it would give workers a sustained organizational base for moving into the political arena.

3. Although the power elite appreciate the value of old-age, disability, and unemployment insurance, they worry that politicians might allow these programs to become too generous. In fact, these programs expanded in response to the turmoil of the 1960s and 1970s to the point where the Reagan Administration felt it necessary to cut them back in order to reduce inflation and make corporations more profitable (Piven and Cloward 1982).

4. The government can tighten labor markets by limiting immigration. The immigration of low-wage labor has been essential to the corporate community throughout American history. When conservative Republicans began to think about passing anti-immigration legislation in the mid-1990s and in recent years, as called for in their campaign rhetoric, they were met with a barrage of employer opposition, particularly from leaders in agribusiness, and quickly retreated both times.

5. Government can reduce unemployment and tighten labor markets by raising interest rates through the operations of the Federal Reserve System. This fact has been made obvious to a large percentage of the public by the way in which the Federal Reserve increases unemployment by increasing the interest rates whenever the unemployment rate dips too low. Although the issue is cast in terms of "inflation," in fact the economics of inflation are often the politics of labor markets.

Due to the many ways in which the government could tighten labor markets, and thereby increase the economic power of American workers and reduce corporate profits, it is clear once again that structural economic power is not enough to sustain corporate dominance of the economy. It is understandable that the corporate community would be fearful of the government it dominated as of the end of the Bush Administration.

THE LIMITS OF CORPORATE DOMINATION

Involvement in government is the final and most visible aspect of corporate domination, which has its roots in the class structure, control of the investment function, and the operation of the policy-planning network. If government officials did not have to wait on corporate leaders to decide when and where there will be financial investment, and if government officials were not further limited by the general public's acceptance of policy recommendations from the policy-planning network, then power elite involvement in elections and government would have counted for a lot less than they have up until this point. This analysis is supported by the way in which corporate dominance was called into question by the collapse of the financial system during the summer and fall of 2008. The need for government bailouts and the economic anxieties of a restive electorate played a big role in the replacement of the corporate–Christian Right coalition housed in the Republican Party with the corporate moderate-liberal-labor-minority coalition that formed within the Democratic Party.

Domination by the power elite does not negate the reality of continuing conflict over government policies, but few twentieth-century conflicts, as shown in this chapter, involved liberal-labor challenges to the rules that create privileges for the upper class and the corporate community. Most of the numerous battles within the interest-group process, for example, were only over specific spoils and favors; they often involved disagreements between competing business interests.

Similarly, conflicts within the policy-making process usually concerned differences between the moderate conservatives and ultraconservatives in the power elite. Many issues that at first appeared to be legislative defeats for the corporate community turned out to be situations where the moderate conservatives decided for their own reasons to side with the liberal-labor coalition in times of disruption. At other times the policy disagreements involved issues where the needs of the corporate community as a whole came into conflict with the needs of specific industries, which is what happened on trade policies and also on some environmental legislation.

The single most consequential loss for the corporate community, the National Labor Relations Act of 1935, played a role in creating a strong labor movement in the North over the next four decades. This loss occurred in a context of great labor militancy and a willingness on the part of Southern plantation capitalists to side with liberal Democrats in exchange for the exclusion of their own labor force. The defeat, although tempered by later legislation, had a major effect on the nature of the American power structure. It suggests that limits can be placed on corporate power under some conditions. As these paragraphs are being written in early 2009, it is an open question as to whether new constraints of a more extensive and enduring nature will emerge from the present economic crisis. This issue is discussed further in the final chapter. But first the findings and conclusions up to this point are put into a larger theoretical and historical context in the next chapter.

8

The Big Picture

The introductory chapter began with two seeming paradoxes. How can the owners and managers of highly competitive corporations develop the policy unity to shape government policies? And how can large corporations have such great power in a democratic country? The step-by-step argument and evidence presented in previous chapters provide the foundation for a theory that can explain these paradoxes—a *class-domination theory of power* in the United States.

Domination means that the commands of a group or class are carried out with relatively little resistance, which is possible because that group or class has been able to establish the rules and customs through which everyday life is conducted. Domination, in other words, is the institutionalized outcome of great distributive power ("power over"). The upper class of owners and high-level executives, based in the corporate community, is a dominant class in terms of this definition because the cumulative effect of its various distributive powers leads to a situation where most Americans generally accept its policies. The routinized ways of acting in the United States follow from the rules and regulations needed by the corporate community to continue to grow and make profits.

The overall distributive power of the dominant class is first of all based in its structural economic power, which falls to it by virtue of being owners and high-level executives in corporations that sell goods and services for a profit in a market economy. The power to invest or not invest, and to hire and fire employees, leads to a political context where elected officials try to do as much as they can to create a favorable investment climate to avoid being voted out of office in the event of an economic downturn. This structural power is augmented by the ability to create new policies through a complex policy-planning network, which it was possible to institutionalize over many decades because common economic interests and social cohesion give the corporate community enough unity to sustain such an endeavor.

But even these powers might not have been enough to generate a system of extreme class domination if the bargains and compromises embodied in the Constitution had not led unexpectedly to a two-party system in which one party was controlled by the Northern rich and the other by the Southern rich. This in turn reinforced a personality-oriented candidate-selection process that is heavily dependent on large campaign donations—now and in the past as well. The system of party primaries is the one adaptation to this constrictive two-party system that has provided some openings for insurgent liberals and trade unionists.

Structural economic power and control of the two parties, along with the elaboration of an opinion-shaping network, resulted in a polity where there is little or no organized public opinion on specific legislative issues that is independent of the limits and obfuscations created by debates within the power elite itself. Opponents of corporate domination could not create an organizational base from which they could advocate a more egalitarian economic system and until recently there were no openings within the political system that would make it possible for them to carry an alternative message to government.

Finally, the fragmented and constrained system of government carefully crafted by the Founding Fathers led to a relatively small federal government that is easily entered and influenced by wealthy and well-organized private citizens, whether through Congress, the separate departments of the executive branch, or a myriad of regulatory agencies. The net result is that the owners and managers of large income-producing properties have very high scores on all three power indicators: *who benefits, who governs,* and *who wins.* They have a greater proportion of wealth and income than their counterparts in any other capitalist democracy, and through the power elite they are vastly over-represented in key government positions and decision-making groups. They win far more often than they lose on those issues that make it to the government for legislative consideration, although their lack of unity in the face of worker militancy in the 1930s made it possible for organized workers to have far more independence, income, and power for the next 40 years than they ever had before or since.

Despite their lack of power, many Americans feel a sense of empowerment because they have religious freedom, free speech, the right to vote, and the hope that they can make more money or rise in the class structure if they try hard enough. Those with educational credentials and/or secure employment still experience a degree of dignity and respect because there is no tradition of public degradation for those of average or low incomes. Then, too, liberals and leftists retain hope because they had success in expanding individual rights and freedom—for women, for people of color, and most recently for gays and lesbians. But individual rights and freedoms do not necessarily add up to distributive power. In the same time period between 1965 and 2000 when individual rights and freedoms expanded, corporate power also became greater because unions were decimated, the Civil Rights Movement dissipated, and the liberal-labor coalition splintered. This analysis suggests class domination actually increased in recent decades despite a widening of individual freedom and the right to vote. The many social scientists who seem to equate individual rights and freedom with power, which is perhaps especially true of most economists and many pluralists in political science, are wrong to claim that there cannot possibly be class domination in a society based on classical liberal values.

A CRITIQUE OF ALTERNATIVE THEORIES

It is now possible to assess the three alternative theories sketched out in the introductory chapter—pluralism, historical institutionalism, and elite theory—in the light of the empirical findings and arguments presented throughout this book. Pluralists put great weight on the power of public opinion to influence elected officials, but there are few voluntary associations where it is even considered proper to discuss political issues and thereby formulate any group opinions. Furthermore, the evidence pluralists present for the influence of public opinion is almost entirely correlational, which means that it can tell us nothing about causality. Pluralist claims based on correlations overlook the role of the opinion-shaping network (outlined in Chapter 5) as well as the fact that the public's liberal preferences on a wide range of economic programs—government employment of the unemployed, government-supported health insurance, a higher minimum wage—never have been fulfilled.

The additional pluralist claim that voting in elections has a major influence on legislation is based in good part on theoretical arguments and the experience of other countries, not evidence about elections in the United States. It does not take into account the several factors shown in Chapter 6 to dilute this potential influence. In particular, it ignores the way in which a two-party system leads candidates to blur policy differences as they try to win the centrist voters, leaving elected officials relatively free to say one thing in the campaign and do another once in office. It also downplays the major role of the Southern rich in the Democratic Party until very recently, as well as the veto power of the conservative voting bloc in Congress, which is currently exercised through minority Republican filibusters in the Senate.

The pluralist idea that corporate owners and managers are too divided among themselves to dominate government is refuted by the evidence presented in Chapter 3 for the assimilation of corporate managers into the upper class through a wide range of social occasions and economic incentives. Their claim that corporations are only organized into narrow interest groups that argue among themselves misses the high degree of unity generated through common ownership, interlocking directorships, and participation in the policy-planning network outlined in Chapter 4.

The most recent statement of pluralism suggests a *new liberalism* has arisen in which citizen's lobbies, meaning various nonprofit and voluntary groups, proliferate (Berry 1999). This neopluralist view puts great emphasis on the battles between liberals and the Christian Right over cultural values, noting that the liberals often win, but this type of liberal success is irrelevant in analyzing corporate power. The new version of pluralism grants that major foundations, especially the Ford Foundation, funded many of the citizen groups at their outset, but claims they are now independent due to money raised through direct mailings and other outreach efforts. In fact, as documented in Chapters 4 and 5, most of the liberal groups, including the advocacy groups for low-income minority groups, are still very dependent on foundation money. More generally, minimizing the role of foundation grants overlooks the importance of discretionary money in the functioning of any organization.

All environmental groups are counted as part of the new pluralism, but as noted in Chapter 2, conflicts between the corporate community and the growth coalitions over clean air in major cities like Pittsburgh and Los Angeles gave environmentalists their first real opening (Gonzalez 2005). And as Chapter 4 shows, the key groups as far as the formulation of environmental policy are still funded by large foundations and are part of the policy-planning network. Strong environmentalists have had great success in sensitizing public opinion on environmental issues. They have been able to create watchdog groups whose reports receive great attention in the mass media when they are released. They have developed new ideas and technologies for controlling pollution that have been grudgingly accepted by the corporate community. Their activism has been crucial in stopping many specific development projects and in saving old forests. But from 1975 through 2008 they were not able to pass any legislation opposed by the

Business Roundtable. The environmental movement as a whole, and its liberal wing in particular, is more marginal in a power sense than its public reputation would suggest (Dowie 1995; Gonzalez 2001). The fact that this may change during the Obama Administration now that the human-generated climate crisis has been acknowledged by all but a few ultraconservatives does not negate the fact that pluralists have been wrong on this issue for the past forty years.

The consumer movement that developed out of the activism of the civil rights and antiwar movements of the 1960s is also held out as evidence for the success of the new pluralism. Inspired in good part by the efforts of Ralph Nader, the movement led to the passage of many new consumer protection laws between 1967 and 1974. When Jimmy Carter became president in 1976, he appointed the leader of the Consumer Federation of America as an undersecretary of agriculture and the head of one of Nader's congressional watchdog groups as the chair of the National Highway Traffic Safety Administration. In addition, a respected academic researcher was put in charge of the Occupational Safety and Health Administration and a Senate staff member who helped to draft many of the new consumer safety laws became chair of the Federal Trade Commission.

However, there is less evidence of liberal power in this story than meets the eye because the relevant business groups either agreed with the legislation or forced modifications to make it acceptable. Although the U.S. Chamber of Commerce registered its usual protestations, there was little or no business opposition to any of the consumer protection legislation of the 1960s. The important exception is the automobile industry's objections to the National Traffic and Motor Vehicle Safety Act, an effort to force them to make safer cars (Domhoff 1990, chapter 9; Luger 2000).

The profound weakness of the consumer movement was exposed as long ago as 1978 when it could not win enactment for its cautious plan for an Agency for Consumer Advocacy. The proposed agency would not have had any power to enforce laws or issue regulations, but only to gather information and help consumer groups when they approached federal agencies or asked for judicial reviews of agency actions. Nevertheless, the Business Roundtable and other corporate organizations strongly opposed the idea through the Consumer Issues Working Group. Although the act passed both houses of Congress in 1975, a final version was not sent to the White House because President Gerald Ford warned he would veto it. Two years later, despite support from the newly elected Democratic president, the conservative voting bloc in the House rejected the bill.

The movement also failed in all its efforts to legislate greater corporate responsibility. Congress refused to consider the idea of federal charters for corporations, leaving them free to continue to incorporate in states with very weak laws governing corporations. Plans to increase shareholder rights and strengthen the laws on corporate crime were rejected. A flurry of new initiatives at the Federal Trade Commission led to a strong reaction by Congress when it was inundated by complaints from the car dealers, funeral directors, and other business groups that felt put upon and harassed. Every reform was lost. In the early 1980s the ultraconservatives tried to abolish the Federal Trade Commission entirely, but it was saved with the help of corporate moderates who believe it has some uses (Pertschuk 1982).

Surveying the successes and failures of consumer activists from the vantage point of the 1990s, the most detailed study of this movement concludes that pluralists are wrong to claim that the "new" regulation starting in the 1970s is different from earlier forms of regulation, even though it usually covers a wider array of industries. More generally, its authors conclude that business is the dominant force in the interest-group community despite the increase in non-business interest groups in the 1970s (Maney and Bykerk 1994).

When all is said and done, the only significant defeat for a united corporate community since the 1960s was the establishment of the Occupational Safety and Health Administration by the Nixon Administration in 1970. Although the legislation was not nearly as consequential as the National Labor Relations Act was, and the standards created by the corporate community's own American National Standards Institute were written into it as a starting point, the agency was strongly opposed by corporate leaders as both a possible precedent for enlarging government regulation and a potential stronghold for unions. The ensuing history of this new agency is instructive in terms of corporate power, making it possible to go beyond the pluralists' emphasis on success and failure on a specific piece of legislation to demonstrate the overall domination of government by the power elite. By the 1980s, as detailed studies show, the corporations had turned the agency into a captive agency through delays in providing information, legislative amendments that limited its power, legal victories that further reduced its power, and budget cuts that made inspections fewer and more superficial (Noble 1986). One sociologist who studied the agency in depth called it a "political prisoner" (Szasz 1984). As if to make this case even more difficult for pluralists, these changes occurred despite strong public sentiment in favor of enforcing workplace safety laws.

Although it is hard to imagine that the Occupational Safety and Health Administration could be even more ineffective than it had been in the past, it did even less during the George W. Bush Administration. For example, a set of rules to stem the return of tuberculosis in the workplace was cancelled, along with several unfinished plans for new regulations. Responses to complaints took longer to process and there were fewer enforcement actions. Political appointees consistently overruled the scientific staff, even on very small issues (Goldsein and Cohen 2004; Smith 2008).

Historical institutionalist theory, which emphasizes the independent power of government, is a useful general starting point because historical and comparative studies suggest that the government indeed has the potential for autonomy (Mann 1984; Mann 1986; Skocpol 1979). However, this book shows that this potential does not manifest itself in the United States. Government autonomy is only possible when a government is unified and relatively impermeable to the employees and representatives of private organizations, but the American government is neither. For historical reasons explained in the next section, it is a fragmented government completely open to outside agents and therefore vulnerable to domination through the electoral process explained in Chapter 6 and through the appointments from the corporate community and policy-planning network documented in Chapter 7. The movement by members of the power elite between the private sector and government blurs the line between the corporate community, the policy-planning network, and the state, which does not fit with the idea of government independence.

Historical institutionalists stress that the institutional structure of the government—e.g., whether it is parliamentary or presidential, centralized or decentralized—has an important role in shaping party systems and political strategies (Hooks 1991; Skocpol 1992). This is a helpful insight that fits well with a class-dominance theory in the case of the United States. As shown in Chapter 6, the existence of an independent executive branch and the election of Congress on a state-by-state and district-by-district basis accounts for the strength of the two-party system, which made it difficult for the liberal-labor coalition to develop its own organizational base in the past. Moreover, the historic lack of large planning staffs in most executive departments made it possible for a private policy-planning network to flourish. Then, too, the division of American government into national, state, and local levels helps to explain why growth coalitions can be so powerful in most cities.

Historical institutionalists believe a growing budget and an increasing number of employees are indicators of the power of an agency or department within government. More generally, the alleged continued expansion of the federal government is sometimes said to be good evidence for the power of state officials. But the historical institutionalists are wrong for three reasons when they use increases in federal budgets and number of agency employees as power indicators. First, the size of a government does not necessarily say anything about how it is controlled. The government could grow and still be controlled by the power elite, as shown by the fact that corporate leaders working within the policy planning network supported the creation of the Federal Trade Commission, the Office of Management and Budget, the Agricultural Adjustment Administration, and the Social Security Administration. For that reason, there is no substitute for historical studies tracing the origins of any new agencies of government. Second, the growth of government from the 1960s through the 1990s was at the state and local levels, which does not fit with the image of an independently powerful federal government that aggrandizes more resources to itself. Third, as the most detailed and sophisticated study of federal government budgets reveals, budgets actually declined in size from 1950 to 1977 by 8.8 percent as a percentage of gross domestic product when various biasing factors such as inflation are taken into account (Berry and Lowery 1987). That decline continued from 1980, when federal spending was 21.6 percent of gross domestic product, to 2000, when the figure was 18.7 percent. The percentage rose during the Bush Administration in good part due to the massive increases in defense spending that began even before the wars in Afghanistan and Iraq, and also due to increased costs for Medicare, but no one would claim that the Bush Administration is evidence for government autonomy from the corporate community.

Information on the number of federal government employees also contradicts the expectations of the historical institutionalists because the number of federal civilian and military employees declined in the 1990s, both in absolute numbers and as a percentage of the nation's total population. The main finding that emerges from a comparison of the departments in the executive branch is that the Department of Defense dwarfs all others, employing over half of all federal employees when military personnel are included. When only civilian employees are counted, that department is still three to seven times bigger than its nearest rivals.

The claim by historical institutionalists that experts have an independent role in developing new public policies is refuted by the fact that most of these experts are part of the policy-planning network discussed in Chapter 4. Historical institutionalists are right that experts provide many of the new policy ideas, but they do not see that the most important experts are selected and sponsored by one or more of the organizations within the policy network and that their ideas are discussed and criticized by corporate leaders before appearing in reports and proposals.

Elite theorists, with their emphasis on the organizational basis of power, contribute important insights to the understanding of modern-day power structures. Organizations are indeed the basis of power because their leaders command great resources, have more information than those below them in the hierarchy, and can reward followers and punish critics. They can shape lower-level jobs so that the flexibility and information available to employees is limited. They can make alliances with the leaders of other organizations to strengthen their own positions. At the same time, elite theorists remind us that conflicts between organizational elites often arise and have to be carefully managed if continuing dominance of nonelites is to be maintained. Elite theorists rightly emphasize that dominance by the corporate community is open to challenge by other elite interests and that average citizens sometimes have the ability to set limits on the actions of elites, especially when the elites are in conflict among themselves (Burton and Higley 1987b; Higley and Burton 2006; Higley and Lengyel 2000).

However, elite theorists do not fully appreciate the degree to which corporate-based owners and managers dominate other organizational elites in the United States. As shown in Chapters 4 and 5, virtually all other organizations in the country, with the exception of labor unions, are funded and directed by the corporate rich. As demonstrated in Chapter 6, most elected officials are dependent upon wealthy families and corporate leaders for their initial financial support. As shown in Chapter 7, members of the corporate community have been overrepresented in the executive branch of the federal government and have control over military elites through civilian control of the Department of Defense. Nor do elite theorists fully appreciate the class bias that is built into the policy-planning network and other nonprofit organizations in the United States, making the leaders and experts within those organizations secondary to the leaders in the corporate community. The lack of attention to class also leads elite theorists to underestimate the differences between corporate-dominated organizations and organizations based in the working class, especially unions. The leaders of unions do work with the leaders of corporate-oriented organizations once their unions are established, as elite theorists emphasize, but many of their objectives remain class-based. Moreover, the union leaders have been defeated again and again by the corporate community since the late 1930s, as explained in Chapter 7, making them a secondary elite at best.

Thus, as this book shows, it is the combination of insights from class and organizational theories that explains the strength of the American power elite. Capitalism creates an ownership class that has great economic resources and the potential for political power. It also generates ongoing class conflict over wages, profits, works rules, taxes, and government regulation. But a wide range of nonprofit organizations give corporate owners institutional resources that incorporate and legitimate their class resources, making it possible for them to contain class conflict. It is the interaction of class and organizational imperatives at the top of all American organizations, including government institutions, that leads to class domination in the United States.

To conclude this brief discussion of the three alternative theories, it can be added that none of them can account for the strong findings in this book on all three of the power indicators. They do not explain why the wealth and income distributions would be so highly skewed if the corporate owners are not disproportionately powerful, or why men and women from the power elite would be overrepresented in key government positions and decision-making groups. Finally, the pluralist and historical institutionalist views do not have the historical and comparative scope to explain why the corporate community is so powerful in the United States.

WHY IS THE CORPORATE COMMUNITY SO POWERFUL?

How is such a high concentration of corporate power possible? This question can be answered with the insights gained by comparing America's history to the histories of democratic countries in Europe. There are two separate but intertwined historical reasons for class domination in the United States. First, the corporate community in America is stronger because it did not have to contend with feudal aristocrats, strong states, and the hierarchy of an established church, all of which had a pervasive influence in Western European history (Mann 1986). Second, those who work for wages and salaries are weaker as a class than in other democratic countries because they never have been able to establish an organizational base in either the economy or the political system.

The historical factors leading to a decentralized and relatively powerless federal government are especially important in understanding modern corporate dominance. The pre-Revolutionary history of the United States as a set of separate colonial territories, only lightly overseen by the appointed governors representing the British crown, left plenty of room for the development of wealthy merchants and slaveholders, primarily because the colonial governments were so small. The Founding Fathers, as the representatives of the separate colonial capitalist classes, were therefore able to create a government with divided and limited powers that was designed to accommodate the concerns of both Southern slave owners and Northern merchants and manufacturers. They took special care to deal with the fears of the Southern rich, who rightly worried that a strong federal government might lead to the abolishment of slavery in an industrializing society.

Although the plan failed in that their differences over the expansion of slavery into western territories led to a murderous Civil War, the Southern and Northern rich were once again able to work together after they fully compromised their differences through a series of trade-offs in 1877. These compromises made it possible for them to oppose any federal program or agency that might aid those who work with their hands in factories or fields, an opposition that came to be known as the conservative voting bloc during the 1930s (Schwartz 1976; Woodward 1966). From that point on, however, the Southern plantation capitalists were the junior partners in the ownership class even though they were able to build up considerable political power through their strongholds in Congress.

The federal government also remained small because of the absence of any dangerous rival nations along the country's borders. In addition, the British navy provided a deterrent against invasion by any other European states throughout most of the nineteenth century and U.S. involvement in World War I was relatively brief, with no postwar European military obligations (Mills 1956, chapter 8, for what remains the best brief overview). Thus, the United States did not have a permanent military establishment until World War II when corporate leaders came to Washington at no salary to oversee its development and ensure control of it (Domhoff 1996, chapter 6; Waddell 2001). By contrast, the nation-states that survived the severe competition among rival groups in Europe were the ones with strong central governments and large military organizations. These countries came into the modern era with strong states that intertwined with the old aristocracy, so capitalists had to compete for power. The result is a more complex power equation in most European countries (Lachman 2000; Mann 1993).

Within this context, it is very important that there were big corporations by the second half of the nineteenth century, well before there was any semblance of a "big government" at the national level. These corporations and their associated policy-planning organizations were able to play the major role in creating new administrative agencies and regulatory bodies that became important in the twentieth century, as overviewed in Chapter 4. As noted in Chapter 7, efforts within the policy-planning network also led to the establishment of a reorganized Department of Defense, a new National Security Council in the White House, and the Central Intelligence Agency.

For all the early divisions between property owners in the North and South, ordinary Americans were even more divided from the beginning—free white farmers and artisans in the North and black slaves in the South. These divisions were exacerbated by the arrival of immigrants from eastern and southern Europe in the late nineteenth century, who were viewed by entrenched skilled workers of northern

European origins as a threat to the tight labor markets they enjoyed (e.g., Mink 1986). To make matters worse, there was no good way to overcome these divisions because bold activists could not develop strong trade unions in the North, where capitalists dominated state and local governments.

Despite these problems, the working class movement in the Northern United States was very similar to the ones in Britain and France between the 1830s and the 1880s. Then highly organized and violence-prone employers defeated its attempts at classwide organization. In doing so they had the support of the local and state governments controlled by the political parties they dominated. In that atmosphere, only skilled workers were able to unionize, usually in business sectors where there were a large number of highly competitive small owners, such as construction, coal mining, and garment making. By contrast, capitalists in Britain and France were forced by government, still dominated by landed aristocrats and bureaucracies, to compromise with unions (Hamilton 1991; Voss 1993).

More generally, most large-scale attempts at union organizing between the 1880s and 1936 were broken up by government troops or the armed private police forces controlled by corporations. More violence was directed against the American labor movement than any other labor movement in a Western democracy. It was not until early 1937, shortly after the landslide reelection of Franklin D. Roosevelt to the presidency, along with the election of liberal governors in Pennsylvania and Michigan, that industrial unions were able to organize in some Northern states. Braced by their electoral victories, and facing highly organized union activists, these elected officials refused to send federal troops or state police to arrest workers when they took over factories (Bernstein 1969; Fine 1969).

This refusal to honor repeated requests from corporate leaders for armed intervention—on the grounds that sit-down strikes were a form of trespassing on private property—marked the first time in American history that government force was not used to break a major strike. The result was a victory for union organizers in the automobile, rubber, and other heavy industries. Just a year later, however, state police in Ohio, Indiana, and Illinois helped owners defeat strikers who were trying to organize the steel industry (Piven and Cloward 1977, chapter 3). By 1939, the growth in union membership had been brought to a halt. Only the need for national solidarity during World War II made it possible for unions to resume growth due to government intervention on their behalf. This sequence of events is often obscured in studies of the union movement by pro-labor authors, who ignore or downplay the role of the government in making unionization possible. They instead focus almost exclusively on the courage of the workers and the skillful leadership provided at the grassroots by leftists. Skillful leaders and militant workers are indeed necessary, but as a Marxist historian who specialized in leftist social movements concluded, "the central importance of government mediation, and of the alliance with the Democrats, has been glossed over" in many Marxist accounts of the surge in union growth (Weinstein 1975, pp. 80–81).

Nor could workers gain a toehold in the political system because the government structure and electoral rules pulled everyone into a two-party system, as explained in Chapter 6. Thus, there was no way for people to come together to create programs that might help to transcend the white/black and old immigrant/new immigrant divisions. Once again, the situation was different in European countries, mainly because their parliamentary systems made the development of a labor or socialist party more feasible.

Workers in America also suffered from the fact that they were unable to form a solid alliance with middle-class and well-off liberals. This difficulty had its roots in two atypical factors not present in European countries. First, the small trade union movement that developed in the late nineteenth century was strongly antigovernment because it saw government as controlled by capitalists. It was therefore suspicious of the liberals' desire to use government to tame and reform the big corporations. Second, due to the absence of a liberal or labor party, there was no meeting ground where the potential allies could work out their differences and develop a common program (Skocpol 1992). Only after 1935 did the Democratic Party fill part of this need, when the leadership of the new industrial union movement and liberals formed the liberal-labor coalition within the context of the larger New Deal coalition (Brinkley 1995). Lacking an organizational base in unions and a party that could formulate and popularize a more communal and pro-government ethos, there was little possibility for the American working class to overcome the strong individualism and racial prejudice that pervades the United States. Thus, these divisive orientations persist among nonunionized white workers and continue to matter in terms of union organizing and voting patterns.

How much have these relatively unique American historical features mattered in terms of class dominance? The impact is in part revealed in a comparison of the wealth shares held by the top 10 percent in the United States and in several major countries around the world for which information is available. As shown in Table 8.1, the United States, where the top 10 percent have 69.8 percent of the wealth, has by far the highest concentration of wealth of any of the large countries. By contrast, the top 10 percent have 44.4 percent in Germany and 39.3 percent in Japan. The United Kingdom is in an intermediary position at 56.0 percent and France is second to the United States at

Table 8.1 Percentage of Wealth Held by the Top 10 Percent of Families in Selected Countries in 2004

Country	Wealth Owned by Top 10%
United States	69.8%
France	61.0%
United Kingdom	56.0%
Canada	53.0%
India	52.9%
Italy	48.5%
Australia	45.0%
Germany	44.4%
China	41.0%
Japan	39.3%

Note: The estimate for the top 10 percent in the United States in this table is 1.4 percentage points lower than a figure provided in Chapter 1 because the two different studies that are drawn upon use slightly different methods. (Adapted from Davies, Shorrocks and Wolff, 2006, Table 9.) The top 10 percent is used in this table instead of the top 1 percent because reliable information on the top 1 percent does not exist for some countries.

61.0 percent (Davies, Shorrocks and Wolff 2006, Table 9). When the higher poverty rates and weaker social nets in the United States compared to European countries are added to the picture, it seems likely that class dominance is greater in the United States than in other fully industrialized democratic countries (Baker 2007; Smeeding 2008).

In closing this discussion of why the corporate community is so powerful in the United States, it needs to be emphasized that the strong case for class domination in the United States does not demonstrate that there is class domination everywhere. In fact, the ubiquity of class domination is in great dispute in the social sciences. The Marxist theoretical school argues that the dominant power group is usually the economic class that owns the "means of production," but it does underscore that in times of large-scale societal transitions there can be temporary government autonomy or mixed power structures (Miliband 1977; Oppenheimer 2000). Marxism also claims that class struggle between owners and nonowners is the major determinant of historical change, relegating other power networks to a secondary role.

Non-Marxist class-dominance theorists doubt that class domination and class conflict are always at the center of the power equation. They believe that governmental, military, and religious power have an independent status and that they have been important in some times and places in Western history. For example, they argue that state rulers, not property owners, dominated the empires at the dawn of civilization and that the military had greater power than owners in the Roman Empire (Mann 1986). Even after the development of capitalism, the non-Marxists continue, feudal lords and state leaders remained powerful longer than Marxists believe (Hamilton 1991). More generally, they see many aspects of European history from the 1860s through the 1930s as a refutation of Marxist theory, including its analysis of the rise of fascism (Mann 1993; Mann 2004). This book does not try to adjudicate these longstanding theoretical disagreements. They are tangential to its primary purpose, which is to demonstrate and explain class domination in the United States.

Nor does this book imply that the extreme degree of class domination found in the United States is inevitable in the future. It recognizes that power structures do change, as demonstrated most dramatically by the nonviolent collapse of the Soviet Union in 1990–1991 and the relatively peaceful replacement of white rule and a repressive system of apartheid in South Africa in the 1980s. Rather obviously, nothing so large-scale seems likely in the United States, but the potential for changes in the American power structure created by events over the past 45 years are explored in the final chapter.

9

Potential Challenges to Class Domination

THE TRANSFORMATION OF AMERICAN POLITICS

With the Northern rich dominating the Republicans and the Southern rich dominating the Democrats, and a conservative voting coalition of Northern Republicans and Southern Democrats controlling Congress on class issues, there was little chance of egalitarian social change through the electoral system between 1877 and 1965. Those who were opposed to class domination or racial exclusion therefore resorted to social movements outside of the electoral system to try to win new rights, including in some cases the right to vote.

The largest, most sustained, and best known of these social movements, the Civil Rights Movement of the 1950s and 1960s, not only transformed the lives of African-Americans in the South and made possible the growth of a black middle class throughout the nation, it dynamited the power arrangements that persisted from the New Deal to the mid-1960s. Those power arrangements rested on the acceptance of African-American exclusion—10–12 percent of the country's population—by the liberal-labor coalition in the North as well as by the Northern Republicans and Southern Democrats. However, as mentioned in the Introduction, the Voting Rights Act of 1965 made it possible for African-Americans to help defeat open segregationists and other ultraconservatives in Democratic primaries in the South, thereby hastening their shift to the Republican Party. Black voters' pressure on conservative Democrats was complemented by the fact that the gradual industrialization of the South since World War II had made the situation of the Southern segment of the ownership class even more similar to that of its Northern counterpart. When the Democratic Party could no longer fulfill its main historical function, namely, keeping African-Americans powerless, it was relatively easy for wealthy white conservatives to become Republicans.

The changing political economy of the South also made the complete oppression of African-Americans less crucial for the white rich, but civil rights did not come easily or simply. The Civil Rights Acts of 1964 and 1965 would not have passed without the social disruption created by the Civil Rights Movement. The conservative voting bloc in the Senate, backed by most of the corporate community, was not prepared to budge because it had the 34 votes needed in that era to continue a filibuster (Bloom 1987). The Northern Republicans did not abandon the Southern Democrats on this issue until moderate conservatives in the power elite, confronted with the potential for ongoing social turmoil in inner cities across the nation, decided to move in an accommodating direction to bring the South more in line with practices in the rest of the country. It was only at this juncture that enough Republicans finally broke with the Southern Democrats to end a 13-week filibuster, the longest in Senate history (Whalen and Whalen 1985).

The enactment of civil rights legislation and the exodus of the Southern segment of the ownership class from the Democratic Party created the possibility that the Democratic Party could be transformed into an organizational base for a nationwide liberal-labor coalition that included African-Americans as well as new immigrants from Latin America and Asia. But something very different happened instead, short-circuiting any possibilities for egalitarian economic change for the next 40 years.

The problems for the creation of an expanded liberal-labor coalition began when the Southern white ownership class used appeals to racial resentments to carry middle- and low-income white Southerners into the Republican Party with them. As already stated in Chapter 6, Republican presidential candidate Barry Goldwater emphasized his belief in states' rights in 1964 to capture the four traditionally Democratic states of South Carolina, Georgia, Alabama, and Mississippi, which have been Republican strongholds ever since. The openly segregationist Democratic governor of Alabama, George Wallace, used race as a wedge issue to win 13.5 percent of the vote nationwide in his third-party presidential race in 1968, thereby taking away enough traditional white Democratic voters in the South and Midwest to give the Republican candidate, Richard Nixon, a very narrow victory over his Democratic opponent Hubert Humphrey (43.4 percent to 42.7 percent in the popular vote, which translated into an electoral college vote of 301 for

Nixon, 191 for Humphrey, and 46 for Wallace) (Carter 2000). In 1972 President Nixon solidified the former Wallace voters for the Republicans at the presidential level, especially in the South, paving the way for the Reagan-Bush era from 1980 to 1992 and the Bush-Cheney Administration from 2000 to 2008 (Carmines and Stimson 1989; Carter 1996).

As a result of this racial animus, later supplemented by emotional appeals on other social issues, Republicans held the presidency for all but 12 of the years between 1968 and 2008 and gradually consolidated a nationwide conservative Republican majority that gained control of Congress. The abandonment of the Democrats at the congressional level did not happen at a faster pace primarily because the seniority enjoyed by many Southern Democrats gave them considerable power in national politics as long as that party maintained a majority in Congress. Wherever possible, then, Southern whites continued to control the Democratic Party at the local level while voting Republican at the national level. The result was a split party system in the South from 1968 to 1994. Once the Republicans took control of Congress in 1994, most of the remaining white Southern Democrats quickly consolidated within the Republican Party, including several elected Southern Democrats in the House and Senate who switched parties.

But it was not just racial conflict in the South that destroyed any possibility of an expanded liberal-labor coalition within the Democratic Party. There was also racial resentment and conflict in the North. The arguments and buzz words later used by ultraconservatives in the Republican Party to appeal to Northern whites were already being used by trade unionists and machine Democrats in the early 1960s as part of their resistance to renewed demands for greater integration in the North (Sugrue 2001; Sugrue 2008). There were a few notable exceptions, of course, and many leaders of industrial unions supported the Civil Rights Movement at the legislative level, but enough of the rank-and-file and other middle-income white voters resisted integration in housing, schooling, and unions to put the Democrats on the defensive in the North as well as the South. This point is seen most dramatically in the votes for Governor Wallace of Alabama in Democratic presidential primaries as early as 1964—30 percent in Indiana, 34 percent in Wisconsin, and 47 percent in the former slave state of Maryland, where he won 16 of 23 counties, the state capital, and the white ethnic neighborhoods of Baltimore (Carter 2000, p. 215). In the 1972 Democratic primaries, mixing tirades against busing and welfare with revivalist religious appeals, Wallace then presaged the more coded and symbolic politics of the ultraconservatives within the Republican Party by winning majorities in Michigan and Maryland just before he was forced to drop out of the race by an assassination attempt that left him paralyzed and in excruciating pain.

Nor was it simply racial conflict that caused many Northern whites to oppose liberals of all colors. Many of them did not like the feminists or environmentalists either, who were seen as a danger to their jobs or threats to their status as proud white males. Moreover, many did not like what they saw as the anti-Americanism of the anti-war movement. All of these factors contributed to the disintegration of the liberal-labor coalition and made it possible for President Nixon and his ultraconservative allies to attract more and more white middle-income voters (blue collar and white collar, union and non-union) into the Republican Party, using the same social issues that were still being employed by Republican candidates in 2008 (Edsall 2006; Edsall and Edsall 1992).

For several reasons, then, enough white voters switched to the Republicans to solidify a corporate-conservative coalition within that party. This created further problems for the expansion of the liberal-labor coalition because white trade unionists did not fully appreciate that their unions were now at risk because of the renewed corporate attack on them triggered by the conflict over outsourcing at the National Labor Relations Board (Gross 1995). They did not realize that the strong unions they had built over the previous 35 years could be dismantled very quickly by moving production out of the country at a record-breaking pace. Nor did they realize that the Republicans who had been courting their vote would aid the corporations in their attack through antiunion appointments to the National Labor Relations Board. As explained as part of the discussion of the decline of the Committee for Economic Development in Chapter 7, the nationwide white turn to the Republicans also made it possible for the moderate conservatives to make a right turn on other policy issues in the 1970s once inner cities were calm and the corporations were faced with new economic problems due to rising oil prices and inflation. The result was a "new class war," culminating in the Reagan Administration's cutbacks in various social support programs (Piven and Cloward 1982). This renewed class war also led to the step-by-step deregulation of the financial sector that prepared the ground for the stock market and housing market bubbles that buoyed the economy for most of the years between 1997 and 2006 (Baker 2007; Baker 2009).

The frayed liberal-labor coalition was slowly rebuilt in the early 1990s because women and people of color had solidified many of the individual rights they had fought for and a new generation of younger white workers had come to accept many of these changes. Furthermore, the union movement itself gradually became more diverse as it began to include women and Latino workers, but it was much smaller and weaker than it had been in the past. Weary of twelve uninterrupted years of Republican rule, the liberal-labor coalition was grateful for the few gains it obtained from the centrist Clinton Administration. But it received no support for union organizing and suffered defeats on welfare policies (Clinton ended the New Deal's welfare program) and on the expansion of trade with low-wage countries that further undercut unions. The Clinton Administration also actively supported further financial deregulation that supposedly was no longer necessary in the new business climate.

Despite some demographic trends that liberal journalists claimed to be in the party's favor, there was nothing inevitable about the turn to the Democrats in the presidential and congressional elections in 2008. The South and the Great Plains states were still a strong starting point for any Republican presidential candidate and the key swing states of Ohio and Florida had voted for President Bush in both 2000 and 2004. Instead, it was the massive failures of the Bush Administration in several realms, combined with the appealing, centrist, and reassuring image and message that President Obama was able to present to the country, that ushered in the current Democratic administration.

WILL THE OBAMA ADMINISTRATION CHALLENGE CLASS DOMINATION?

As this book is being written, the obvious question is how the Obama Administration and the large Democratic majorities in the House and Senate are going to respond in the face of the many serious problems they have inherited. As a best guess, readers are likely to find that they have satisfied most of their supporters on feminist and environmental issues, and restored basic constitutional rights that were threatened by the Bush Administration's methods of dealing with those imprisoned as suspected terrorists. Scientific research and findings will be taken seriously once again. It may even be that they can wind down the war in Iraq by admitting the fact that the Iranian government cannot be pressured or overthrown and by tacitly accepting the strong influence it now has in Iraq in exchange for help in stabilizing Afghanistan and Pakistan. The Obama Administration may even decide to negotiate in Afghanistan rather than risk the defeat or long occupation that is likely to be the outcome of a renewed war effort there, if the failures of the British in that rugged tribal land long ago and of the late Soviet Union more recently are any indication. The fact that a large American military presence in the area might lead to fragmentation and an anti-American government in Pakistan also might force the foreign policy establishment within the power elite to acknowledge the limits of American power.

But President Obama and the Democrats face potentially polariz-
ing choices on every economic issue that will be under debate because
they are intertwined with class domination and class conflict. Will they
be sympathetic to the corporate community to which they are closest
in terms of class and educational backgrounds, and most dependent
upon for financial support, or will they lean in the liberal-labor direction, which in every case means that the power of the upper class and
the corporate community will have to be challenged? Many of these
issues are bellwether power indicators that may have registered their
verdict by the time that you are reading this book.

First and foremost, as stressed in Chapter 7, the treatment of legislation to strengthen trade unions will reveal which way the Democrats
are leaning in the ongoing battles between the corporate community
and the liberal-labor coalition. The gradual elimination of private-
sector unions since the 1970s, and the concurrent movement of production facilities out of the country, played a significant role in the
declining share of income that goes to those who work for wages and
salaries (Baker 2007). Most economists focus on the overall economic
advantages of the new production practices, including the benefits for
people in the low-income countries with new production facilities, but
this book is concerned with power, not economics. From a power vantage point, the decline in union strength has meant a decline in power
as well as stagnating incomes for average Americans. This includes
many people who are not members of unions whose wages were often
pulled upwards by union wages. For all their many faults as bureaucracies that sometimes become fiefdoms for self-serving leaders, as is
the case with any large organization, unions provided a measure of
security and dignity to many people's lives. The Democrats will have to
decide if they are going to support unions or practice forms of paternalism, including some improvements in health insurance and other
social benefits, which would be the preference of the moderate conservatives in the corporate community who supported Democratic candidates in 2008.

The treatment of tax issues will also be an early sign of which way
the Democrats are leaning. Take the issue of slightly higher income
taxes on those who make more than $250,000, which President Obama
promised to enact when he was on the campaign trail. Increased government spending based on such tax increases would be a good way
to stimulate the economy because it would put money into circulation
that wealthy people would be unlikely to spend or invest in the current
economic crisis. Will that tax be enacted even though the Republicans
are against it, or will the administration wait for the Bush tax cuts to
expire in 2010 to win favor with Republicans? There is another tax
issue that is simple and crucial. The Democrats could place a small

tax on every stock market transaction. A transaction tax of 0.5 percent on each financial trade would have the benefit of reducing destabilizing speculative trading as well as raising large sums of money, an estimated $100 billion a year. Such a tax, proposed many times by liberal economists over the decades, is opposed by the financial services industry (Pollin, Baker and Schaberg 2001/2008).

The mortgage crisis provides another telltale indicator. Homeowners had lost over $8 trillion by the end of 2008 and many people had lost their houses as well because they could not make their monthly payments. But most plans to deal with the problem provide bailouts for the banks that simply include clauses calling for the bankers to renegotiate loan payments and interest rates. As might be expected, these clauses will help few if any families because they leave complete control of the issue in the hands of the bankers, who have little or no incentive to renegotiate. Instead of propping up these companies by giving them money and hoping they treat homeowners well, it would be possible to give homeowners the right to stay on as renters at the market rate, which would encourage bankers to negotiate more realistically and allow people to continue with their normal routines (Baker 2009). The government also could buy mortgages that people can no longer afford and issue new government mortgages to them at a much lower interest rate, which is what was done to deal with the housing crisis during the New Deal (Gotham 2000; Gotham 2002). That would provide a bailout for homeowners as well as financial institutions, but the corporate community does not like the idea of the government having even more control over mortgages than it does now.

The way in which any changes in Social Security are handled will also be highly revealing. Although the corporate community, backed by reports from both the Brookings Institution and the American Enterprise Institute, has claimed for two decades that Social Security faces a crisis, in fact any small shortfalls it faces could be fully funded for the 75-year planning period simply by taxing all earned income instead of the first $106,800 that will be taxed in 2009 (see Rogne, Estes, Grossman, Hollister and Solway 2009, for information on how the corporate community has misled the public on Social Security even though moderate conservatives helped create it in the 1930s). But such a change would mean an increase in taxes for those few with high earned incomes. The real issue, which will be an acid test for the integrity of the Obama Administration, is that any alleged reforms that involve decreases in Social Security benefits over the long run would legitimize one of the most massive peaceful transfers of wealth from the middle class to the upper class in Western history. That's because any cuts in payments or increases in the age of retirement would mean that the people who started paying higher payroll taxes in 1983 that were supposed to guarantee their security until 2042 (through the purchase of Treasury bonds by the Social Security Administration) will find that their money has been used to finance the very large tax cuts to the corporate rich over the past 25 years. In other words, the money the government has received from increased payroll taxes since 1983 has been used to help fund the federal government's yearly expenses, making lower taxes for high-income people possible without running even larger deficits. Put still another way, if benefits are cut, it is the equivalent of defaulting on some of the $1.2 trillion in Treasury bonds that President Reagan and other political leaders, both Democrats and Republicans, assured taxpayers in the 1980s that they were purchasing with payroll taxes (Baker 2001; Baker and Weisbrot 1999).

And yet a step in the direction of such reforms seemed to be emerging early in the Obama Administration when the president talked with Senate Republicans about setting up a bipartisan task force to propose changes that might lead to later retirement ages, higher payroll taxes for average workers, and even caps on the amount that could be spent for Social Security (Calmes 2009; Greider 2009). Such a task force, which would have been staffed by economists from the policy-planning network, some of them already working in the Obama Administration, was strongly opposed by representatives of the liberal-labor coalition, which generated opposition by liberals in the House and Senate. But according to one *New York Times* columnist, the hope for a bipartisan bargain is not completely dead. Based on conversations with "four senior members of the administration" he concluded that President Obama is "extremely committed to entitlement reform and is plotting politically feasible ways to reduce Social Security as well as health spending" (Brooks 2009, p. A23). He added that he "had the impression they'd be willing to raise taxes on the bottom 95 percent of earners as part of an overall package."

How will unemployment be dealt with? Will there be slightly larger unemployment checks for slightly longer periods of time, or will the government provide money to state and local government to rehire the many essential employees who have been laid off and also to hire the many additional teachers and social service employees who are needed if people with average and low incomes, or no income at all, are to lead full and productive lives? And if the Great Recession continues into 2010 or beyond, will the Obama Administration create the kind of government agencies and work programs that carried out reforestation programs and built improvements in national parks during the New Deal (Rose 1994)?

In the case of health care, there were many plans on the table in early 2009, but they cannot solve the problems facing large numbers of Americans without cutting into the power and profits of the insurance companies, drug companies, and other profit-making institutions in the medical-industrial complex (e.g., Krugman 2007; Krugman and Wells 2006). One of the ways to do that would be to create government insurance plans to compete with private plans, or to extend Medicare to people who retire before age 62 or lose their employer-sponsored insurance because they are laid off. Republicans oppose these options because they think such programs would have unfair advantages over private health insurance.

The willingness of the Democrats to take the liberal-labor side on labor and economic issues may be revealed by how they deal with the Republican minority in the Senate, which can mount a successful filibuster if all forty-one Republicans maintain solidarity or if the ultraconservative Republicans gain the support of the few conservative Democrats. Will President Obama and the majority of Senate Democrats make serious efforts to overcome filibusters? Or will they use Republican objections as a way to compromise liberal-labor proposals without having to take the blame? Will they consider abolishing the Senate custom called the filibuster, which has no standing in law, with a call for a majority vote on putting an end to it? The battle is most likely to be joined on the Employee Free Choice Act, an issue on which Democrats might agree to surrender if Republicans promise not to block other aspects of their program (Greider 2008).

CHALLENGES TO CLASS DOMINANCE THROUGH SOCIAL DISRUPTION

If the Democrats take centrist, pro-corporate positions on most of the crucial domestic economic issues, the liberal-labor coalition and social movement activists will face the problem of how to respond, if at all. It might be that they will simply wait to see if the Democrats can win the three or four Senate seats in 2010 that seem likely to come their way. It is here that all the unknowns come into the picture and the answer as to what opponents of class dominance might do becomes the usual "it all depends." First and foremost, the state of the economy is likely to be the major determinant of how the liberal-labor coalition responds. If the economy is showing signs of recovery and a majority of citizens feel hopeful, then it will be difficult to challenge the centrist Democrats and the corporate community. If the recession continues to deepen and it looks like it will last for several years, then the liberal-labor coalition might be able to gain support from most Democrats and the few remaining moderate Republicans in the Senate for a bolder plan for intervention into the economy. Several liberal advocates have suggested ways that the government could support the creation of a more egalitarian market economy that is not dominated by corporations and their owners (e.g., Baker 2009; Krugman 2007; Kuttner 2009).

But at some point in a long and deep recession, the people who are suffering the most from job losses, low incomes, mortgage fore-closures, and a lack of health insurance might take matters into their own hands through direct action, aided by the social movement activists who have been working at the grassroots level on these issues for many years. Average Americans already know from the events of the 1930s and the 1960s, as well as from some of their own efforts on smaller and more specific recent issues, that sit-downs, sit-ins, strikes, boycotts, and blockades can be effective. They also know that the average worker in Canada and Europe receives more government support and job opportunities than they do, including health insurance. Sit-ins that close banks, insurance offices, health-care offices, or government offices might become the order of the day. Eviction notices and bill collectors might be ignored through collective efforts.

If such efforts began to emerge, there would be a contagion effect that might lead to new methods of resistance and disruption that those who are at a distance from the lived experience of the insurgents could not predict beforehand. However, the new efforts would face one great danger, the self-defeating resort to violent methods, which would alienate potentially sympathetic independents and moderates who are necessary to the long-term success of disruptive social protests in the United States. Then, too, any use of violence would play into the hands of local and state-level officials looking for reasons to employ force to restore "law and order." At this point, activists in the tradition of strategic nonviolence that was successfully utilized by Martin Luther King, Jr., and Cesar Chavez in the 1960s and 1970s would have to be able to control or marginalize those who advocate violent strategies.

In the context of large nonviolent protest movements, a federal government headed by the first African-American president (himself a former community organizer) and staffed by people of all races, ethnicities, and religions, might be reluctant to take repressive measures, especially when it is likely that the protestors would include many people of color. Faced with the choice between incarcerating large numbers of people or making major economic concessions, the Obama Administration might be forced to institute far-reaching reforms that make use of both market mechanisms and government-owned enterprises to provide meaningful gainful employment for everyone, as well as the level of social benefits that have long existed in Canada and Western Europe.

In other words, as was stressed at the end of the previous chapter, social change often occurs in unanticipated ways. No social scientist could have predicted that there would be a New Deal in the face of the

Great Depression, leading to the creation of the liberal-labor coalition, or that a massive nonviolent Civil Rights Movement would come roaring out of the Silent Fifties, generating antiwar, feminist, environmental, and gay and lesbian movements in its train. Nor could anyone have predicted the impact the Christian Right would have from the 1970s onwards through its opposition to the liberal social agenda. Most of all, the idea that the Democrats would be in a position even to imagine making egalitarian changes in the economic system was unthinkable as recently as September 2008.

Social scientists and historians can outline the structure of power and analyze trends. They can say that social movements often (but not always) emerge in reaction to economic, military, or cultural shocks. However, the only thing anyone knows for sure is that unexpected conflicts and crises often occur, which give rise to the possibility that activists with the right mix of programs, strategies, and tactics could effectively challenge class dominance. The analysis presented in this book is based on this open-ended view of history.

APPENDIX

Indicators
of Upper-Class Standing

Coed and Boys' Schools

Asheville (Asheville, N.C.)
Buckley (New York, N.Y.)
Cate (Carpinteria, Calif.)
Catlin Gabel (Portland, Ore.)
Choate (Wallingford, Conn.)
Country Day School (St. Louis, Mo.)
Cranbrook (Bloomfield Hills, Mich.)
Deerfield (Deerfield, Mass.)
Episcopal High (Alexandria, Va.)
Gilman (Baltimore, Md.)
Groton (Groton, Mass.)
Hill (Pottstown, Pa.)
Hotchkiss (Lakeville, Conn.)
Kent (Kent, Conn.)
Lake Forest (Lake Forest, Ill.)
Lakeside (Seattle, Wash.)
Lawrenceville (Lawrenceville, N.J.)
Middlesex (Concord, Mass.)
Milton (Milton, Mass.)
Pomfret (Pomfret, Conn.)
Punahou (Honolulu, Hawaii)
Portsmouth Priority (Portsmouth, R.I.)
St. Andrew's (Middlebury, Del.)
St. Christopher's (Richmond, Va.)
St. George's (Newport, R.I.)
St. Mark's (Southborough, Mass.)
St. Paul's (Concord, N.H.)
Shattuck (Fairbault, Minn.)
Taft (Watertown, Conn.)
Thatcher (Ojai, Calif.)
University School (Cleveland, Ohio)

Webb (Bell Buckle, Tenn.)
Westminster (Atlanta, Ga.)
Woodberry Forest (Woodberry Forest, Va.)

Girls' Schools

Abbot Academy (Andover, Mass.)
Agnes Irwin (Wynnewood, Pa.)
Anna Head (Berkeley, Calif.)
Annie Wright (Tacoma, Wash.)
Ashley Hall (Charleston, S.C.)
Baldwin (Bryn Mawr, Pa.)
Berkeley Institute (Brooklyn, N.Y.)
Bishop's (La Jolla, Calif.)
Brearly (New York, N.Y.)
Brimmer's and May (Chestnut Hill, Mass.)
Brooke Hill (Birmingham, Ala.)
Bryn Mawr (Baltimore, Md.)
Chapin (New York, N.Y.)
Chatham Hall (Chatham, Va.)
Collegiate (Richmond, Va.)
Concord Academy (Concord, Mass.)
Convent of the Sacred Heart (New York, N.Y.)
Dalton (New York, N.Y.)
Dana Hall (Wellesley, Mass.)
Emma Willard (Troy, N.Y.)
Ethel Walker (Simsbury, Conn.)
Foxcroft (Middleburg, Va.)
Garrison Forest (Garrison, Md.)
Hathaway Brown (Cleveland, Ohio)
Hockaday (Dallas, Tex.)
Katherine Branson (Ross, Calif.)
Kingswood (Bloomfield Hills, Mich.)
Kinkaid (Houston, Tex.)
Lake Forest Country Day (Lake Forest, Ill.)
Laurel (Cleveland, Ohio)
Louise S. McGehee (New Orleans, La.)
Madeira (Greenway, Va.)
Marlborough (Los Angeles, Calif.)
Mary Institute (St. Louis, Mo.)
Master's (Dobbs Ferry, N.Y.)
Miss Hall's (Pittsfield, Mass.)
Miss Hewitt's (New York, N.Y.)
Miss Porter's (Farmington, Conn.)
Mt. Vernon Seminary (Washington, D.C.)
Rosemary Hall (Greenwich, Conn.)
Salem Academy (Winston-Salem, N.C.)
Shipley (Bryn Mawr, Pa.)
Spence (New York, N.Y.)
St. Agnes Episcopal (Alexandria, Va.)

St. Catherine's (Richmond, Va.)
St. Mary's Hall (San Antonio, Tex.)
St. Nicholas (Seattle, Wash.)
St. Timothy's (Stevenson, Md.)
Stuart Hall (Staunton, Va.)
Walnut Hill (Natick, Mass.)
Westminster (Atlanta, Gal)
Westover (Middlebury, Conn.)
Westridge (Pasadena, Calif.)

Country and Men's Clubs

Arlington (Portland, Ore.)
Bohemian (San Francisco, Calif.)
Boston (New Orleans, La.)
Brook (New York, N.Y.)
Burlingame Country Club (San Francisco, Calif.)
California (Los Angeles, Calif.)
Chagrin Valley Hunt (Cleveland, Ohio)
Charleston (Charleston, S.C.)
Chicago (Chicago, Ill.)
Cuyamuca (San Diego, Calif.)
Denver (Denver, Colo.)
Detroit (Detroit, Mich.)
Eagle Lake (Houston, Tex.)
Everglades (Palm Beach, Calif.)
Hartford (Hartford, Conn.)
Hope (Providence, R.I.)
Idlewild (Dallas, Tex.)
Knickerbocker (New York, N.Y.)
Links (New York, N.Y.)
Maryland (Baltimore, Md.)
Milwaukee (Milwaukee, Wis.)
Minneapolis (Minneapolis, Minn.)
Pacific Union (San Francisco, Calif.)
Philadelphia (Philadelphia, Pa.)
Piedmont Driving (Atlanta, Ga.)
Piping Rock (New York, N.Y.)
Racquet Club (St. Louis, Mo.)
Rainier (Seattle, Wash.)
Richmond German (Richmond, Va.)
Rittenhouse (Philadelphia, Pa.)
River (New York, N.Y.)
Rolling Rock (Pittsburgh, Pa.)
Saturn (Buffalo, N.Y.)
St. Cecelia (Charleston, S.C.)
St. Louis County Club (St. Louis, Mo.)
Somerset (Boston, Mass.)
Union (Cleveland, Ohio)
Woodhill Country Club (Minneapolis, Minn.)

Women's Clubs

Acorn (Philadelphia, Pa.)
Chilton (Boston, Mass.)
Colony (New York, N.Y.)
Fortnightly (Chicago, III.)
Friday (Chicago, III.)
Mt. Vernon Club (Baltimore, Md.)
Society of Colonial Dames
Sulgrave (Washington, D.C.)
Sunset (Seattle, Wash.)
Vincent (Boston, Mass.)

References

Abbate, Janet. 1999. *Inventing the Internet*. Cambridge: MIT Press.

Albrecht, Stephen and Michael Locker. 1981. *CDE Stock Ownership Directory No. 5. Fortune* 500. New York: Corporate Data Exchange, Inc.

Allen, Michael Patrick. 1992. Elite social movement organizations and the state: The rise of the conservative policy-planning network. *Research in Politics and Society* 4:87–109.

Almond, Gabriel. 1998. *Plutocracy and politics in New York City*. Boulder, CO: Westview Press.

Alpert, Irvine and Ann Markusen. 1980. Think tanks and capitalist policy. In *Power Structure Research*, ed. G. W. Domhoff, 173–197. Beverly Hills: Sage Publications.

Alston, Lee J. and Joseph P. Ferrie. 1999. *Southern paternalism and the American welfare state*. New York: Cambridge University Press.

Altemeyer, Bob. 1996. *The authoritarian specter*. Cambridge: Harvard University Press.

Anderson, Sarah, John Cavanagh, Chuck Collins, Sam Pizzigati, and Mike Lapham. 2008. *Executive excess: 15th annual CEO compensation survey*. Washington, DC: Institute for Policy Studies.

Andrews, Suzanna. 2003. Shattered dynasty: Legal wrangling between Jay Pritzker's family members over inheritance. *Vanity Fair*, May 1, pp. 80–97.

Armstrong, Christopher. 1974. Privilege and productivity: The cases of two private schools and their graduates. Ph.D. diss., University of Pennsylvania.

Auerbach, Jerold S. 1966. *Labor and liberty: The LaFollette Committee and the New Deal*. Indianapolis: Bobbs Merrill.

Baer, Kenneth. 2000. *Reinventing Democrats: The politics of liberalism from Reagan to Clinton*. Lawrence: University Press of Kansas.

Bagdikian, Ben H. 2004. *The new media monopoly*. Boston: Beacon Press.

Bailey, Stephen K. 1950. *Congress makes a law: The story behind the Employment Act of 1946*. New York: Columbia University Press.

Baker, Dean. 2001. *Defaulting on the Social Security Trust Fund bonds: Winner and losers*. Washington, DC: Center for Economic and Political Research.

———. 2007. *The United States since 1980*. New York: Cambridge University Press.

———. 2008. Bill Gates' secret to success: Cheating. Beat the press, *The American Prospect*. http://prospect.org/csnc/blogs/beat_the_press.

———. 2009. *Plunder and blunder: The rise and fall of the bubble economy*. Sausalito, CA: PoliPoint Press.

Baker, Dean and Mark Weisbrot. 1999. *Social Security: The phony crisis*. Chicago: University of Chicago Press.

Baltzell, E. Digby. 1958. *Philadelphia gentlemen: The making of a national upper class*. New York: Free Press.

———. 1964. *The Protestant establishment: Aristocracy and caste in America*. New York: Random House.

Balz, Dan and Jon Cohen. 2008. The bad economy helps Obama. *The Washington Post*, national weekly edition. Sept. 29–Oct. 5, pp 13–14.

Barboza, David. 1999. Is the sun setting on farmers? *The New York Times*. Nov. 28, sec. C1.

Barker, Lucius and Ronald W. Walters. 1989. *Jesse Jackson's 1984 presidential campaign: Challenge and change in American politics*. Urbana: University of Illinois Press.

Barnes, Roy C. and Emily R. Ritter. 2001. Networks of corporate interlock: 1962–1995. *Critical Sociology* 27:192–220.

Barnes, Roy C. and Emily Sweezea. 2006. Bohemians and beyond: Social clubs and the corporate elite. A paper presented to the annual meetings of the Southern Sociological Society. New Orleans.

Barrow, Clyde W. 1990. *Universities and the capitalist state: Corporate liberalism and the reconstruction of American higher education, 1894–1928*. Madison: University of Wisconsin Press.

Barshay, Jill and Kathryn Wolfe. 2004. Special interests strike gold in richly targeted tax bill. *CQ Weekly*, Oct. 16, pp. 24–34.

Baum, Lawrence. 1998. *The Supreme Court*. Washington, DC: CQ Press.

Becker, Jo and Christopher Drew. 2008. The long run: Pragmatic politics, forged on the South Side. *The New York Times*, May 11, sec. A1.

Bellant, Russ. 1991. *The Coors connection: How Coors family philanthropy undermines democratic pluralism*. Boston: South End Press.

Belz, Herman. 1991. *Equality transformed*. New Brunswick: Transaction Books.

Benoit, Denise. 2007. *The best-kept secret: Women corporate lobbyists, policy, & power in the United States*. Piscataway: Rutgers University Press.

Berger, Warren. 2000. Source of classic images now struggles to be seen. *The New York Times*, Nov. 20, sec. D6.

Bergthold, Linda. 1990. *Purchasing power in health: Business, the state, and health care politics*. New Brunswick: Rutgers University Press.

Bernstein, Irving. 1969. *Turbulent years: A history of the American worker, 1933–1941*. Boston: Houghton Mifflin.

Berry, Jeffrey. 1999. *The new liberalism*. Washington, DC: Brookings Institution Press.

Berry, William Dale and David Lowery. 1987. *Understanding United States government growth: An empirical analysis of the post-war era*. New York: Praeger.

Birnbaum, Jeffrey H. 2007. Consistently conservative small-business lobby reaches out to Democrats. *The Washington Post*, Jan. 23, sec. A15.

Birnbaum, Jeffrey H. and Ellen McCarthy. 2005. Stottlemyer to head business lobby. *The Washington Post*, Nov. 5, sec. D1.

Bloom, Jack M. 1987. *Class, race, and the Civil Rights Movement*. Bloomington: Indiana University Press.

Bluestone, Barry and Bennett Harrison. 1982. *The deindustrialization of America: Plant closings, community abandonment, and the dismantling of basic industry*. New York: Basic Books.

Bonacich, Phillip. 1972. Technique for analyzing overlapping memberships. In *Sociological Methodology*, ed. H. Costner. San Francisco: Jossey-Bass.

Bonacich, Phillip and G. William Domhoff. 1981. Latent classes and group membership. *Social Networks* 3:175–196.

BondGraham, Darwin. 2007. The direction of higher education: A network analysis of university regents and trustees. Unpublished manuscript. Department of Sociology, University of California, Santa Barbara.

Bourdieu, Pierre. 1986. Forms of capital. In *Handbook of theory and research for the sociology of education*, ed. J. G. Richardson, 241–258. Westport, CT: Greenwood Press.

Breiger, Ronald L. 1974. The duality of persons and groups. *Social Forces* 53: 181–190.

Brinkley, Alan. 1995. *The end of reform: New Deal liberalism in recession and war*. New York: Knopf.

Broad, David. 1996. The Social Register: Directory of America's upper class. *Sociological Spectrum* 16:173–181.

Brooks, David. 2009. When Obamatons respond. *The New York Times*, March 6, sec. A23.

Brown, Michael K. 1999. *Race, money and the American welfare state*. Ithaca: Cornell University Press.

Browne, William, Jerry Skees, Louis Swanson, Paul Thompson, and Lauren Unnevehr. 1992. *Sacred cows and hot potatoes*. Boulder, CO: Westview Press.

Browning, Lynnley. 2004. Foreign tax havens costly to U.S., study says. *The New York Times*, Sept. 27, sec. C2.

———. 2009. Pressured by I.R.S., UBS is closing secret accounts. *The New York Times*, Jan. 9, sec. B1.

Bruce, Robert V. 1959. *1877: The year of violence*. Indianapolis: Bobbs-Merrill.

Bruck, Connie. 1988. *The predators' ball: The junk-bond raiders and the man who staked them*. New York: Simon & Schuster.

Bumiller, Elizabeth. 2008. Research groups boom in Washington. *The New York Times*, Jan. 30, sec. A12.

Bunting, David. 1983. Origins of the American corporate network. *Social Science History* 7:129–142.

———. 1987. *The rise of large American corporations 1889–1919*. New York: Garland.

Burch, Philip H. 1972. *The managerial revolution reassessed: Family control in America's large corporations*. Lexington, MA: Lexington Books.

———. 1980. *Elites in American history: The New Deal to the Carter administration*, Vol. 3. New York: Holmes & Meier.

———. 1981a. *Elites in American history: The Civil War to the New Deal*, Vol. 2. New York: Holmes & Meier.

———. 1981b. *Elites in American history: The Federalist years to the Civil War*, Vol. 1. New York: Holmes & Meier.

Burris, Val. 2005. Interlocking directorates and political cohesion among corporate elites. *American Journal of Sociology* 111:249–283.

———. 2008. The interlock structure of the policy-planning network and the right turn in U.S. state policy. *Research in Political Sociology* 17:3–42.

Burton, Michael G. and John Higley. 1987a. Elite settlements. *American Sociological Review* 52:295–307.

Burton, Michael and John Higley. 1987b. Invitation to elite theory: The basic contentions reconsidered. In *Power elites and organizations*, ed. G. W. Domhoff and T. Dye, 219–238. Beverly Hills, CA: Sage.

Callahan, David. 1999. *$1 billion for ideas: Conservative think tanks in the 1990s*. Washington, DC: National Committee for Responsive Philanthropy.

Calmes, Jackie. 2009. Obama finds resistance in his party on addressing Social Security. *The New York Times*, February 23, sec. A15.

Carmines, Edward G. and James A. Stimson. 1989. *Issue evolution: Race and the transformation of American politics*. Princeton, NJ: Princeton University Press.

Carp, Robert and Ronald Stidham. 1998. *Judicial process in America*. Washington, DC: CQ Press.

Carter, Dan T. 1996. *From George Wallace to New Gingrich: Race in the conservative counterrevolution, 1963–1994*. Baton Rouge: Louisiana State University Press.

———. 2000. *The politics of rage: George Wallace, the origins of the new conservatism, and the transformation of American politics*. Baton Rouge: Louisiana State University Press.

Cartwright, Dorwin and Alvin Frederick Zander. 1968. *Group dynamics: Research and theory*. New York: Harper and Row.

Celsi, Teresa. 1992. *Jesse Jackson and political power*. Brookfield, CT: Millbrook Press.

Chomsky, Noam and Edward Herman. 1988. *The manufacture of consent: The political economy of the mass media*. New York: Pantheon.

Clausen, Aage R. 1973. *How congressmen decide: A policy focus*. New York: St. Martin's Press.

Clawson, Dan, Alan Neustadtl, and Denise Scott. 1992. *Money talks: Corporate PACs and political influence*. New York: Basic Books.

Clawson, Dan, Alan Neustadtl, and Mark Weller. 1998. *Dollars and votes: How business campaign contributions subvert democracy*. Philadelphia: Temple University Press.

Coleman, Richard Patrick, Lee Rainwater, and Kent A. McClelland. 1978. *Social standing in America: New dimensions of class*. New York: Basic Books.

Collins, Chuck. 1997. *Born on third base: The sources of wealth of the 1996 Forbes 400*. Boston: United for a Fair Economy.

Coltrane, Scott. 2001. Marketing the marriage "solution": Misplaced simplicity in the politics of fatherhood. *Sociological Perspectives* 44:387–418.

Colwell, M. 1980. The foundation connection: Links among foundations and recipient organizations. In *Philanthropy and cultural imperialism: The foundations at home and abroad*, ed. R. F. Arnove, 413–452. Boston: G. K. Hall & Co.

———. 1993. *Private foundations and public policy: The political role of philanthropy*. New York: Garland.

Conason, Joe. 1997. The Starr in Richard Scaife's eyes. *The Washington Post*, Mar. 18, sec. C4.

Cookson, Peter W. and Caroline Hodges Persell. 1985. *Preparing for power: America's elite boarding schools*. New York: Basic Books.

Cortner, Richard. 1964. *The Wagner Act cases*. Knoxville: University of Tennessee Press.

Covington, Sally. 1999. *Moving a public policy agenda: The strategic philanthropy of conservative foundations*. Washington, DC: National Committee for Responsive Philanthropy.

CQ. 1996. Will the rise of "blue dogs" revive the partisan right? *Congressional Quarterly*, December 21, pp. 3436–3438.

Daalder, Ivo and James Lindsay. 2003. *America unbound*. Washington, DC: Brookings Institution.

Dahl, Robert A. 1961. *Who governs? Democracy and power in an American city*. New Haven: Yale University Press.

Dalzell, Robert F. 1987. *Enterprising elite: The Boston Associates and the world they made*. Cambridge: Harvard University Press.

Daniels, Arlene Kaplan. 1988. *Invisible careers: Women civic leaders from the volunteer world*. Chicago: University of Chicago Press.

Davidson, Chandler, Tanya Dunlap, Gale Kenny, and Benjamin Wise. 2004. *Republican ballot security programs: Vote protection or minority vote suppression—or both?* Washington, DC: Center for Voting Rights and Protection.

Davies, James B., Anthony Shorrocks, and Edward Wolff. 2006. *The world distribution of household wealth*. Helsinki: The World Institute for Development Economics Research.

Davis, Allison, Burleigh Gardner, and Mary Gardner. 1941. *Deep South*. Chicago: University of Chicago Press.

Davis, Gerald F., Mina Yoo, and Wayne Baker. 2002. The small world of the American corporate elite, 1982–2001. *Strategic Organization* 1:301–326.

Day, Kathleen. 2000. A voice for stockholders. *The Washington Post* national weekly edition, Sept. 4, pp. 18–19.

de Figueiredo, John and James S. Snyder. 2003. Why is there so little money in U.S. politics? *Journal of Economic Perspectives*. http://opensecrets.org.

Dellinger, David. 1993. *From Yale to jail: The life story of a moral dissenter*. New York: Pantheon Books.

Demers, David. 1996. *The menace of the corporate newspaper: Fact or fiction?* Ames: University of Iowa Press.

Deutsch, Claudia. 2003. The revolution that wasn't: 10 years later, corporate oversight is still dismal. *The New York Times*, Jan. 26, sec. C1.

DiTomaso, Nancy. 1980. Organizational analysis and power structure research. In *Power Structure Research*, ed. G. W. Domhoff, 255–268. Beverly Hills, CA: Sage.

Dobrzynski, Judith H. 1996a. Investor group's leadership vote is a rebuff to union members. *The New York Times*, Apr. 2, sec. C2(N), D23(L).

———. 1996b. Shareholder-rights group faces a fight over its own leadership. *The New York Times*, Apr. 1, sec A1(N), D2(L).

Domhoff, G. W. 1967. *Who rules America?* Englewood Cliffs, NJ: Prentice Hall.

———. 1970. *The higher circles*. New York: Random House.

———. 1975. Social clubs, policy-planning groups, and corporations: A network study of ruling-class cohesiveness. *The Insurgent Sociologist* 5:173–184.

———. 1983. *Who rules America now?* New York: Simon & Schuster.

———. 1987. Where do government experts come from? The CEA and the policy-planning network. In *Power elites and organizations*, ed. G. W. Domhoff and T. Dye, 189–200. Beverly Hills, CA: Sage.

———. 1990. *The power elite and the state: How policy is made in America*. Hawthorne, NY: Aldine de Gruyter.

———. 1996. *State autonomy or class dominance? Case studies on policy making in America*. Hawthorne, NY: Aldine de Gruyter.

———. 1998. *Who rules America? Power and politics in the year 2000*. Mountain View, CA: Mayfield Publishing Company.

———. 2005. Who really ruled in Dahl's New Haven? http://whorulesamerica.net [retrieved Mar. 3, 2009].

———. 2006. *Who rules America? Power, politics, and social change*. New York: McGraw-Hill.

Dowie, Mark. 1995. *Losing ground: American environmentalism at the close of the twentieth century*. Cambridge, Mass.: MIT Press.

Dreier, Peter. 1982. The position of the press in the U.S. power structure. *Social Problems* 29:298–310.

Dreier, Peter, John Mollenkopf, and Todd Swanstrom. 2004. *Place matters: Metropolitics for the twenty-first century*. Lawrence: University Press of Kansas.

Dreiling, Michael. 2001. *Solidarity and contention: The politics of class and sustainability in the NAFTA conflict*. New York: Garland Press.

Dreiling, Michael and Derek Darves. 2007. *Coporate unity in American trade policy: A network analysis of corporate-dyad political action*. Paper presented to the annual meetings of the American Sociological Association. New York.

Dreyfuss, Robert. 2008. Obama's evolving foreign policy. *The Nation*, July 21/28, pp. 20–27.

———. 2009. Obama's hawk. *The Nation*, January 5, pp. 6–7.

Driscoll, Dawn-Marie and Carol R. Goldberg. 1993. *Members of the club: The coming of age of executive women*. New York: Free Press.

Dye, Thomas R. 1995. *Who's running America? The Clinton years*. Englewood Cliffs, N.J.: Prentice Hall.

Edsall, Thomas B. 2006. *Building red America: The new conservative coalition and the drive for permanent power*. New York: Basic Books.

Edsall, Thomas B. and Mary D. Edsall. 1992. *Chain reaction: The impact of race, rights, and taxes on American politics*. New York: Norton.

Eliasoph, N. 1998. *Avoiding politics: How Americans produce apathy in everyday life*. New York: Cambridge University Press.

Erikson, Robert and Kent Tedin. 2005. *American public opinion: Its origins, content, and impact*. New York: Pearson Education.

Ermann, M. David. 1978. The operative goals of corporate philanthropy: Contributions to the Public Broadcasting Service, 1972–1976. *Social Problems* 25:504–514.

Ernst, Morris Leopold. 1973. *The great reversals: Tales of the Supreme Court*. New York: Weybright and Talley.

Eulau, Heinz and John D. Sprague. 1984. *Lawyers in politics: A study in professional convergence*. Westport, CT: Greenwood Press.

Ewen, Stuart. 1996. *PR!: A social history of spin*. New York: Basic Books.

Faiola, Anthony, Ellen Nakshima, and Jill Drew. 2008. What went wrong: Washington policy makers disagreed about intervention in markets. *The Washington Post*, national weekly edition, Oct. 15, pp. 6–9.

Fine, Sidney. 1969. *Sit-down: The General Motors strike of 1936–1937*. Ann Arbor: University of Michigan Press.

Flacks, Richard. 1988. *Making history: The radical tradition in American life*. New York: Columbia University Press.

Foner, Philip S. 1977. *The great labor uprising of 1877*. New York: Pathfinder Press.

Fontenay, Charles L. 1980. *Estes Kefauver: A biography*. Knoxville: University of Tennessee Press.

Frederick, William. 1981. Free market vs. social responsibility: Decision time at the CED. *California Management Review* 23:20–28.

Gamson, William A. 1992. *Talking politics*. New York: Cambridge University Press.

Gans, Herbert. 1985. Are U.S. journalists dangerously liberal? *Columbia Journalism Review*, November/December:29–33.

Gendron, Richard and G. William Domhhoff. 2009. *The leftmost city: Power and progressive politics in Santa Cruz*. Boulder, CO: Westview.

Ghiloni, Beth. 1987. The velvet ghetto: women, power, and the corporation. In *Power elites and organizations*, ed. G. W. Domhoff and T. Dye, 21–36. Beverly Hills, CA: Sage.

Ghiloni, Beth Wesley. 1986. New women of power: An examination of the ruling class model of domination. Ph.D. diss. University of California, Santa Cruz.

Gitelman, H. M. 1988. *Legacy of the Ludlow massacre*. Philadelphia: University of Pennsylvania Press.

Glynn, C., S. Herbst, G. O'Keefe, and R. Shapiro. 1999. *Public opinion*. Boulder, CO: Westview.

Goertzel, Ted. 1985. Militarism as a sociological problem. *Research in Political Sociology* 1:119–139.

Gold, Howard J. 1992. *Hollow mandates: American public opinion and the conservative shift*. Boulder, CO: Westview Press.

Goldman, Jacob. 2000. Innovation isn't the Microsoft way. *The New York Times*, June 10, sec. A27.

Goldstein, Amy and Sarah Cohen. 2004. The rules that apply: Under the Bush Administration, OSHA is friendly with business. *The Washington Post*, national weekly edition Aug. 23–29, pp. 6–9.

Goldstein, Kenneth M. 1999. *Interest groups, lobbying, and participation in America*. New York: Cambridge University Press.

Gonzalez, George A. 2001. *Corporate power and the environment: The political economy of U.S. environmental policy*. Lanham, MD: Rowman and Littlefield.

———. 2005. *The politics of air pollution*. Albany: State University of New York Press.

Goodstein, Eban. 1999. *The trade-off myth: Fact and fiction about jobs and the environment*. Washington, DC: Island Press.

Gordon, Michael. 1969. Changing patterns of upper-class prep school college placements. *Pacific Sociological Review* 12:23–26.

Gordon, Stacy. 2005. *Campaign contributions and legislative voting behavior: A new approach*. New York: Routledge.

Gotham, Kevin Fox. 2000. Racialization and the state: the Housing Act of 1934 and the creation of the Federal Housing Administration. *Sociological Perspectives* 43:291–317.

———. 2002. *Race, real estate, and uneven development*. Albany: State University of New York Press.

Granfield, Robert. 1992. *Making elite lawyers: Visions of law at Harvard and beyond*. New York: Routledge.

Greenberg, Daniel. 2007. *The perils, rewards, and delusions of campus capitalism*. Chicago: University of Chicago Press.

Greenhouse, Steven. 2008. Unions look for new life in world of Obama. *The New York Times*, Dec. 29, sec. A1.

———. 2009. Bill easing unionization under heavy attack. *The New York Times*, Jan. 8, sec. A14.

Greider, William. 1989. *Secrets of the temple: How the Federal Reserve runs the country*. New York: Simon & Schuster.

———. 2008. Stop Senator No. *The Nation*, Dec. 29, pp. 6–7.

———. 2009. The looting of Social Security. *The Nation*, March 2, pp. 12–15.

Gross, James A. 1974. *The making of the National Labor Relations Board*. Albany: State University of New York Press.

———. 1981. *The reshaping of the National Labor Relations Board*. Albany: State University of New York Press.

———. 1995. *Broken promise: The subversion of U.S. labor relations policy*. Philadelphia: Temple University Press.

Guttsman, W. L. 1969. *The English ruling class*. London: Weidenfeld & Nicholson.

Hacker, Andrew. 1961. The elected and the anointed: Two American elites. *American Political Science Review* 55:539–549.

Hamilton, Richard F. 1972. *Class and politics in the United States*. New York: Wiley.

———. 1975. *Restraining myths: Critical studies of U.S. social structure and politics*. New York: Sage Publications.

———. 1991. *The bourgeois epoch: Marx and Engels on Britain, France, and Germany*. Chapel Hill: University of North Carolina Press.

Harrison, Bennett. 1994. *Lean and mean: The changing landscape of corporate power in the age of flexibility*. New York: Basic Books.

Hartz, Louis. 1955. *The liberal tradition in America: An interpretation of American political thought since the Revolution*. New York: Harcourt, Brace.

Hawthorne, Fran. 2008. The family office, granting every wish. *The New York Times*, Mar. 18, sec. H2.

Hendrix, Steve and Michael D. Shear. 2008. Rahm Emanuel, Obama's pit bull. *The Washington Post*, national weekly edition, Nov. 17–23, pp. 9–10.

Herman, Edward. 1975. *Conflicts of interest: Commercial bank trust departments*. New York: Twentieth Century Fund.

Herman, Edward S. 1981. *Corporate control, corporate power*. New York: Cambridge University Press.

Hernandez, Raymond and David Chen. 2008. Gifts to pet charities keep lawmakers happy. *The New York Times*, Oct. 19, sec. A1.

Hewitt, Christopher. 1977. The effect of political democracy and social democracy on equality in industrial societies: A cross-national comparison. *American Sociological Review* 42:450–464.

Higley, John. 2003. Force to the fore: The Bush elite and America's post-9/11 democracy. *Australasian Journal of American Studies* 22:25–40.

Higley, John and Michael Burton. 2006. *Elite foundations of liberal democracy*. Lanham, MD: Rowman and Littlefield.

Higley, John and Michael G. Burton. 1989. The elite variable in democratic transitions and breakdowns. *American Sociological Review* 54:17–32.

Higley, John and Gyorgy Lengyel. 2000. *Elites after state socialism*. New York: Rowman & Littlefield.

Himmelstein, Jerome L. 1990. *To the right: The transformation of American conservatism*. Berkeley: University of California Press.

———. 1997. *Looking good and doing good: Corporate philanthropy and corporate power*. Bloomington: Indiana University Press.

Hirsch, Glenn K. 1975. Only you can prevent ideological hegemony: The Advertising Council and its place in the American power structure. *The Insurgent Sociologist* 5:64–82.

Hoffman, Paul. 1973. *Lions in the Street*. New York: Saturday Review Press.

Hofstadter, Richard. 1969. *The idea of a party system: The rise of legitimate opposition in the United States, 1780–1840*. Berkeley: University of California Press.

Hogg, Michael. 1992. *The social psychology of group coehsiveness*. New York: New York University Press.

Hollingshead, August and Fredrick C. Redlich. 1958. *Social class and mental illness: A community study*. New York: Wiley.

Hooks, Gregory. 1991. *Forging the military-industrial complex: World War II's battle of the Potomac*. Urbana: University of Illinois Press.

Horowitz, Juliana. 2008. *Winds of political change haven't shifted public's ideology balance*. Philadelphia: Pew Research Center for the People and the Press.

Horrock, Nicholas. 1976. Reagan resists financial disclosure. *The New York Times*, Aug. 13, sec. A10.

Hundt, Reed E. 2000. *You say you want a revolution: A story of information age politics*. New Haven: Yale University Press.

Huntington, Samuel. 1961. *The common defense*. New York: Columbia University Press.

Huthmacher, J. Joseph. 1968. *Senator Robert F. Wagner and the rise of urban liberalism*. New York: Atheneum.

Iyengar, Shanto and Richard Reeves. 1997. *Do the media govern? Politicians, voters, and reporters in America*. Thousand Oaks, CA: Sage Publications.

Iyengar, Shanto and Adam F. Simon. 2000. New perspectives and evidence on political communication and campaign effects. *Annual Review of Psychology*:149.

Jacobs, David C. 1999. *Business lobbies and the power structure in America: Evidence and arguments*. Westport, CT: Quorum Books.

Jacobs, Lawrence and Benjamin Page. 2005. Who influences U.S. foreign policy? *American Political Science Review* 99:107–123.

Jacobs, Lawrence and Robert Shapiro. 2000. *Politicians don't pander*. Chicago: University of Chicago Press.

Johnson, Stephen. 1976. How the West was won: Last shootout for the Yankee-Cowboy theory. *Insurgent Sociologist* 6:61–93.

Johnston, David. 2000. Study finds that many large companies pay no taxes. *The New York Times*, Oct. 20, sec. C2.

Johnston, David Cay and Joseph Treaster. 2007. Insurers want U.S. to curb competitors' fund transfers to Bermuda. *The New York Times*, Sept. 26, sec. B1.

Jost, John T. and Brenda Major. 2001. *The psychology of legitimacy: Emerging perspectives on ideology, justice, and intergroup relations*. New York: Cambridge University Press.

Jost, John T. and Jim Sedanius. 2004. *Political psychology: The key readings*. New York: Psychology Press.

Kahn, Jonathan. 1997. *Budgeting democracy: State building and citizenship in America, 1890–1928*. Ithaca: Cornell University Press.

Kaiser, Robert and Ira Chinoy. 1999. The right's funding father. *The Washington Post*, national weekly edition, May 17, p. 6.

Kanter, Rosabeth Moss. 1993. *Men and women of the corporation*. New York: Basic Books.

Kaplan, Esther. 2009. Can American labor revive the American dream? *The Nation*, Jan. 26, pp. 10–14.

Kazee, Nicole, Michael Lipsky, and Cathie Jo Martin. 2008. Outside the big box: Who speaks for small business? *Boston Review*, July/August, http://bostonreview.net/BR33.4/kazee.php.

Kendall, Diana. 2002. *The power of good deeds: Privileged women and the social reproduction of class*. Lanham, MD: Rowman and Littlefield.

———. 2008. *Members only: Elite clubs and the process of exclusion*. Lanham, MD: Rowman and Littlefield.

Kerbo, Harold R. 2000. *Social stratification and inequality: Class conflict in histori-cal, comparative, and global perspective*. Boston: McGraw-Hill.

Kesiter, Lisa. 2005. *Getting rich: A study of wealth mobility in America*. New York: Cambridge University Press.

Kessler, David. 2000. *A question of intent: How a small government agency took on America's most powerful and deadly industry*. New York: Public Affairs Press.

Key, V. O. 1949. *Southern politics in state and nation*. New York: Random House.

Koenig, Thomas and Robert Gogel. 1981. Interlocking corporate director-ships as a social network. *The American Journal of Economics and Sociology* 40:37–50.

Konigsberg, Eric. 2008. Advising, and calming, the worried super-rich. *The New York Times*, Oct. 24, sec. A17.

Krehely, Jeff, Meaghan House, and Emily Kernan. 2004. *Axis of ideology: Conserva-tive foundations and public policy*. New York: National Committee for Respon-sive Philanthropy.

Krugman, Paul. 2007. *The conscience of a liberal*. New York: Norton & Co.

Krugman, Paul and Robin Wells. 2006. The health care crisis and what to do about it. *New York Review*, Mar. 23, pp. 38–43.

Kuo, David. 2006. *Tempting faith: An inside story of political seduction*. New York: Simon & Schuster.

Kuttner, Robert. 2009. *Obama's moment: America's economic crisis and the power of a transformative presidency*. White River Junction, VT: Chelsea Green Publishing.

Labaton, Stephen. 2000. Congress severely curtails plan for low-power FM stations. *The New York Times*, Dec. 19, p. 1.

Lachman, Richard. 2000. *Capitalists in spite of themselves: Elite conflict and eco-nomic transformation in early modern Euope*. New York: Oxford University Press.

Lakoff, George. 1996. *Moral politics: What conservatives know that liberals don't*. Chicago: University of Chicago Press.

Lane, Robert Edwards. 1962. *Political ideology: Why the American common man believes what he does*. New York: Free Press of Glencoe.

Lazarsfeld, Paul. 1966. Concept formation and measurement. In *Concepts, Theory, and Explanation in the Behavioral Sciences*, ed. G. DiRenzo, 144–202. New York: Random House.

Leeman, Nicholas. 2008. Worlds apart: Obama, McCain, and the future of foreign policy. *The New Yorker*, Oct. 13, pp. 110–121.

Levere, Jane. 2002. An Ad Council campaign sells freedom, but some call it propa-ganda. *The New York Times*, July 1, sec. C8.

Levine, Rhonda F. 1988. *Class struggle and the New Deal*. Lawrence: University of Kansas Press.

Lindblom, Charles. 1977. *Politics and markets: The world's political economic sys-tems*. New York: Basic Books.

Lindsay, D. Michael. 2007. *Faith in the halls of power: How evangelicals joined the American elite*. New York: Oxford University Press.

———. 2008. Evangelicals in the power elite: Elite cohesion advancing a move-ment. *American Sociological Review* 73:60–82.

Lipset, Seymour Martin. 1963. *The first new nation: The United States in historical and comparative perspective*. New York: Basic Books.

Lipset, Seymour Martin and Gary Wolfe Marks. 2000. *It didn't happen here: Why socialism failed in the United States*. New York: W. W. Norton & Co.

Livingston, James. 1986. *Origins of the Federal Reserve System: Money, class, and corporate capitalism, 1890–1913*. Ithaca: Cornell University Press.

Lizza, Ryan. 2008. Miking it: How Chicago shaped Obama. *The New Yorker*, July 21, pp. 49–65.

Lobao, Linda and Katherine Meyer. 2001. The great agricultural transition. *Annual Review of Sociology* 27:103–124.

———. 2004. Farm power without farmers. *Contexts* 3:12–21.

Logan, John and H. Molotch. 2007. *Urban fortunes: The political economy of place*. Berkeley: University of California Press.

Lovejoy, Allen F. 1941. *La Follette and the establishment of the direct primary in Wisconsin, 1890–1904*. New Haven: Yale University Press.

Lowenstein, Roger. 1995. *Buffett: The making of an American capitalist*. New York: Random House.

Luger, Stan. 2000. *Corporate power, American democracy, and the automobile industry*. New York: Cambridge University Press.

Luo, Michael. 2008a. In banking, top Obama aide made money and connections. *The New York Times*, Dec. 3, sec. A1.

———. 2008b. Study: Many Obama small donors really weren't. *The New York Times*, Nov. 24, sec. A12.

Luo, Michael and Karen Cullotta. 2008. Even workers surprised by success of factory sit-in. *The New York Times*, Dec. 13, sec. A9.

Luo, Michael and Sarah Wheaton. 2008. List of McCain fundraisers includes prominent lobbyists. *The New York Times*, Apr. 21, sec. A17.

MacLeod, Margo. 1984. *Influential women volunteers: Rexamining the concept of power*. Paper presented to the annual meetings of the American Sociological Association. San Antonio.

Magat, Richard. 1999. *Unlikely partners: Philanthropic foundations and the labor movement*. Ithaca, NY: ILR Press.

Main, Jackson Turner. 1965. *The social structure of Revolutionary America*. Princeton: Princeton University Press.

Malbin, Michael. 2008. Reality check: Obama received about the same percentage from small donors in 2008 as Bush in 2004. Washingon, DC: Campaign Finance Institute.

Maney, Ardith and Loree Gerdes Bykerk. 1994. *Consumer politics: Protecting public interests on Capitol Hill*. Westport, CT: Greenwood Press.

Mann, Michael. 1984. The autonomous power of the state: Its origins, mechanisms, and results. *Archives of European Sociology* 25:185–213.

———. 1986. *The sources of social power: A history of power from the beginning to A.D. 1760*, Vol. 1. New York: Cambridge University Press.

———. 1993. *The sources of social power: The rise of classes and nation-states, 1760–1914*, Vol. 2. New York: Cambridge University Press.

———. 2004. *Fascists*. New York: Cambridge University Press.

Manza, J. and C. Brooks. 1999. *Social cleavages and political change: Voter alignments and U.S. party coalitions*. New York: Oxford University Press.

Mariolis, Peter. 1975. Interlocking directorates and control of corporations. *Social Sciences Quarterly* 56:425–439.

Marquez, Benjamin. 1993. Mexican-American community development corporations and the limits of directed capitalism. *Economic Development Quarterly* 7:287–295.

———. 2003. Mexican-American political organizatons and philanthropy: Bankrolling a social movement. *Social Service Review* 77:329–348.

Marsh, Ann. 1996. The Forbes four hundred. *Forbes*, Oct. 14, p. 100(5).

Massey, Douglas. 2005. *Return of the "L" word: A liberal vision for the new century*. Princeton: Princeton University Press.

Matthews, Donald R. 1967. *The social background of political decision-makers*. New York: Random House.

Mauss, Marcel. 1924/1969. *The gift: Forms and functions of exchange in archaic societies*. London: Cohen & West.

Mayer, William. 1996. *The divided Democrats*. Boulder, CO: Westview Press.

McCammon, Holly J. 1990. Legal limits on labor militancy: U.S. labor law and the right to strike since the New Deal. *Social Problems* 37:206–229.

———. 1993. "Government by injunction": The U.S. judiciary and strike action in the late 19th and early 20th centuries. *Work and Occupations* 20:174–204.

———. 1994. Disorganizing and reorganizing conflict: Outcomes of the state's legal regulation of the strike since the Wagner Act. *Social Forces* 72: 1011–1049.

McCammon, Holly J. and Melinda D. Kane. 1997. Shaping judicial law in the post–World War II period: When is labor's legal mobilization successful? *Sociological Inquiry* 67:275–298.

McCarty, Nolan, Keith Poole, and Howard Rosenthal. 2006. *Polarized America: The dance of ideology and unequal riches*. Cambridge, MA: MIT Press.

McConnell, Grant. 1966. *Private power and American democracy*. New York: Knopf.

McIntyre, Robert S. 2004. *Corporate income taxes in the Bush years*. Washington, DC: Citizens for Tax Justice.

McQuaid, Kim. 1979. The frustration of corporate revival in the early New Deal. *Historian* 41:682–704.

———. 1982. *Big business and presidential power from FDR to Reagan*. New York: Morrow.

Melber, Ari. 2008. Obama's iSuccess. *The Nation*, Oct. 27, p. 8.

Mendell, David. 2007. *Obama: From promise to power*. New York: HarperCollins.

Miethe, T. D. 1999. *Whistleblowing at work: Tough choices in exposing fraud, waste, and abuse on the job*. Boulder, CO: Westview Press.

Miliband, Ralph. 1977. *Marxism and politics*. Oxford: Oxford University Press.

Miller, Berkeley and William Canak. 1995a. Laws as a cause and consequence of public employee unionism. *Industrial Relations Research Association Series*, 346–357.

———. 1995b. There should be no blanket guarantee: Employers' reactions to public employee unionism, 1965–1975. *Journal of Collective Negotiations in the Public Sector* 24:17–35.

Miller, Mark C. 1995. *The high priests of American politics: The role of lawyers in American political institutions*. Knoxville: University of Tennessee Press.

Miller, Warren and J. Merrill Shanks. 1996. *The new American voter*. Cambridge: Harvard University Press.

Miller, William. 1949. American historians and the business elite. *Journal of Economic History* 9:184–208.

Mills, C. Wright. 1956. *The power elite*. New York: Oxford University Press.

Mink, Gwendolyn. 1986. *Old labor and new immigrants in American political development, 1870–1925*. Ithaca: Cornell University Press.

Mintz, Beth. 1975. The president's cabinet, 1897–1972: A contribution to the power structure debate. *Insurgent Sociologist* 5:131–148.

————. 1998. The failure of health care reform: The role of big business in policy formation. In *Social Policy and the Conservative Agenda*, ed. C. Lo and M. Schwartz, 210–224. Malden, MA: Blackwell.

Mintz, Beth and Michael Schwartz. 1983. Financial interest groups and interlocking directorates. *Social Science History* 7:183–204.

Miroff, Bruce. 2007. *The liberal's moment: The McGovern insurgency and the identity crisis of the Democratic Party*. Lawrence: University of Kansas Press.

Mishel, Larry, Jared Bernstein, and Sylvia Allegretto. 2007. *The state of working America 2006/2007*. Ithaca, NY: ILR Press.

Mitchell, Greg. 1992. *The campaign of the century: Upton Sinclair's race for governor of California and the birth of media politics*. New York: Random House.

Mitchell, Robert. 1991. From conservation to environmental movement: The development of the modern environmental lobbies. In *Governmental and Environmental Politics*, ed. M. Lacey, 81–113. Baltimore: Johns Hopkins University Press.

Mizruchi, M. 1982. *The American corporate network, 1904–1974*. Beverly Hills, CA: Sage Publications.

Mizruchi, M. 1992. *The structure of corporate political action: Interfirm relations and their consequences*. Cambridge: Harvard University Press.

————. 1996. What do interlocks do? An analysis, critique, and assessment of research on interlocking directorates. *Annual Review of Sociology* 22:271–298.

Mizruchi, M. and D. Bunting. 1981. Influence in corporate networks: An examination of four measures. *Administrative Science Quarterly* 26:475–489.

Molotch, Harvey. 1970. Oil in Santa Barbara and power in America. *Sociological Inquiry* 40:131–144.

————. 2004. Spilling out (again). In *Enriching the sociological imagination: How radical sociology changed the discipline*, ed. R. F. Levine, 87–90. Boston: Brill.

Molotch, Harvey and Marilyn Lester. 2004. Accidents, scandals, and routines: Resources for insurgent methodology. In *Enriching the sociological imagination: How radical sociology changed the discipline*, ed. R. F. Levine, 91–104. Boston: Brill.

Mooney, Chris. 2008. *Doubt is their product: How industry's assault on science threatens your health*. Chicago: University of Chicago Press.

Moore, G., Lawrence Raffalovich, J. Allen Whitt, Sarah Sobieraj, Scott Dolan, and Daniel Beaulieu. 2003. *Ties that bind: Exploring the neglected role of nonprofits in corporate and government networks*. Paper presented to the annual meetings of the American Sociological Association. Atlanta, GA.

Moore, G., S. Sobieraj, J. Whitt, O. Mayorova, and D. Beaulieu. 2002. Elite interlocks in three U.S. sectors: Nonprofit, corporate, and government. *Social Science Quarterly* 83:726–744.

Moore, Gwen. 2007. From Vietnam to Iraq: American elites' views on the use of military force. *Comparative Sociology* 6:215–231.

Morin, Richard. 1995. What informed opinion? A survey trick points out the hazards facing those who take the nation's pulse. *The Washington Post*, national weekly edition, Apr. 10, p. 36.

Morlan, Robert L. 1985. *Political prairie fire: The Non-Partisan League, 1915–1922*. St. Paul: Minnesota Historical Society Press.

Morris, David. 2004. How to write a prize-winning essay on inequality. In www.inequality.org.

Mosk, Matthew and Sarah Cohen. 2008. Big donors drive Obama's money edge. *The Washington Post*, Oct. 22, sec. A1.

Mosk, Matthew and Alec MacGillis. 2008. Big donors among Obama's grass roots: Bundlers have a voice in campaign. *The Washington Post,* Apr. 11, sec. A1.

Mucllcr, John E. 1973. *War, presidents, and public opinion.* New York: Wiley.

———. 1984. Reflections on the Vietnam antiwar movement and on the curious calm at the war's end. In *Vietnam as history: Ten years after the Paris Peace Accords,* ed. P. Braestrup, 151–157. Washington, DC: University Press of America.

———. 2005. The Iraq syndrome. *Foreign Affairs,* November/December, pp. 44–54.

Murray, Shailagh. 2008. In Obama's circle, Chicago remains the tie that binds. *The Washingon Post,* July 14, sec. A1.

NCEE. 1997. *EconomicsAmerica: Directory.* New York: National Council for Economic Education.

Nelson, Robert L. 1988. *Partners with power: The social transformation of the large law firm.* Berkeley: University of California Press.

Neustadtl, Alan, Denise Scott, and Dan Clawson. 1991. Class struggle in campaign finance? Political action committee contributions in the 1984 elections. *Sociological Forum* 6:219–238.

Nixon, Richard. 1978. *RN: The memoirs of Richard Nixon.* New York: Grosset & Dunlap.

Noble, Charles. 1986. *Liberalism at work: The rise and fall of OSHA.* Philadelphia: Temple University Press.

NRDC. 1990. *Twenty years defending the environment: NRDC 1970–1990.* New York: Natural Resources Defense Council.

Olsen, Marvin E. and Martin N. Marger. 1993. *Power in modern societies.* Boulder, CO: Westview Press.

Olson, Elizabeth. 2006. Amassing the troops for political battle. *The New York Times,* May 4, sec. C7.

Oppenheimer, Martin. 2000. *The state in modern society.* New York: Humanity Books.

Ostrander, Susan A. 1980. Upper-class women: Class consciousness as conduct and meaning. In *Power Structure Research,* ed. G. W. Domhoff, 73–96. Beverly Hills, CA: Sage.

———. 1984. *Women of the upper class.* Philadelphia: Temple University Press.

———. 1987. Elite domination in private social agencies: How it happens and how it is challenged. In *Power elites and organizations,* ed. G. W. Domhoff and T. Dye, 85–102. Beverly Hills: Sage.

———. 1995. *Money for change: Social movement philanthropy at Haymarket People's Fund.* Philadelphia: Temple University Press.

Page, B. and R. Y. Shapiro. 1992. *The rational public: Fifty years of trends in Americans' policy preferences.* Chicago: University of Chicago Press.

Page, Benjamin. 2008. *The foreign policy disconnect: What Americans want from our leaders but don't get.* Chicago: University of Chicago Press.

Page, Benjamin and Lawrence Jacobs. 2009. *Class war? What Americans really think about economic inequality.* Chicago: University of Chicago Press.

Palmer, Donald. 1983. Interpreting corporate interlocks from broken ties. *Social Science History* 7:217–231.

Palmer, Robert R. 1959. *The age of the democratic revolution: A political history of Europe and America, 1760–1800.* Princeton, NJ: Princeton University Press.

Parker-Gwin, Rachel and William G. Roy. 1996. Corporate law and the organization of property in the United States: The origin and institutionalization of New Jersey corporation law, 1888–1903. *Politics & Society,* 24:111–136.

Patterson, James T. 1981. *Congressional conservatism and the New Deal: The growth of the conservative coalition in Congress, 1933–1939.* Lexington: University of Kentucky Press.

Pear, Robert. 2009. House passes two measures on job bias. *The New York Times,* Jan. 9, sec. A13.

Pederson, Morgens. 1972. Lawyers in politics: The Danish Folketing and United States legislatures. In *Comparative Legislative Behavior,* ed. S. Patterson and J. Wahlke, 25–63. New York: Wiley & Sons.

Peoples, Clayton. 2007. Class dominance and policymaking in the U.S. House. Paper presented to the annual meetings of the Pacific Sociological Association. Oakland, CA.

Peoples, Clayton and Michael Gortari. 2008. The impact of campaign contributions on policymaking in the U.S. and Canada: Theoretical and public policy implications *Research in Political Sociology* 17:43–64.

Perlstein, Rick. 2001. *Before the storm: Barry Goldwater and the unmaking of the American consensus.* New York: Hill and Wang.

Pertschuk, Michael. 1982. *Revolt against regulation: The rise and pause of the consumer movement.* Berkeley: University of California Press.

Peschek, Joseph G. 1987. *Policy-planning organizations: Elite agendas and America's rightward turn.* Philadelphia: Temple University Press.

Pessen, Edward. 1984. *The log cabin myth: The social backgrounds of the presidents.* New Haven: Yale University Press.

Phillips, Peter. 1994. A relative advantage: Sociology of the San Francisco Bohemian Club. Ph.D. diss., University of California, Davis.

Pilisuk, Marc and Thomas Hayden. 1965. Is there a military-industrial complex which prevents peace? *Journal of Social Issues* 21:67–117.

Piven, Frances Fox and Richard A. Cloward. 1971/1993. *Regulating the poor: The functions of public welfare.* New York: Vintage Books.

———. 1977. *Poor people's movements: Why they succeed, how they fail.* New York: Random House.

———. 1982. *The new class war: Reagan's attack on the welfare state and its consequences.* New York: Pantheon Books.

POGO. 2004. The politics of contracting. Washington, DC: Project on Government Oversight.

Pollin, Robert, Dean Baker, and Marc Schaberg. 2001/2008. Securities transaction taxes for U.S. financial markets. Amherst, MA: Political Economy Research Institute.

Poole, Keith T. and Howard Rosenthal. 1997. *Congress: A political-economic history of roll call voting.* New York: Oxford University Press.

Potter, David. 1972. *The South and the concurrent majority.* Baton Rouge: Louisiana State University Press.

Prothro, James. 1954. *The dollar decade: Business ideas in the 1920s.* Baton Rouge: Louisiana State University Press.

Rae, Douglas. 1971. *The political consequences of electoral laws.* New Haven: Yale University Press.

Ramirez, Bruno. 1978. *When workers fight.* Westport, CT: Greenwood.

Riddiough, Christine and David Card. 2008. 2007 congressional voting record. Washington, DC: Americans for Democratic Action

Rising, George. 1997. *Clean for Gene: Eugene McCarthy's 1968 presidential campaign.* Westport, CT: Praeger.

Robinson, Marshall. 1993. The Ford Foundation: Sowing the seeds of a revolution. *Environment*, pp. 10–20.

Rogne, Leah, Carroll L. Estes, Brian R. Grossman, Brooke A. Hollister, and Erica S. Solway. 2009. *Social insurance and social justice: Social Security, Medicare, and the campaign against entitlements*. New York: Springer Publishers.

Rose, Nancy Ellen. 1994. *Put to work: Relief programs in the Great Depression*. New York: Monthly Review Press.

Rosen, Jeffrey. 2008. Supreme Court Inc.: How the nation's highest court became increasingly receptive to the arguments of American business. *The New York Times Magazine*.Mar. 16, pp. 20–26.

Rosenstone, Steven J., Roy L. Behr, and Edward H. Lazarus. 1996. *Third parties in America: Citizen response to major party failure*. Princeton, NJ: Princeton University Press.

Rossi, Peter and Robert Dentler. 1961. *The politics of urban renewal*. New York: Free Press.

Rothschild, Joyce and Terance Miethe. 1994. Whistleblowing as resistance in modern work organizations. In *Resistance and power in organizations*, ed. J. Jermier, D. Knights, and W. Nord, 252–273. New York: Routledge.

Roy, William G. 1983. Interlocking directorates and the corporate revolution. *Social Science History* 7:143–164.

———. 1997. *Socializing capital: The rise of the large industrial corporation in America*. Princeton, NJ: Princeton University Press.

Russell, Bertrand. 1938. *Power: A new social analysis*. London: Allen and Unwin.

Russell, John. 2005. *Funding the culture wars: Philanthropy, church, and state*. New York: National Council for Responsive Philanthropy.

Ryan, William. 1971. *Blaming the victim*. New York: Random House.

Salzman, Harold and G. William Domhoff. 1980. The corporate community and government: Do they interlock? In *Power structure research*, ed. G. W. Domhoff, 227–254. Beverly Hills, CA: Sage.

———. 1983. Nonprofit organizations and the corporate community. *Social Science History* 7:205–216.

Sanders, Jerry. 1983. *Peddlers of crisis: The committee on the present danger and the politics of containment*. Boston: South End Press.

Savage, Charlie. 2008a. Obama fundraiser knocks down cabinet rumors. *The New York Times*, Nov. 20, sec. A25.

———. 2008b. Shepherd of a govenment in exile. *The New York Times,* Nov. 7, sec. A18.

Schlesinger, Joseph A. 1966. *Ambition and politics: Political careers in the United States*. Chicago: Rand McNally.

Schneider, William. 1998. And lo, the momentum shifted. *National Journal*, Oct. 3, p. 2350.

Schuby, T. D. 1975. Class, power, kinship and social cohesion: A case study of a local elite. *Sociological Focus* 8:243–255.

Schudson, Michael. 1995. *The power of news*. Cambridge, MA: Harvard University Press.

Schwartz, Michael. 1976. *Radical protest and social structure: The Southern Farmers' Alliance and cotton tenancy, 1880–1890*. New York: Academic Press.

Schweizer, Peter and Rochelle Schweizer. 2004. *The Bushes: Portrait of a dynasty*. New York: Doubleday.

Sennett, Richard and Jonathan Cobb. 1973. *The hidden injuries of class*. New York: Norton.

Shaiko, R. and M. Wallace. 1999. From Wall Street to Main Street: The National Federation of Independent Business and the new Republican majority. In *After the revolution: PACs, lobbies, and the Republican Congress*, ed. R. Biersack, P. Herrnson, and C. Wilcox, 18–35. Boston: Allyn and Bacon.

Shear, Michael D. 2009. Obama pledges entitlement reform: President-elect says he'll reshape Social Security, Medicare programs. *The Washington Post*, Jan.16, sec. A1.

Shear, Michael D. and Jeffrey H. Birnbaum. 2008. The anti-lobbyist surrounds himself with lobbyists. *The Washington Post*, national weekly edition, Mar. 3–9, p. 13.

Sherwood, Jessica. 2004. Talk about country clubs: Ideology and the reproduction of privilege. Ph.D. diss., North Carolina State University.

Shoup, Laurence and William Minter. 1977. *Imperial brain trust*. New York: Monthly Review Press.

Silk, Leonard Solomon and David Vogel. 1976. *Ethics and profits: The crisis of confidence in American business*. New York: Simon & Schuster.

Silverstein, Ken. 2006. Barack Obama, Inc.: The birth of a Washingon machine. *Harper's*, November, pp. 14–29.

Skocpol, T. 1992. *Protecting soldiers and mothers: The political origins of social policy in the United States*. Cambridge: Harvard University Press.

Skocpol, Theda. 1979. *States and social revolutions: A comparative analysis of France, Russia, and China*. New York: Cambridge University Press.

Smeeding, Timothy. 2008. Poorer by comparison: Poverty, work, and public policy in comparative perspective. *Pathways* 1:3–5.

Smith, R. Jeffrey. 2008. Under Bush, OSHA Mired in Inaction. *The Washington Post*, Dec. 29, sec. A1.

Stauber, John C. and Sheldon Rampton. 1995. *Toxic sludge is good for you: Lies, damn lies, and the public relations industry*. Monroe, ME: Common Courage Press.

Steinhauer, Jennifer. 2008. Phoenix Club expels member over his press interview. *The New York Times*, July 31, sec. A19.

Stephens, John. 1979. *The transition from capitalism to socialism*. London: Macmillan.

Sterngold, James. 1996. A swift transformation. *The New York Times*, Dec. 16, p. 1.

———. 1997. GM sells unit to Raytheon as arms mergers continue. *New York Times*, Jan. 17, sec. A1.

Stewart, James B. 1991. *Den of thieves*. New York: Simon & Schuster.

Stolberg, Sheryl Gay. 2009. For a power lawyer, a new high-wire act. *The New York Times*, Jan. 16, sec. A12.

Stone, Peter. 2000. A Bermuda brouhaha for insurers. *National Journal*, Oct. 14, pp. 3262.

Street, Paul. 2008. *Barack Obama and the future of American politics*. Boulder, CO: Paradigm Publishers.

Sugrue, Thomas. 2001. Breaking through: The troubled origins of affirmative action in the workplace. In *Color lines: Affirmative action, immigration, and civil rights options for America*, ed. J. Skrentny, 31–52. Chicago: University of Chicago Press.

———. 2008. *Sweet land of liberty: The forgotten struggle for civil rights in the North*. New York: Random House.

Sweezy, Paul. 1953. The American ruling class. In *The Present as History*, ed. P. Sweezy, 120–138. New York: Monthly Review Press.

Szasz, Andrew. 1984. Industrial resistance to occupational safety and health regulation: 1971–1981. *Social Problems* 32:103–116.

Tittle, Diana. 1992. *Rebuilding Cleveland: The Cleveland Foundation and its evolving urban strategy*. Columbus: Ohio State University Press.

Tomkins, Sylvan. 1964. Left and right: A basic dimension of personality and ideology. In *The study of lives*, ed. R. W. White, 388–411. New York: Atherton Press.

Toobin, Jeffrey. 2008. *The nine: Inside the secret world of the Supreme Court*. New York: Random House.

Trejos, Nancy. 2008. Take two on time off: Sweeping changes debated for landmark Family and Medical Leave Act. *The Washington Post*, Apr. 24, sec. D1.

UCS. 2007. *Smoke, mirrors, and hot air*. Cambridge, MA: Union of Concerned Scientists.

Useem, Michael. 1978. The inner group of the American capitalist class. *Social Problems* 25:225–240.

———. 1980a. Corporations and the Corporate Elite. *Annual Review of Sociology* 6:41–77.

———. 1980b. Which business leaders help govern? In *Power Structure Research*, ed. G. W. Domhoff, 199–225. Beverly Hills, CA: Sage.

———. 1984. *The inner circle: Large corporations and the rise of business political activity in the U.S. and U.K.* New York: Oxford University Press.

Useem, Michael and Jerome Karabel. 1986. Pathways to top corporate management. *American Sociological Review* 51:184–200.

Vaughn, James C. 2006. The culture of the Bohemian Grove: The dramaturgy of power. *Michigan Sociological Review* 20:85–121.

Vogel, David. 1978. Why businessmen mistrust their state: The political consciousness of American corporate executives. *British Journal of Political Science* 8:45–78.

———. 1989. *Fluctuating fortunes: The political power of business in America*. New York: Basic Books.

Voss, Kim. 1993. *The making of American exceptionalism: The Knights of Labor and class formation in the nineteenth century*. Ithaca: Cornell University Press.

Waddell, Brian. 2001. *The war against the New Deal: World War II and American democracy*. DeKalb: Northern Illinois University Press.

Wala, Michael. 1994. *The Council on Foreign Relations and American foreign policy in the early Cold War*. Providence: Berghahn Books.

Walsh, Mary W. 2004. Leader quits corporate governance group amid clashes. *The New York Times*, Sept. 22, sec. C8..

Warburg, James P. 1964. *The long road home: The autobiography of a maverick*. New York: Doubleday.

Washburn, Jennifer. 2005. *University, Inc.: The corporate corruption of American higher education*. New York: Basic Books.

Webber, Michael. 2000. *New Deal fat cats: Business, labor, and campaign finance in the 1936 presidential election*. New York: Fordham University Press.

Weber, Max. 1998. Class, status, and party. In *Social class and stratification: Classic statements and theoretical debates*, ed. R. F. Levine, 43–56. Lanham, MD: Rowman and Littlefield.

Wehr, Kevin. 1994. The power elite at the Bohemian Grove: Has anything changed in the 1990s? *Critical Sociology* 20:121–124.

Weinstein, James. 1968. *The corporate ideal in the liberal state*. Boston: Beacon Press.

———. 1975. *Ambiguous legacy: The Left in American politics*. New York: Franklin Watts.

Whalen, Charles W. and Barbara Whalen. 1985. *The longest sebate: A legislative history of the 1964 Civil Rights Act*. Washington: Seven Locks Press.

White, Lawrence J. 2002. Trends in aggregate concentration in the United States. *Journal of Economic Perspectives* 16:137–160.

Wolff, Edward. 2007. Recent trends in household wealth in the United States: Rising debt and the middle-class squeeze. Annandale-on-Hudson, NY: Levy Economics Institute.

Woodward, Bob. 2000. *Maestro: Greenspan's Fed and the American boom*. New York: Simon & Schuster.

Woodward, C. Vann. 1966. *Reunion and reaction: The compromise of 1877 and the end of Reconstruction*. Boston: Little, Brown.

Wright, Erik Olin. 1998. Class analysis. In *Social class and stratification: Classic statements and theoretical debates*, ed. R. F. Levine, 141–165. Lanham, MD: Rowman and Littlefied.

Wrong, Dennis. 1995. *Power: Its forms, bases, and uses*. New Brunswick, NJ: Transaction Publishers.

WSJ. 1976. Rehabilitation project: Once-mighty CED panel of executives seeks a revival, offers advice to Carter. *The Wall Street Journal*, Dec. 17, p. 38.

Yaqub, Reshma. 2002. Getting inside the ivory gates. *Worth Magazine*, pp. 10–20.

Yuen, Eddie, Daniel Burton-Rose, and George Katsiaficas. 2001. The battle for Seattle. New York: Soft Skull Press.

———. 2004. *Confronting capitalism: Dispatches from a global movement*. Brooklyn: Soft Skull Press.

Zaller, John. 1992. *The nature and origins of mass opinion*. New York: Cambridge University Press.

Zeller, Shawn. 2000. Cassidy captures the gold. *National Journal*, Oct. 21, pp. 3332–3334.

Zweigenhaft, Richard. 1975. Who represents America? *Insurgent Sociologist* 5:119–130.

Zweigenhaft, Richard and G. William Domhoff. 2006. *Diversity in the power elite: How it happened, why it matters*. Lanham, MD: Rowman and Littlefield.

Zweigenhaft, Richard and G. William Domhoff. 1982. *Jews in the Protestant establishment*. New York: Praeger.

———. 2003. *Blacks in the white elite: Will the progress continue?* Lanham, MD: Rowman and Littlefield.

Index